The Proficient Pil

Volume 1

Also by Barry Schiff

*Flight 902 is Down!**

*The Vatican Target**

Golden Science Guide to Flying

The Boeing 707

All About Flying

Basic Meteorology

The Pilot's Digest

The Proficient Pilot, Volume 2

Flying Wisdom: The Proficient Pilot, Volume 3

*Air Navigation***

*in collaboration

**in progress

The Proficient Pilot

Volume 1

Barry Schiff

Foreword by Ernest K. Gann

Aviation Supplies & Academics, Inc.
Newcastle, Washington

The Proficient Pilot, Volume 1
by Barry Schiff

Aviation Supplies & Academics, Inc.
7005 132nd Place SE
Newcastle, Washington 98059-3153

Published 1997 by Aviation Supplies & Academics, Inc.
First published 1980, Aircraft Owners and Pilots Association
1985 MacMillan. 1994 Thomasson-Grant, Inc.

Printed in the United States of America

9   8   7   6   5   4   3   2

ASA-PP1
ISBN 1-56027-281-3

Library of Congress Cataloging-in-Publication Data:

Schiff, Barry J.
    The proficient pilot / Barry Schiff.
        p.   cm.
    Originally published: Rev. and enl. ed.
    New York: Macmillan: London: Collier
Macmillan, c1985.
    "An Eleanor Friede book."
    ISBN 1-56566-075-7 (h/c):
    1. Airplanes—Piloting. I. Title.
TL710.S293 1994
629.132'52—dc20 94-14249

Dedication

This book is dedicated to my first dozen instructors for whose patience and understanding I am eternally grateful.

Mike Walters
Steve Occhipinti
Bill Tolman
R. "Pete" Peterson
Richard Kersey
Frank Rosenstein
Joe DeBona
Charles Gress
Jimmy Most
Ila Pimlott
Paul Bell
Paul Blackman

Contents

Foreword

There are all kinds of pilots aloft these days, and they are as individual as they are individuals. Alas, not when it comes to flying. For all of us have entered upon an upper world that is not obliging even when sparsely inhabited. There are regulations that even the bureaucrats themselves cannot interpret with any consistency. It is best to surrender and just suppose that all of the regulations are cut "for our own good."

As a consequence, the old "seat-of-the-pants" aviator has become almost as extinct as the auk — almost!

The trouble begins with flight instruction, which is too often the case of the blind leading the blind. "If you descend to W feet at X knots and turn right at Y and descend at Z feet per minute for two minutes and thirty seconds..." Hallelujah! You have now completed the primary requirement of the future aviator. You must make just as many successful landings as takeoffs.

Thus do you learn to drive an airplane rather than fly it. You buy a new windbreaker and timing watch. Male or female, you swagger just a bit. But you are not an aviator. You have just become someone "interested" in aviation and reasonably capable of safe flight, provided all goes dandy. ("Air person," Amelia, whom I knew well, would have been amused.) If you intend to become a true airman and stay that way, you have to know a lot more than following the numbers, and the best host I know of to that altocumulus of flying know-how is Barry Schiff. He not only understands the theories, but he knows how to make them work, which makes him a rare bird indeed.

Now, in my fiftieth year of flying everything from the Goodyear blimp to the U-2, the F-15, F-106, 747, and even pre-World War I types while accumulating some 20,000 hours plus, I recommend you heed Schiff's messages because they are written by a true aviator. He knows, he has done it, and is doing it. And best of all, he thinks. While that has not always been absolutely necessary in a true aviator or aviatrix, it should be part of everyone's survival kit.

There is a well-established nest of curiously obtuse thinkers who insist beyond all comprehensible logic that single-engine airplanes are safer than the multi-engine variety. Welcome to the Land of Oz! Statistics prove that the average pilot is not skilled enough to continue flight if one engine quits, which compounds the nonsense. There are no statistics to cover the number of lives saved by having 50 percent of your power remaining (at night, or on instruments, or any old time), rather than 0 percent. The anti-multi-engine people say, "If your one engine quits, your choice is made for you. Land immediately." I, for one, prefer to postpone a hasty decision. I'm sure Barry Schiff agrees with me, even though he also flies single-engine when he's not at the helm of a 747.

Schiff is a true pro, and he covers the whole lofty field of airmanship with the skill and dignity it deserves. Beginner or veteran, you cannot avoid improving your overall comprehension of the flying business if you share some hours with such an aviator. The "X" approach to landing becomes a skilled numerical exercise if on instruments, as it should be. Yet because of the understanding you should receive from this book, you will also know the pure joy of the old "non-mumbling" approach. Your eyes will transfer to your brain a few hundred minor factors at full computer speed. You'll evaluate the apparent surface wind from countless sources, the influence of other aircraft on your decisions, the temperature effect, the glare effect, the airspeed effect plus spending of altitude, the effect of load aboard, the surrounding terrain, and the condition of the runway or grass strip; all of these matters will be brought to your attention in seconds while you slide gracefully down that invisible banister and touch down exactly where you intended. And that is flying.

There is one vital truth involved in any kind of flying, and the process separates the airmen from the drivers. Schiff's very superior book squeezes the essence of that truth drop by drop into your busy brain without your actually realizing it.

"Think ahead of your airplane" is one of the oldest adages in aviation. It is also the most forgotten by the drivers. If your aircraft cruises at 100 miles per hour, then think about your situation at least 5 miles ahead. If it is cruising at 350, then stretch that advance thinking to 20 or 30 miles. While the figures are as variable as the perceived situation, maybe, when you have arrived there, you are still flying the airplane. It is not flying you. We mourn for the countless nice guys and gals who forgot this venerable ceremony.

Barry Schiff's book does these honors in such a way that even I can understand his messages, which all add up to thinking ahead of your airplane. So to a great reading and thinking experience, and fair winds from the ancient pelican...

Ernest K. Gann
Friday Harbor, Washington

Ernest K. Gann is the author of many books, among them *The High and the Mighty, Twilight for the God, The Aviator, The Magistrate,* and *Fate is the Hunter.*

Section 1

The Dynamics of Flight

In the beginning, God created the heaven and the earth, but it is doubtful if He had intended for man to travel between the two, otherwise man would have been born with wings.

Author Unknown

Chapter 1 **The Miracle of Lift**

This antiquated piece of philosophy is, of course, fallacious. Otherwise, so the rebuttal goes, if God had intended for man to drive upon the earth, man would have been provided with little wheels on his feet.

When man observed that birds had wings, he was jealous. But as centuries passed, jealousy evolved into curiosity and eventually into challenge.

It was natural for man to emulate the birds, and he contrived all manner of flapping-wing devices in a valiant effort to mimic his feathered friends. These contrivances were called ornithopters. None were successful.

Ornithopter proponents argued vehemently that "Nature must know best" and that experiments with flapping wings should continue. But these arguments were illogical; otherwise, the great sailing vessels would have spanned the seven seas by wiggling their rudders like fish, and stagecoaches would have had legs instead of wheels.

Nature's suggested method of flight was eventually and fortunately discarded in favor of the nonflappable wing.

The modern, fixed wing truly is the heart and soul of the airplane. Without it, flight as we know it would be impossible. It is ingeniously designed to produce awesome quantities of lift, yet it has no moving parts.

The shapely, sculptured lines of a wing perform miraculous feats, but only a handful of pilots can properly explain how lift is created. There are all manner of half-truths and concocted explanations to be heard, many of which unfortunately originate in some otherwise highly respected training manuals. Accuracy is sacrificed for simplicity.

There is, for example, this amusing fable: "Air flowing above the wing has a greater distance to travel (because of camber) than air flowing beneath the wing. Therefore, air above the wing must travel faster so as to arrive at the wing's trailing edge at the same time as air flowing underneath."

This is pure nonsense. How could the air molecules flowing above and below the wing gain the anthropomorphic intelligence to determine that they must arrive simultaneously at the trailing edge? The truth is that, because of viscosity, once the airflow divides at the wing's leading edge, the separated air particles never again meet (unless by coincidence in some typhoon over the South China Sea).

There are those who contend that a pilot doesn't need to know how a wing creates lift. They say that this knowledge is as useless to a pilot as a study of the laws of buoyancy is to a swimmer. But I disagree.

Pilots are a generally curious, intelligent breed who desire to learn as much as possible about the science of flight. This separates them from most automobile drivers, who don't know and couldn't care less about the difference between a distributor and a differential.

Pilots use lift; their lives depend on it. They read and talk about it, are quizzed about it, and even try explaining this miracle of flight to their lay friends. The problem is that most pilots really don't know how lift is created; they only think they do.

Early pioneers did learn something from the birds—with the help of Sir Isaac Newton and his third law of motion: "To every action there is an equal and opposite reaction." Experimenters realized quite early in their studies that birds created lift (a reaction) by beating down air (the action). The principle is very much like what happens when a rifle is fired. The bullet is propelled from the barrel (an action) causing kickback (or recoil), an equal and opposite reaction.

Ornithopter devotees were on the right track. They tried every possible way to design a pair of wings that could flap sufficiently to force down enough air to lift a man and his machine.

The modern wing, working silently and much more efficiently than any ornithopter ever did, does much the same thing. It is designed to force down great quantities of air, which in turn causes the reaction called lift.

To learn how this is accomplished requires traveling a somewhat circuitous route. Our aerodynamic journey begins at a familiar location: the Venturi tube. It terminates in the Land of Crystal Clarity, an aeronautical Shangri-La where everything is easily understood.

Almost every pilot is familiar with a Venturi tube, that hollow chamber with the narrow throat (Figure 1).

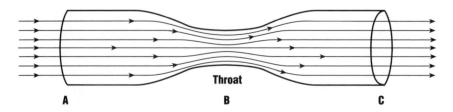

Throat

A   B   C

Figure 1. Venturi tube

"Aha!" you say. "I know all about that thing. Airspeed increases in the center of the tube causing a reduction in atmospheric pressure against the inside of the tube."

"And aha! to you," I say. "But do you know why the pressure against the inside of the tube decreases?"

The mysterious workings of the Venturi tube can be explained partially, using a flow of water as an example. It's easy to see that whatever amount of water enters the inlet (A) certainly must come out the other end (C). If this were not true, the water would have to bunch up in the throat (B) and become compressed. But since water is virtually incompressible, this simply cannot happen.

The same amount of water, therefore, must pass point B as passes points A and C. Since there is less room in the throat, the water is compelled, therefore, to accelerate and travel more rapidly.

A more graphic example is what happens when you partially block the outlet of a garden hose with your thumb or add a nozzle to the hose. In either case, a Venturi-type constriction (or throat) is created, and the water escapes much faster than it normally would.

What many do not fully appreciate is that air and water behave similarly; both are fluids. And since free-flowing subsonic air also is considered incompressible, the same thing happens to it when flowing through a constriction: it accelerates.

Up to this point, everything should seem quite plausible—nothing really new or exciting. But now the stinger, the question rarely answered except in sophisticated textbooks. Why does an increase in airspeed produce a decrease in pressure inside the Venturi tube? The answer, to be fully appreciated, requires a slight detour.

There are many different forms of energy, the most familiar being light, heat, sound, and electricity. Two other forms of energy are not quite so well known: kinetic and static.

Kinetic energy is a form of energy contained by an object in motion. An automobile speeding along the highway possesses kinetic energy; the faster it moves, the more kinetic energy it has. When the brakes are applied, this kinetic energy (of motion) does not simply disappear. Instead, it is converted to another form of energy, heat, which can be felt on the brake linings. Also, some of the kinetic energy is converted to heating the tires (and sometimes to melting the rubber).

The process of energy conversion works in reverse, too. A car at rest has no kinetic energy because it is not in motion. But when the driver depresses the accelerator pedal, fuel is burned and some of its chemical energy is converted to kinetic energy. The car is again in motion.

The point to remember is that energy can neither be created nor destroyed; it simply changes form. Another example of energy conversion is the light bulb, which changes electrical energy to light and heat.

Air in motion (like any other object) possesses kinetic energy. The second form of energy possessed by air is static pressure. An inflated toy balloon is an excellent example of static pressure (energy) being stored. If the air inside is allowed to escape, the static pressure (one form of energy) changes to kinetic energy (another form of energy). The air pressure inside decreases (causing the balloon to deflate), and the airspeed increases while the air escapes through the balloon's "nozzle."

Two very important pieces of the lift puzzle, therefore, state that: (1) energy can neither be created nor destroyed, and (2) air entering a Venturi tube consists of two significant forms of energy; kinetic energy (of motion) and static (atmospheric) pressure.

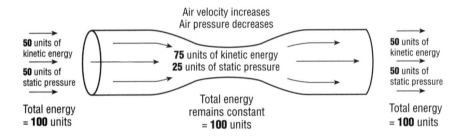

Figure 2. Kinetic energy plus static pressure = total energy

The air entering the Venturi tube (Figure 2) has a given amount of total energy, equal to the sum of its kinetic energy and its static pressure.

As the airflow approaches the Venturi constriction, its velocity increases. This represents an increase in kinetic energy. Yet it has been stated earlier that energy cannot be created. It would seem as though the law regarding the conservation of energy has failed. But, as you may have guessed, it has not.

What happens is that some of the air's pressure energy is sacrificed (or converted) into kinetic energy. In this manner, the total energy content of the air remains unchanged. This process of energy conversion is identical to what happens when air escapes from a balloon: air velocity increases and air pressure decreases. Within the Venturi tube, static air pressure is sacrificed to accelerate the airflow, resulting in reduced pressure against the inside of the Venturi tube.

It should now be easier to understand why airspeed and air pressure are so closely related and why an increase (or decrease) of one results in a decrease (or increase) of the other. This relationship between airspeed and pressure originally was expressed by Daniel Bernoulli, an eighteenth century Swiss physicist, and has come to be known as Bernoulli's Principle.

Figure 3 shows the "circulation" or airflow pattern about a wing. Notice that the wing's cambered (curved) upper surface is shaped much like the bottom half of a Venturi tube. The upper half of this imaginary tube is simply the undisturbed airflow at some distance above the wing.

Notice also what happens to the air flowing over the wing's upper surface. As it enters the constriction formed by the wing's camber, the air accelerates just the way it does when passing through a conventional Venturi tube. The result is a corresponding decrease in pressure along the upper surface of the wing.

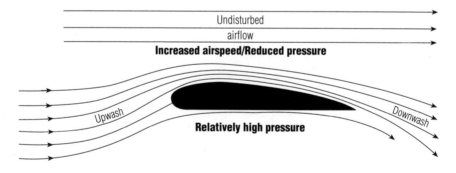

Figure 3. Airflow pattern about a wing

This reduced air pressure is frequently and erroneously called suction. Actually, the amount of pressure reduction is quite small, much less than that created by an infant suckling its mother's breast. A fully loaded Cessna 177 Cardinal, for example, has a gross weight of 2,500 pounds and a wing area of 172.4 square feet. Dividing the weight by the wing area results in the Cardinal's wing loading of 14.5 pounds per square foot. In other words, each square foot of wing is responsible for lifting 14.5 pounds of weight. Since there are 144 square inches in a square foot, it is easily determined that each square inch of wing creates only 0.1 pound, or less than 2 ounces, of lift.

It seems logical that the relatively high-pressure air beneath the wing would attempt to flow to the area of reduced pressure above the wing. After all, this is what happens in the free atmosphere; air always moves from a high to a low. But in the case of an airplane, a wing separates the regions of high and low pressure, and the wing is forced to rise into the low-pressure region above it. (Some of the relatively high-pressure air actually does curl around the wingtip in an attempt to "fill the low" created above the wing. This curling of air about the wingtip breeds that hazard known as the wingtip vortex and also is responsible for induced drag.)

The explanation of lift often ends at this point, but this still leaves the serious student far short of his destination.

Notice how the airflow in Figure 3 completes its journey across the wing. It flows not only rearward, but downward as well. This action is called downwash. Remember the lessons of Sir Isaac Newton and, more specifically, of the birds? When air (or anything else for that matter) is deflected downward, there must be an equal and opposite reaction. The reaction to downwash is, in fact, that misunderstood force called lift. If it were possible to determine and add together the vertical component of force with which each particle of air is deflected downward, the total would exactly equal the lift being created by the entire wing. Welcome to the Land of Crystal Clarity.

Once this is accepted, it should be obvious that additional lift can be created only by increasing the downwash of air behind the wing. Aerodynamicists are well aware of this fact of flight and try to get as much air above the wing as possible because all of it is ultimately directed downward from the wing's trailing edge. This is accomplished by an ingenious application of the rules already discussed.

The low (or reduced) pressure area above the wing is required because this influences the air approaching the wing's leading edge. This air is attracted to the area of reduced pressure and flows not only from in front of the wing, but also from below the wing. This increases the "mass airflow" above the wing, and therefore, the downwash behind it.

Parenthetically, there is a stagnation point on the wing's leading edge where the air seemingly can't make up its mind as to whether it should flow over or under the wing.

When the wing is flown at a large angle of attack, a more highly constricted "Venturi tube" is created. The effects of increased airspeed and reduced pressure over the wing are increased. Larger quantities of air are attracted over the wing's leading edge and, as a result, considerably more downwash is created. Lift is increased. (The reaction produced by downwash is particularly significant when you consider that each cubic yard of sea-level air weighs 2 pounds.)

When air strikes the bottom of the wing (during flight at a large angle of attack) it, too, is deflected downward and creates even more reaction and contributes to total wing lift.

This deflection of air from the bottom of the wing is particularly significant at large angles of attack and explains the flight of a kite or the planing of water skis. Air (or water) is deflected downward, causing an upward reaction. This is why it can be said truthfully that, given enough power, anything can be made to fly...including the proverbial barn door.

Anyone who doesn't believe in the tremendous forces created by hurling air downward in large quantities has only to stand beneath a hovering helicopter. The downward blast of air is precisely what occurs during fixed-wing flight.

The rotors of a helicopter create lift identically to the manner in which a fixed wing creates lift. The only significant difference is that helicopter wings rotate and create relative wind without any movement of the helicopter. Fixed wings encounter relative wind only when the airplane is in motion.

Man has learned much from the birds, but he still watches them with envy. We have more, much more, to learn.

Chapter 2 **All About Stalls**

A Golden Rule of Flight is: "Maintain thy airspeed lest the earth shall arise and smite thee."

This platitude has survived for a century of manned flight, and although it is certainly well intended, it can be grossly misleading. This is because airspeed is related only indirectly to the stall. Most pilots know that an airplane can be made to stall at any airspeed while being flown in any attitude.

A stall, we have been taught, results only from an excessive angle of attack. To relate a stall to airspeed can be as erroneous as the advice given by Daedalus to his impetuous son: "Don't fly too high, Icarus, lest the heat of the sun shall melt your waxen wings and thee shall plummet from the skies."

Figure 4 shows air flowing smoothly about a wing, caressing it fondly to produce lift. In the second case, the air (relative wind) strikes the wing at such a large angle of attack that it cannot negotiate a change in direction quickly enough to hug the wing's upper surface. Instead, the air separates from above the wing and burbles; lift is destroyed.

Air, like every other mass, has inertia and resists making sharp turns.

Consider an athlete sprinting around a race track at maximum speed. As long as the track consists of straightaways and gentle curves, he has no difficulty following the oval course. But ask the runner to make a sharp, 90-degree turn without slowing down, and we ask the impossible. There is no way it can be done without either overshooting the corner or toppling in the attempt. Airflow about a wing behaves similarly; it can make only gradual changes in direction.

The elevator controls angle of attack. With it, a pilot determines the angle at which he would like the air to meet the wings. When the control wheel (or stick) is brought aft, the angle of attack increases. With sufficient back pressure on the wheel, the angle of attack reaches a critical value, an angle at which the air can no longer "make the turn." The air is asked to perform the impossible. The result is a rebellious stall, irrespective of airspeed and attitude. (In an effort to make some aircraft "stall-proof," designers simply limit up-elevator travel.)

The purpose here is not to belabor the significance of angle of attack. This drum is beaten loudly by every flight instructor and in every training

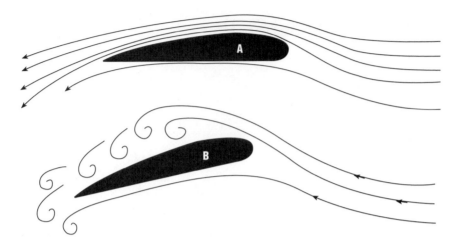

Figure 4. Lift production and lift destruction

manual. Unfortunately, these sources often drop the ball as soon as the pilot gets interested. The subject is presented like a striptease act; rarely do we get to see the whole picture.

A major problem arises when a stall is illustrated as in the second example in Figure 4. The pilot is given the impression that when a specific angle of attack is reached, the entire wing stalls. This is seemingly verified in flight when, during a practice stall, all lift seems to disappear suddenly. But this is not the way it works.

The figure is misleading because it shows only an airfoil, a narrow, cross-sectional slice of wing. It represents what occurs at a specific point along the wing, but not what happens along the entire span. In other words, the pilot sees only one small, albeit important, piece of the puzzle. He is not shown the big picture.

One of the best ways to learn the stall characteristics of an entire wing is to actually observe airflow behavior. Since this is difficult without a wind tunnel, settle for second best: a tufted wing. By attaching small strands of yarn to a wing's upper surface, the development or erosion of lift can be seen at various angles of attack.

A low-wing airplane works best. Similar tests can be conducted with a high-wing airplane, but without mirrors the pilot would have difficulty observing the tuft patterns above the wing.

Although tufting a wing is not difficult, it is simplified with the help of a volunteer. My partner during one series of stall investigation tests was NASA's Cal Pitts, who was particularly interested in observing the stall characteristics of the subject airplane, a Piper Cherokee 180.

Armed with two skeins of black yarn, a large roll of masking tape and a pair of scissors, we began the tufting process. After two hours of wrapping, taping and snipping, Cal and I stood back to admire the Cherokee's quaintly attired left wing. We couldn't help but wonder what it would be like to work for Boeing's flight test department and have to tuft the wing of a 747.

During the subsequent takeoff roll, neither of us paid much attention to the mechanics of flying; we were preoccupied watching the tufts line up with the relative wind, watching the fruits of our effort come to life.

Prior to takeoff, Pitts also attached a 10-foot strand of yarn to the right wingtip. During climbout, it whipped about like a small cyclone, describing a long cone in revolution. There it was, for all to see: a wingtip vortex. It makes a believer of you. It is one thing to read about vortices, but it is quite another to see one in action.

We began a stall series high above the smog oozing from the nearby Los Angeles basin. Throttle retarded and wings level, Pitts slowly raised the nose. With the wing flying at a relatively small angle of attack, we noticed a stall developing at the wingroot near the trailing edge. The tufts there were no longer lying flush with the wing. Instead, they had flipped forward, wriggling and writhing, reacting to the burbling, turbulent eddies of air. The airflow had separated from this area of the wing. We were witnessing the strangulation of lift.

Raising the nose farther, we could see the stall spread or propagate forward and spanwise, stealing larger and larger chunks of lift.

The stall warning came alive, and the familiar buffet was felt. With the control wheel fully aft, the Cherokee bucked lightly and the nose pitched downward.

When the wing had been flown at the maximum angle of attack, we noted that only the inboard half of the wing had stalled. During this and subsequent stalls, it was apparent that at no time did the entire wing stall.

Such a demonstration raises this question: If a stall develops progressively and the wing is always developing some lift, what causes the sudden "break" or "nose drop" associated with a stall?

The answer is only incidental to the loss of lift. In normal flight, downwash from the wing (Figure 5) strikes the upper surface of the horizontal tailplane. This action helps the elevator-stabilizer combination to produce a

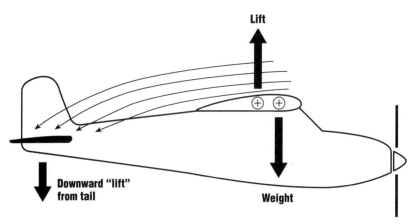

Figure 5. The effect of downwash

downward force that keeps the nose up in straight-and-level flight. Without "tailfeathers," a conventional aircraft would dive uncontrollably.

As a stall is approached, turbulent air from above the stalled portion of wing strikes the tail (and sometimes the aft fuselage). This is usually the cause of the familiar stall buffet. In other words, the wing doesn't buffet, the tail does. When enough of the wing stalls, insufficient downwash remains to keep the tail down. In a sense, the horizontal stabilizer stalls, too. This, in addition to the air striking the bottom of the stabilizer (at large angles of attack), causes the tail to rise.

As a result, the nose drops, a form of longitudinal stability that automatically assists stall recovery.

The stall pattern demonstrated by the Cherokee 180 wing is typical of a rectangular wing. Other wing shapes (Figure 6) exhibit different stall patterns. The stall of a swept wing, for example, begins at the outboard tip of the trailing edge and propagates inboard and forward.

The rectangular wing has the most ideal stall pattern (that is, an aft root stall). Such a stall provides a tail buffet to warn of an impending stall and allows the wingtips to remain flying as long as possible. This is, of course, where the ailerons are, and it is important for these controls to remain as effective as possible.

A tip stall, on the other hand, is bad news. The tailplanes are not behind the stalled portion of the wings and therefore may not provide the warning buffet. The ailerons become ineffective early in the stall and cannot be counted upon to provide roll control during flight at minimum airspeed. Also, the stabilizing effect of a nose-down pitching moment may not occur during a tip stall. A tip stall on a swept wing can be particularly hazardous because a loss of aft lift on the wing could produce a nose-up pitching moment and drive the airplane into a deeper stall.

For obvious reasons, aircraft designers go to great lengths to make certain that their aircraft exhibit optimum stall patterns that begin at or near the wingroot. Four methods are commonly used to achieve this.

Wing twist. The wings of high-wing Cessnas are twisted slightly so that the angle of attack of an inboard wing section is always larger than that of the outboard wing section. This is also called "washing out" a wing. For example, the wing twist of a Cessna 172 is 3 degrees. When the inboard section of a 172 wing is at an angle of attack of 14 degrees, the outer wing section has an angle of attack of only 11 degrees. Such a scheme forces the root to stall before the tip.

A stall strip is a narrow length of metal usually having a triangular cross section that is mounted spanwise on the leading edge of a wing. At large angles of attack, the strip interferes with airflow at the leading edge and induces a stall to form behind. In this manner, the initial stall pattern of a wing can be placed almost anywhere along the wing. A similar, but more expensive technique, is to sharpen the leading edge near the wingroot.

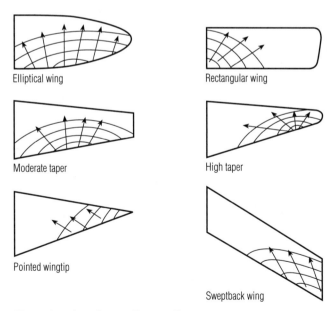

Figure 6. Wing shape affects stall pattern

Variable airfoil wings behave much like twisted wings. Such a wing incorporates two or more airfoils, an airfoil being a wing's cross-sectional shape at some given point. The airfoils are selected in such a way that those used near the wingroots have smaller stalling angles of attack than the airfoil(s) used near the tip. The result: a root stall. This sophisticated technique has been used in the design of many aircraft including the Ryan Navion and most jet transports.

Wingtip slots are expensive, which explains why they are uncommon. The Globe Swift, for example, has a moderately tapered wing that might create an unsatisfactory stall pattern were it not for the built-in wing slot on the outboard section of each wing. The slots tend to delay airflow separation behind them. Such slots delay stalling of the outboard wing sections and, as a fringe benefit, increase aileron effectiveness at low airspeed.

With the help of a tufted wing, it is possible also to observe the main difference between power-on and power-off stalls (Figure 7).

During an approach to a power-on stall, propwash flowing over the inboard wing section preserves lift in that area. Additionally, propwash helps to keep the tail flying longer.

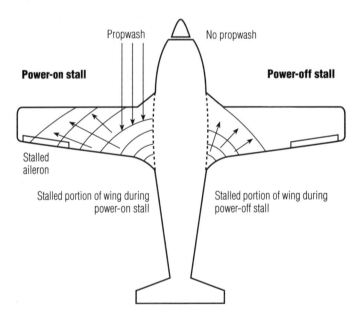

Figure 7. Effect of propwash on stall pattern

Consequently, the airplane can be forced into a deeper stall that involves considerably more wing area. So much of the wing is stalled that it is unable to provide much in the way of lateral stability. As a result, the aircraft often exhibits a surprisingly strong roll toward the wing most deeply involved in the stall, a problem that is compounded when flaps are extended.

A pilot's reaction to such an abrupt roll is to counter with opposite aileron. But since these controls may be located in the stalled portion of the wing, their deflection can have an adverse effect and actually contribute to an increased roll rate.

Without experience in a particular aircraft, it is difficult to predict which wing will drop during a full-power stall. This is because the factors causing one wing to stall before the other might consist of minute flaws on a leading edge such as a dent, a flat spot, or even a landing light.

Engine and propeller forces often cause the left wing to drop during a power-on stall, but only if both wings are identical, exactly identical—a condition rarely found on production airplanes.

Since the elevator usually is in the propwash, it is considerably more effective during an approach to a power-on stall. This, combined with the vertical component of thrust from the engine, results in the ability to force the aircraft into a deeper, more complete stall.

When the power-on stall pays off, the combined pitching and rolling moments are considerably more abrupt than during a power-off stall. The pilot must be prepared to use skillful recovery techniques and be particularly attentive to proper control usage.

Two other factors are noteworthy. During a climbing turn, the outside wing is at a slightly larger angle of attack than the inside wing. If the aircraft is stalled under these conditions, the outside (or high) wing usually stalls first, resulting in an abrupt reversal in the direction of bank. Such a maneuver is called an "over-the-top" stall. Failure to execute a timely recovery can lead to a full roll followed by a conventional spin.

During a descending turn, the converse occurs. The inside wing has the larger angle of attack. This means that if the aircraft stalls while turning and descending, the inside wing would tend to stall first, resulting in an increased bank angle. An attempt to recover using ailerons can aggravate the "under-the-bottom" stall and result in an increased bank angle and possible spin.

The difference between power-on and power-off stalls explains why stalling a conventional twin-engine airplane with a failed engine out can be so vicious. One wing is protected from an early stall by propwash from the operative engine; the wing with the inoperative engine has no such protection. When the angle of attack is increased under these conditions, only one wing stalls, and this can force the aircraft into something similar to a snap roll followed by a spin.

Quite obviously, airspeed—or the lack of it—is not the primary cause of a stall. This has been a rather involved discussion without mentioning knots or miles per hour because any airplane can be made to stall at any airspeed (as long as excessive load factors don't break the machine first).

A stall occurs for only one reason: the pilot has tried to fly the wing at too large an angle of attack. Recovery is just as simple. Reduce the angle of attack.

Chapter 3 **Stalls and Spins**

Although general-aviation accidents can be attributed to numerous causes, the single most frequent and lethal consequence of these continues to be the stall/spin accident. It occurs with distressing, predictable regularity and accounts for almost half of all fatal accidents. According to the National Transportation Safety Board, the stall/spin assassin averages a kill at least once every day. One reason for this is that the very training designed to reduce the frequency of stall/spin accidents appears to be contributing to the fatality rate.

When a student is taught stall entry and recovery, he is introduced to the apparent need for an exceptionally nose-high attitude. These empirical lessons teach that an airplane stalls only when the nose is well above the horizon. Then, usually at some later date, he is informed and expected to believe that a stall can occur with the airplane in any attitude, even when the nose is below the horizon. Some basic aerodynamics and convincing logic compel him to accept this seemingly abstract notion, but it comes across only as an intellectual exercise. The facts are stored away in a cerebral memory bank, only to be recalled when needed during some FAA examination.

Although most pilots acknowledge that stalls can and do occur with the airplane in a nose-low attitude, their training reinforces, for all practical purposes, that a stall—intentional or otherwise—is definitely a nose-high maneuver. They simply are not given an opportunity to develop an awareness based on experience that the most frequent types of stall/spin accident result from a stall that occurs with the nose pointed toward or below the horizon.

Another deficiency with current training methods is the marked contrast between stalls practiced in the training environment and those that occur under critical conditions at low altitude. While receiving stall instruction, for example, the student concentrates solely on the maneuver. And with so much excess altitude usually available, there is no sense of urgency during recovery. The pilot's attitude often is characterized by nonchalance. Also, he rarely performs such an exercise with the poor control coordination and rapid airspeed decay likely to aggravate an unintentional stall.

The FAA recently conducted an in-depth stall-awareness study. One purpose was to create scenarios of flight situations that typically account for the most common stall/spin accidents. These results are extremely valuable. If properly employed by flight instructors, they can be used to teach students the conditions during which inadvertent stall/spins really occur. Pilots can develop an awareness, based on experience (not just theory), that can go a long way toward reducing the number of lives claimed by the stall/spin accident.

Topping the list of scenarios is the cross-controlled turn from base leg to final approach, an unintentional maneuver that historically claims the most victims. Although cross-controlled turns at low altitude most commonly occur while maneuvering toward an emergency landing following an engine failure, they also are induced during conventional approaches when power is available.

Assume that an airplane is slightly low on altitude when turning from base leg to a short final approach. The pilot hesitates to roll into a sufficiently steep bank because of the low altitude, a phenomenon known as ground shyness. Instead, he subconsciously yaws the airplane onto final approach by applying bottom rudder. This excessive rudder application has the added effect of increasing bank angle and forcing the nose down. Usually without realizing it (because his attention is directed outside), the pilot counteracts this by applying opposite aileron and back pressure to the control wheel. If airspeed decay and cross-controlling are sufficient, the airplane simply enters a spin toward the low wing (an under-the-bottom spin). Because of insufficient altitude, recovery usually is impossible.

This is a good example of an incipient spin, that first phase of a spin that begins at the moment of stall and ends when the spin axis becomes vertical (or nearly so) and spin rotation has increased to the fully developed spin rate. For most light airplanes, the incipient spin takes 4 to 6 seconds and approximately two rotations.

Investigators find it difficult—and sometimes impossible—to substantiate that a given accident resulted from an incipient spin. This is because spin motion prior to impact often does not develop sufficiently to either enable an eyewitness to observe the rotation or result in a conspicuous ground-wreckage pattern. Even some who survive such a harrowing experience often do not realize that they caused their aircraft to stall and spin. One reason for this is that the airplane may not attain the nose-high attitude customarily associated with a stall entry. Also, the stall may not be characterized by the familiar stall "break" and rapid, nose-down pitching moment. Instead, airplane attitude simply may approximate level flight, during which time an excessive sink rate develops. The sequence of events can be of such short duration that a pilot has little opportunity to recognize what happened.

Although this scenario deals with a skidding turn to final approach, a cross-controlled slipping turn can be more dramatic and equally lethal.

Consider again a pilot turning from base to final. This time, however, he allows the airplane to overshoot the extended runway centerline (a frequent occurrence at high density altitudes when approach groundspeed is greater than anticipated). He executes an appropriately steep turn to realign the airplane on final approach, but fails to simultaneously apply sufficient bottom rudder (a slipping turn).

The large bank angle results in a nose-down pitching moment and an increased sink rate, which is opposed by the application of up-elevator. If the maneuver is aggravated sufficiently, the airplane is forced into an accelerated (high-speed) stall. And since the airplane is slipping at the time, it may enter a spin opposite to the direction of turn. Such an "over-the-top" spin begins with a complete roll about the airplane's longitudinal axis before evolving into a conventional spin.

Does any of this imply that pilots should receive spin training? No, not at all. Knowing how to recover from a spin at the low altitudes normally associated with stall/spin accidents allows neither the time nor the altitude necessary for extrication. What is suggested, however, is that pilots become more familiar with the conditions that historically have led to stall/spin accidents and develop the knowledge and skill needed to avoid them.

One way to accomplish this is to obtain the services of a competent instructor and practice at altitude the type of stalls generally associated with stall/spin accidents. Two of these, the slipping and skidding turns from base leg to final approach, have been discussed. Other types are described later.

Another way is to recognize that inadvertent stalls most frequently occur when the pilot is distracted from his primary role of controlling the airplane. This is why stall training should require students to perform secondary chores while maneuvering at minimum-controllable airspeed.

The effects of cross-controlling should receive heavy emphasis as well. Although every pilot recognizes that a stall must precede a spin, many do not realize that a spin usually will not develop unless the airplane is either slipping or skidding when stalled. In other words, a spin generally can be avoided by coordinating aileron-rudder application and keeping the slip-skid ball centered between the lubber lines of the instrument. If a pro-spin force is present, the ball will be "out of its cage," and the airplane will tend to spin "away from the ball." In the case of a skidding left turn, for example, the ball is to the right and the spin to the left; during a slipping left turn, the ball is left and the spin is right.

When any pro-spin force is present (due to cross-controlling, or the left-turning tendency of a single-engine airplane, for instance) the likelihood of a spin can be reduced (prior to stall) simply by "stepping on the ball" and returning it to its cage. In other words, if the ball is left, apply left rudder pressure (or right aileron pressure), and vice versa. Restoring the aircraft to a coordinated flight condition usually neutralizes the pro-spin force required for spin entry.

Once a cross-controlled airplane stalls and begins to yaw into a spin, a pilot must be prepared to avert the maneuver by lowering the nose and aggressively applying rudder to prevent the yaw associated with a spin.

One way to obtain proficiency in arresting spin development is to practice a series of oscillation stalls (with a qualified instructor, please). This consists of entering a conventional, power-off, wings-level stall. But instead of recovering, keep the control wheel fully aft and the ailerons neutral. The airplane will oscillate about all three axes and might display a tendency to spin one way and then the other. By aggressively applying rudder to counter any apparent yaw, the airplane can be kept on a relatively even keel. This is best accomplished by keeping the nose pointed at some distant reference point on the horizon.

Do not attempt power-on oscillation stalls, because many airplanes do not have sufficient rudder power to tame the wild gyrations that may develop during such a maneuver. This is why a departure stall at low altitude usually is unsurvivable, especially if sufficient right rudder (to compensate for P-factor) is not being applied as the stall occurs. The left-turning tendency has the effect of skidding the airplane into a power-on, left-hand spin.

Prior to 1949, a student pilot was required to intentionally spin an airplane to qualify for a private pilot certificate. During that era, airplanes were equal to the task. To be certificated, those airplanes had to demonstrate the ability to recover from a six-turn spin by having the test pilot do no more than release the controls.

But spin requirements have changed over the years. Modern single-engine airplanes certificated in the normal category need only be shown capable of recovering from a one-turn or three-second spin (whichever takes longer) in no more than one additional spin upon the application of normal, anti-spin control deflections. Such a requirement is regarded only as an investigation of an airplane's controllability during a delayed stall recovery and not a valid test of spin characteristics. This explains why such an airplane never should be spun intentionally. Not even the manufacturer's test pilot could advise what to expect if recovery were initiated beyond the first spin. To be blunt, a pilot should assume that airplanes placarded against intentional spins may become uncontrollable in a spin.

With respect to modern airplanes, engineers and test pilots seem to agree that the trend toward increased performance has resulted in spin characteristics less favorable than those of older, slower airplanes. And, paradoxically, the newer machines that are difficult to spin intentionally seem to be the most likely to spin inadvertently if mishandled during slow flight.

Since most modern, normal-category airplanes are considered unsafe to spin, it is unlikely that future pilot-certification requirements will reinstate spin training. Instead, emphasis will be placed where it should be, on stall awareness, recognition, and prevention.

In addition to becoming aware of and possibly practicing cross-controlled turns during slow flight (with an instructor), pilots also should become familiar with the following additional situations that result in stall/spin accidents. With a little imagination, instructors can develop these into valuable training exercises.

Go around with full nose-up trim. The pilot establishes a properly trimmed, full-flap descent while approaching a runway at the recommended airspeed. If a go-around is initiated by rapidly applying full power and partially raising the flaps, insufficient forward elevator pressure can lead to an excessively nose-high attitude and a stall, especially if the center of gravity is relatively far aft.

Go around with premature flap retraction. The airplane descends toward the runway, and a landing flare is begun at the appropriate height. After airspeed decays to less than the flaps-up stall speed (the bottom of the green arc on the airspeed indicator), the pilot finds it necessary to go around, but mishandles the procedure by fully and prematurely retracting the flaps. This can result in a full-power stall and settling toward the ground in a nose-high, behind-the-power-curve attitude.

Left-turning tendency (P-factor) during a go-around following an attempted landing into a right crosswind. While on short final approach at the proper speed and trim, the pilot enters a right slip (right wing down and left rudder) to compensate for a right crosswind. He then elects to go around, adds power and raises the nose to climb attitude. If the left-rudder deflection is not neutralized quickly enough, this yawing moment combines with the left-turning tendency produced by the propeller to generate a strong pro-spin force to the left, a particularly hazardous situation if excessive nose-up elevator has been applied.

Recovery from a high sink rate on short final approach. The airplane is in the landing configuration while being flown at only 10 percent above the flaps-down stall speed. The pilot recognizes the need to go around, but is not familiar with the large amount of additional altitude loss required to arrest the high sink rate. In his zeal to begin climbing without losing additional altitude, which usually is not possible, he rotates the nose with impatient abandon, possibly before the engine has an opportunity to react to throttle application. The most likely result is a stall.

Additional scenarios that are known to have contributed to stall/spin statistics include: becoming distracted while attempting to prevent overtaking slower aircraft in the traffic pattern; encountering wind shear, mishandling short-field takeoffs, especially at high density altitudes when the airplane is heavily loaded and departure obstacles are present; mishandling airspeed and attitude immediately following an engine failure after takeoff; and attempting to return to the airport from too low an altitude following an engine failure after takeoff.

There are essentially three ways to prevent stall/spin accidents. The first is to design a stallproof airplane, a concept that does not seem to combine very well with the requirement for high-performance aircraft.

The second is to provide the pilot with sufficient and reliable warning of an impending stall. Of the various devices available, the stall-warning light is the least effective, because most stall-spin accidents occur during daylight hours in VFR conditions, when an illuminated red light commands little attention. Aural warning devices are better, but even these lose effectiveness when a pilot is preoccupied with operational contingencies. A number of pilots who survived stall/spin accidents claim never to have heard the warning.

According to simulator studies, the most effective device is a tactile stickshaker. This was effective in alerting pilots to an impending stall 99 percent of the time (compared to the 84-percent effectiveness of an intermittent horn and 64 percent effectiveness of a steady horn). Stickshakers, however, are expensive and are not yet available for small, single-engine, propeller-driven airplanes.

In the final analysis, the best available stall/spin preventative still appears to be proficiency and awareness, goals to which all pilots should constantly aspire.

Chapter 4 **Turning and Maneuvering**

It has been said the 180-degree turn is one of aviation's most difficult maneuvers. This is because a course reversal usually is contrary to plan and forces a pilot to admit defeat in the face of adversity.

But this is a psychological reason. The maneuver itself is relatively simple. Or is it? An astonishing number of fatal accidents occur annually because many pilots apparently do not appreciate the dynamics of a turning airplane.

Figure 8 reviews two variables associated with turning flight that every student discovered while learning to fly. Unfortunately, however, many seem to have forgotten these early lessons. So it might be appropriate to review them before discussing advanced concepts.

As the angle of bank is increased during a coordinated turn, the load factor also increases, something easily sensed by the gluteus maximus. But a larger G-load causes more than temporary discomfort of the pilot's posterior. It also burdens the wings with additional "weight." At two Gs, for example, the wings must provide twice the lift required during level flight. This, in turn, requires a larger angle of attack, which increases drag and reduces airspeed (unless additional power is applied).

It is interesting to note that an increased load factor results in the same airspeed loss (or requires the same amount of additional power) as if the airplane were loaded with the equivalent excess payload while in level flight.

For example, an airplane in a 40-degree banked turn develops 1.31 Gs. The resultant airspeed loss in such a turn is the same as if the airplane were 31 percent heavier while in level flight. Similarly, the airplane's climb capability

Bank angle in coordinated turn	0°	10°	20°	30°	40°	50°	60°	70°	80°	90°
Load factor	1.0 G	1.02 Gs	1.06 Gs	1.15 Gs	1.31 Gs	1.56 Gs	2.0 Gs	2.92 Gs	5.76 Gs	infinite
Stall speed increase	0%	1%	3%	7%	14%	25%	41%	71%	140%	infinite

Note: Load factor = 1 ÷ cosine of bank angle, and stall speed increase = square root of load factor

Figure 8. Variables of turning flight

is reduced. In other words, as bank angle steepens, the airplane becomes increasingly "heavier" and its performance suffers accordingly.

The lesson here is obvious. When maximum performance is required, don't turn.

Since aircraft weight effectively increases during a turn, it is logical to assume that stall speeds also would rise—which, of course, they do.

Figure 9 illustrates the effects of varying bank angle and airspeed. Not surprisingly, rate of turn at any given airspeed increases as the bank angle steepens. But what is often not considered is that rate of turn decreases as true airspeed increases (for a given bank angle).

The effect of airspeed on turn rate is particularly distressing to pilots of the SR-71, which is probably the world's fastest airplane. When this remarkable machine is rolled into a 30-degree bank while cruising nonchalantly at 2,000 knots, the rate of turn is only 0.3 degrees per second. A 360-degree turn would take nineteen minutes, and the circle would have a diameter that stretches from Dayton, Ohio, across Indiana to Chicago, Illinois. Now that's what is meant by having to plan ahead.

Effect of True Airspeed and Bank Angle on Rate of Turn and Turn Radius

True Airspeed	Bank Angle 10°	20°	30°	40°	50°	60°	70°	80°
50 knots	3.8°/s 1,259 ft.	7.9°/s 610 ft.	12.6°/s 385 ft.	18.3°/s 265 ft.	26.0°/s 186 ft.	37.8°/s 128 ft.	60.0°/s 81 ft.	124°/s 39 ft.
100 knots	1.9°/s 5,037 ft.	4.0°/s 2,440 ft.	6.3°/s 1,538 ft.	9.2°/s 1,058 ft.	13.0°/s 745 ft.	18.9°/s 513 ft.	30.0°/s 323 ft.	61.9°/s 157 ft.
150 knots	1.3°/s 1.9 nm	2.6°/s 5,490 ft.	4.2°/s 3,461 ft.	6.1°/s 2,381 ft.	8.7°/s 1,677 ft.	12.6°/s 1,154 ft.	20.0°/s 727 ft.	41.2°/s 352 ft.
200 knots	1.0°/s 3.3 nm	2.0°/s 1.6 nm	3.1°/s 1.0 nm	4.6°/s 4,234 ft.	6.5°/s 2,981 ft.	9.4°/s 2,051 ft.	15.0°/s 1,293 ft.	30.9°/s 626 ft.
250 knots	.8°/s 5.2 nm	1.6°/s 2.5 nm	2.6°/s 1.6 nm	3.7°/s 1.1 nm	5.2°/s 4,658 ft.	7.6°/s 3,205 ft.	12.0°/s 2,020 ft.	24.8°/s 979 ft.

$$\text{Rate of turn (degrees/second)} = \frac{(1,091)\ (\text{tangent of bank angle})}{(\text{true airspeed in knots})}$$

$$\text{Turn radius} = \frac{(\text{true airspeed in knots})^2}{(11.26)\ (\text{tangent of bank angle})}$$

Figure 9. Effect of true airspeed and bank angle on rate of turn and turn radius

Although an extreme example, this indicates the need to initiate turns from base leg to final approach a little earlier when flying at unusually high approach speeds and when checking out in high-performance aircraft. Failure to plan ahead can result in either overshooting final approach or having to roll into an excessively steep turn at a dangerously low altitude, one of many causes for the infamous stall/spin accident.

Most pilots realize that a standard-rate turn is 3 degrees per second. But this is only for relatively slow airplanes. Such a turn at 500 knots, for example, would require a 54-degree (1.7 G) bank angle. That's why a standard-rate turn in subsonic, jet-powered airplanes is only 1.5 degrees per second.

The variables of turning flight give rise to an interesting problem. Assume that a pilot is flying through a very narrow canyon and has to make a minimum-radius, 180-degree turn without gaining or losing altitude. What technique should he use?

He knows that, for a given bank angle, the greatest rate of turn occurs at the slowest airspeed. He knows also that, for a given airspeed, turn radius decreases as the bank angle steepens. This suggests, therefore, that the canyon turn should be performed with a steep bank angle and minimum airspeed. But could this intrepid aviator complete the turn without stalling? Probably not.

In theory, the minimum-radius, or maximum-performance, turn is achieved by maintaining the airplane's maneuvering speed (V_A) and using the maximum possible bank angle without inducing either a stall or an excessive load factor. For aircraft certificated for 3.8 Gs (most light planes), this is about a 75-degree bank angle. The resultant maneuver is a balance between structural and aerodynamic limits. When turning with a 75-degree bank angle, the load factor would be 3.8 Gs (maximum allowable). Also, with any less airspeed or with additional bank angle, the airplane would stall. Quite obviously, this is a tricky, delicate maneuver.

Most light aircraft, however, are incapable of performing such a turn. At 3.8 Gs, the airplane effectively weighs almost four times as much as when in level flight. Tremendous power is required to maintain altitude in such a configuration, something lacking in most airplanes, especially when operating at high density altitudes. To attempt such a maximum performance maneuver when near the ground, therefore, is to flirt with disaster.

When flying an underpowered airplane, such a turn can be performed only when a pilot is willing to sacrifice altitude. (Curiously, turn radius is slightly less when climbing or descending compared to an identical turn while maintaining altitude.)

Parenthetically, when flying through a narrow valley, it is usually best to fly along the downwind side. If a turn has to be made, it will be into the wind, which decreases turn radius. Conversely, a turn away from the wind increases turn radius and requires considerably more elbow room. Also, flying along the downwind side of a valley often places an airplane in orographically rising air, which improves cruise performance.

Many airplanes lacking sufficient power for maximum-performance turns also are similarly underpowered during moderately steep turns at reduced airspeed. This is because of the increased induced drag that occurs as the angle of attack is enlarged.

Consider an airplane climbing over an obstacle at full power and reduced airspeed. If the pilot enters a 45-degree banked turn, induced drag may double; in a 60-degree banked turn, induced drag can more than triple. As a result, considerable power is required not only to climb, but simply to maintain altitude. Lacking sufficient power, the airplane descends with the throttle wide open. This sensation may not be as dramatic as a stall, but can be just as lethal. Raising the nose farther to arrest the sink rate worsens the dilemma and leads to a stall. The solution? Roll out of the turn.

Accident statistics reveal that such a stall accident most frequently occurs while departing high-elevation airports, when airplane and engine performance may be marginal.

An approach accident of this type can occur when a pilot on base leg fails to recognize that the normal indicated approach airspeed converts to a much higher true airspeed when flying into a high-elevation airport. As a result, he peripherally senses an abnormally fast approach speed through the side window and subconsciously reduces airspeed. Then, because he may still have a faster than normal groundspeed (because of the faster true airspeed), he might overshoot final approach and tighten the turn to line up with the runway. *Voila!* He has just met the admission requirements to join that elite society of flagging fliers. A missed approach isn't good for the ego, but it is much preferred to steep turns near the ground.

Stalls resulting from climbing and descending turns often wreak a unique brand of havoc: initially uncontrollable rolling moments that can lead to inverted flight and possible spinning. During a climbing, turning stall, the angle of attack of the outside wing is larger than that of the inside wing. As a result, the outside, or high wing stalls first and causes a rapid roll opposite to the direction of turn. Such an involuntary maneuver is called an "over-the-top" spin entry, which, if unchecked, results in a complete roll followed by a spin.

During a descending, turning stall, the angle of attack of the inside wing is larger than that of the outside wing. Consequently, the inside, or low wing, stalls first and simply drops lower. Less dramatic than flipping on your back, but equally as dangerous, this is known as an entry to an "under-the bottom" spin.

It must be noted that any attempt to correct either of these situations by applying "opposite" aileron control usually aggravates the crisis.

It is not easy to visualize why the outside wing in a climbing turn and the inside wing in a descending turn have larger angles of attack than their opposite wings. To understand this important concept, it is necessary to analyze the motion of an airplane about all three axes.

In a flat, skidding turn with the wings level, for example, the aircraft is only yawing. But, in a coordinated turn while maintaining altitude, the airplane is yawing and pitching. In the extreme case of a 90-degree banked turn, the airplane is only pitching. But in a normal gliding or climbing turn, the airplane is yawing, pitching, and rolling.

In a gliding turn, the airplane rolls inward, which causes the inside wing to have the larger angle of attack. Similarly, in a climbing turn, the airplane rolls outward, which causes the outside wing to have the larger angle of attack.

Here's another way to look at it. During the descending turn, the inside wing is turning on a smaller radius, which means it is descending in a steeper spiral than the outside wing. The air, therefore, must "rise" to meet the inside wing at a larger angle (of attack) than it does the outside wing. Similar logic explains why the outside wing has a larger angle of attack during climbing turns.

When an airplane is made to stall while turning and maintaining altitude, the bank angle should not change one way or the other. The exception occurs when one wing stalls before the other, because both wings are not physically symmetrical.

The effect that wind has on turning flight during ground-track maneuvers is not always appreciated. (Remember, flying a rectangular traffic pattern is a ground-track maneuver).

For example, assume that a pilot is attempting to fly a perfect circle around a pylon. Unfortunately, a strong northerly wind is doing its best to foil the pilot's plans. To fly a perfect circle during such a condition, the pilot must vary bank angle during the 360-degree turn. At what part of the circle should the turn be the steepest? Where should it be the shallowest?

Most pilots believe that the steepest bank angle is required at the southerly part of the circle to prevent the northerly wind from blowing the aircraft away from the circular ground track. Similarly, the logic continues, the shallowest bank angle is needed on the northerly side to prevent drifting into the circle. This sounds logical, but is wrong.

Figure 10 shows a 100-knot airplane flying counterclockwise about a pylon: a 20-knot breeze is blowing from the north. During no-wind conditions, a constant, 40-degree banked turn would result in a circle with a radius of 1,058 feet. But because of the northerly wind, in this case, the bank angle must vary, as shown in the diagram.

Notice that the steepest bank is required when flying downwind along the western edge of the circle, not at the southern edge. This is because the steepest bank is required when groundspeed is at a maximum. The airplane is flying so rapidly that the rate of turn must be increased to remain on track.

Similarly, the shallowest bank is required when flying upwind on the eastern side of the circle, not when flying crosswind at the northern edge. Groundspeed here is at a minimum. The airplane is flying so slowly that more time is available to turn a given number of degrees. Hence, a shallow bank angle must be used.

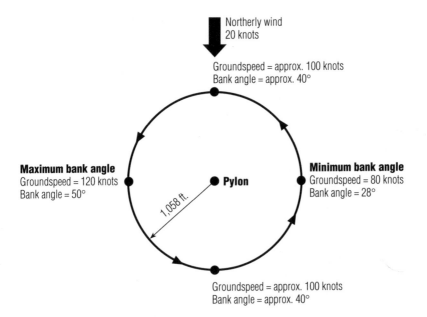

Figure 10. Bank angle varies with groundspeed and wind direction

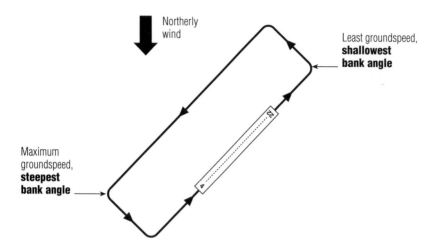

Figure 11. Bank angles vary in the traffic pattern

The same logic applies when flying the traffic pattern. Notice in Figure 11 that, because of a northerly wind, the turn from downwind to base leg results in the highest groundspeed and therefore requires the steepest bank angle (assuming that airspeed is held constant around the pattern). Similarly, turning onto the crosswind leg (after takeoff) results in the lowest ground-speed and suggests a shallower bank angle.

As we have seen, there are numerous circumstances calling for executing steeper-than-anticipated turns while at low altitude. Unless a pilot is very adept at such maneuvering and has a sufficiently powerful engine, such turning can be foolhardy indeed.

It is doubtful that there lives a pilot who has not lost altitude inadvert-ently while practicing steep turns. At altitude, this is not a serious problem. But when near the ground, there may not be sufficient time to apply the proper corrections.

Instructors teach three basic ways to arrest an undesirable sink rate dur-ing a steep turn. One way is to raise the nose; another is to add power. If neither of these corrections is adequate, the third alternative is to decrease bank angle and raise the nose, or roll out of the turn entirely.

Unfortunately, rolling out of a turn to arrest an increasing sink rate usually is regarded as a sign of failure, an inability to control the aircraft. But when operating an airplane at the limits of its performance capability, rolling out of a steep turn can be the only safe way to maintain a healthy reserve of airspeed and power. If a steep turn gets out of hand, it is far wiser to recognize the limitations of plane and pilot than to horse back on the yoke and risk stalling or creating enough of a G-load to warp a wing. Rolling out of an undesirable situation is a safe, professional technique that allows the turn to be repeated at the pilot's leisure; stalling at low altitude might not allow this luxury.

Since prevention is preferable to cure, learn to recognize and avoid situations that induce an apparent need to turn sharply.

Chapter 5 **That Shifting Center of Gravity**

When Lindbergh guided the Spirit of St. Louis across the Atlantic in 1927, he endured many hours of monotony. Some of these were spent contemplating trivial aspects of the flight. At one point, for example, he calculated that his nine-cylinder, Wright Whirlwind engine would have to produce 15 million power strokes during the 33½-hour flight from Roosevelt Field on Long Island, NY, to LeBourget Airport in Paris, France. This staggering figure, he admitted later, gave him cause for concern. After all, how could any engine endure so many punishing "explosions" without failing?

On a lighter note, Lindbergh observed a stowaway housefly aboard his Ryan monoplane. He knew that when the fly was at rest, it added infinitesimally to the payload. But what about when the fly was winging about the cabin? When the housefly supports its own weight, does this relieve the aircraft of having to support the load?

"If this is so," Lindbergh mused, "then perhaps I should not allow the fly to rest and needlessly burden the Spirit of St. Louis." Lindbergh knew, however, that it made no difference whether the fly was airborne or at rest on the instrument panel. When flying, the insect's wing deflected air downward. Eventually, this minute quantity of air pressed against the cockpit floor with a force equal to the weight of the fly. The only way to eliminate such a "load" was to eject the stowaway bug through an open window.

A few years ago, the Lufthansa Airline magazine, *Jet Tales* posed a similar problem: "If a Lufthansa 747 freighter is loaded with 50 tons of live doves, and if all of these birds were to fly around in their containers at the same time, would the jumbo jet lose 50 tons of weight?"

Obviously not. There would be, however, a record number of midair collisions and busted beaks.

This problem leads to another. If all of the birds were to suddenly fly from the floor to the ceiling, would this have any effect on the jumbo's center of gravity? Absolutely.

Assume that the dove-loaded aircraft is cruising at 41,000 feet and all the birds are at rest. When the birds fly toward the ceiling, the center of gravity, or CG, is displaced vertically to a higher location in the aircraft. The new CG could, for example, be 10 feet above the original CG. Now, would this have any effect on the 747's flight path?

It may not be immediately obvious, but fifty tons of cargo rising to the ceiling causes the aircraft to lose as much altitude as is gained by the center of gravity (10 feet, in this case). Everything else being equal, it is the center of gravity that maintains a constant altitude, not the aircraft. If this were not so, then a drowning swimmer could lift himself out of the water by pulling up on his own hair.

When the birds tire of such folly and return to the cabin floor, the CG returns to its original location, and the aircraft gains the altitude previously lost.

It also is interesting to note that the three motions of an airplane— pitch, roll, and yaw—all take place about the center of gravity. In other words, when the CG changes location, so does the airplane's aerodynamic pivot point.

Most pilots are not particularly concerned about the center of gravity's vertical movement, but they do (or should) regard seriously its longitudinal (fore and aft) travel. When CG limits are violated, both plane and pilot may be in jeopardy. But even when specified limits are observed, the location of the CG can significantly alter performance.

For example, does an airplane fly faster with an aft CG, a forward CG, or does this have no effect on airspeed? Initially, the answer seems illogical, but once understood, it provides some insight as to the effects of CG movement.

If the average pilot were to guess, he might suggest that CG location has no effect on airspeed. He would be wrong. Next, he might speculate that a forward CG would improve performance because it would help to keep the

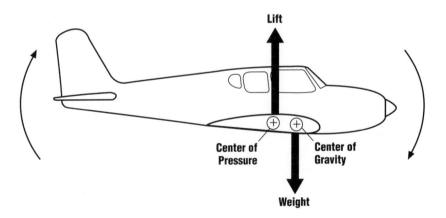

Figure 12. Relative positions of lift and weight

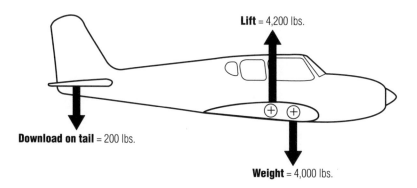

Figure 13. The horizontal stabilizer produces "negative lift"

nose down. An aft CG, he might reason, would cause the tail to sag, resulting in a nose-high attitude and mushing flight. Wrong again. Generally speaking, an aft CG results in the highest airspeed; a forward CG reduces airspeed.

Figure 12 shows a 4,000-pound airplane in cruise flight at a constant airspeed. Notice that the center of gravity is forward of the center of pressure, a theoretical point at which all wing lift appears to be concentrated. For most light airplanes, this is the normal relationship between lift and weight.

If wing lift and gross weight were the only vertical forces present, the airplane would have an overwhelming urge to pitch earthward.

Figure 13 introduces another factor: the horizontal stabilizer. This surface is called upon to produce "negative lift," a downward force on the tail that prevents the nose from pitching down. The wing, therefore, must not only overcome aircraft weight, it also must generate enough additional lift to offset the downward force on the tail. To maintain equilibrium in this case, wing lift must equal the sum of aircraft weight (4,000 pounds) plus the negative tail load (200 pounds, for example), a total of 4,200 pounds.

Figure 14 shows the same airplane after the center of gravity has been moved aft to a point vertically aligned with the center of lift. Since lift and weight are in balance, a download on the tail is unnecessary. As a result, the wing needs to produce only 4,000 pounds of lift compared to 4,200 pounds when the center of gravity was forward.

Since the wing does not need to produce as much lift when the center of gravity is aft, it is flown at a smaller angle of attack As a result, drag is reduced and airspeed increases. Or, the same airspeed can be maintained at a reduced power setting.

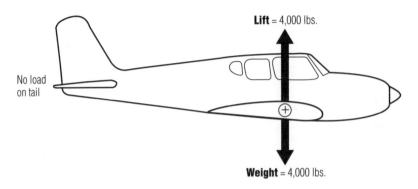

Figure 14. Elimination of tail load when center of gravity is aligned with center of lift

When speed is important, a few knots can often be gained with aft loading. By placing heavier baggage and passengers as far rearward as is legal and practical, tail loading is reduced, which allows the wing to be flown at a smaller angle of attack Several air carriers use this technique on cargo flights. Aft loading saves considerable fuel (and increases range) because cruise speed is achieved with slightly reduced thrust.

When operating some aircraft, a similar result can be achieved by burning fuel from forward tanks. As the flight progresses, the center of gravity gradually moves aft and a slight increase in airspeed can be detected.

Since the wing carries "less weight" when the center of gravity is aft, it might be concluded that stall speeds are reduced at such a time. That's true. And, as the center of gravity moves forward, stall speeds increase.

At least one major airframe manufacturer has been known to take advantage of this little-known fact. Stall speeds shown in its operating handbooks often are valid only for when the center of gravity is at the extreme aft limit. At other times, when the CG is more normal, stall speeds are greater. This, however, cannot be found anywhere in the pilot's handbook. Very sneaky!

It is beneficial, therefore, to fly with an aft center of gravity. But it is possible to have too much of a good thing.

Figure 15 shows an airplane with its center of gravity behind the center of lift. To keep such an airplane in balance, it is necessary for the horizontal stabilizer to develop positive lift. This takes even more load off the wing, which further decreases the required angle of attack and reduces wing drag. But there's a catch. Since the stabilizer is generating lift, it also must create additional drag. As a result, very little may be gained.

In terms of performance, therefore, the best place for the center of gravity is at or very close to the center of lift. The stabilizer is unloaded (with no induced drag of its own), and the wing carries only the airplane's gross weight.

Most of the time, however, the center of gravity is forward of the center of lift, requiring the horizontal stabilizer to produce a balancing and inefficient (in terms of performance) download.

One way to resolve this problem is to move the horizontal stabilizer from the tail to the nose of the airplane. When configured in such a manner, the horizontal stabilizer becomes a small, auxiliary wing because it is called upon—like the main wing—to produce positive lift, a necessity if the airplane is to be kept in balance. This configuration is referred to as a canard airplane, and the forward-located horizontal stabilizer is called a canard surface.

There is nothing new about a canard; it has been applied to various airplane designs for almost a century (beginning with the Wright Flyer). Although the canard surface generally is more efficient than a conventional horizontal stabilizer, inherent difficulties with longitudinal stability have inhibited popularization of the concept. Interest in the canard, however, has been revitalized in recent years. Burt Rutan's revolutionary designs seem to have overcome the canard's critical design aspects.

But those of us who fly with conventional tail surfaces must compensate as much as possible by maintaining an aft center of gravity.

There is nothing wrong with an aft center of gravity as long as it is kept within limits designated by the airframe manufacturer. Violating an aft CG limit, however, can result in an unacceptable decrease in longitudinal (pitch) stability, something far more dangerous than most pilots understand.

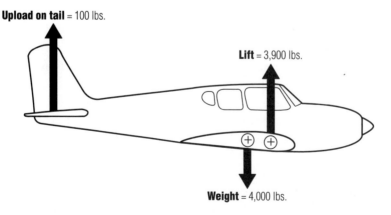

Upload on tail = 100 lbs.

Lift = 3,900 lbs.

Weight = 4,000 lbs.

Figure 15. Effect on tail load when center of gravity is behind center of lift

Simply stated, longitudinal stability is the ability of an airplane to return to its trimmed angle of attack (or airspeed) if disturbed from that angle of attack (or airspeed).

Many forces created by an airplane contribute to longitudinal stability, but the horizontal stabilizer generally is the most influential. In a crude manner of speaking, an airplane's tailfeathers really are like feathers, the feathers of an arrow. Without them, a conventional airplane would wallow and wobble uncontrollably.

The stabilizing role of the horizontal tailfeathers can be appreciated by visualizing an airplane flying steadily at a given angle of attack. Suddenly the plane is assaulted by an updraft, which momentarily increases that angle of attack. The stabilizer also would be flying at a larger and possibly positive angle of attack. As a result, the tail would temporarily create more lift (or less download). Since the horizontal stabilizer is situated way behind the center of gravity, this forces the nose to pitch down, tending to return the aircraft to its original angle of attack. This is longitudinal stability.

Like a wing, the horizontal stabilizer performs only when supplied with a healthy diet of airspeed. Reduce that life-supporting flow of air across the tail, and the forces produced by the stabilizer can change dramatically.

Consider the balanced aircraft as shown in Figure 13. The forces are aligned normally, and the engine is developing cruise power. Propwash flowing across the tail, therefore, is helping the stabilizer to do its job: create negative lift.

Assume now that the pilot suddenly retards the throttle. The amount of propwash flowing across the horizontal stabilizer decreases, which causes a decrease in the negative lift produced by this tail surface. In other words, the download produced by the tail is reduced. As a result, the nose drops.

Conversely, when power is added, the negative lift produced by the stabilizer increases, and the aircraft nose rises. (Other factors also are responsible for these pitching reactions to power changes, but the action of the stabilizer usually is most influential.)

Now consider the potentially critical situation shown in Figure 15. The center of gravity has been shifted beyond its aft limit to a point behind the center of lift. To maintain balance, the horizontal stabilizer obviously must produce upward lift.

If power is reduced at such a time, the horizontal stabilizer receives less propwash and is unable to produce as much lift, and the tail descends. Imagine such a situation! Retard the throttle and the nose goes up.

Perhaps the converse would be even more disastrous. By applying power (such as during a missed approach), the nose would plunge earthward. (The lofty horizontal stabilizers of some T-tailed aircraft are above the propwash and do not react as abruptly to power changes.)

The trend is clear: as the center of gravity moves aft, longitudinal stability decreases. Eventually, instability sets in. Flying such a machine would be a fatiguing, full-time, dangerous operation. This is why airplanes have center of gravity limits that must be strictly observed.

Additional problems created by an excessively aft CG include potentially violent stall characteristics, a tendency for normal spins to develop into flat spins (from which recovery may not be possible), and a reduction of control wheel forces that make it easier for a pilot to overcontrol and overstress the airplane.

On the other hand, an excessively forward center of gravity introduces another set of adverse flight characteristics. These include faster stalling speeds, decreased performance, and excessive longitudinal stability that increases the control wheel forces required to control pitch. So much up-elevator may be required to maintain equilibrium that there may not be enough left over to safely flare during landing. This can result in an overly stressed nosewheel or prevent a taildragger from making a three-point landing (which is why you should not solo a Piper J-3 Cub from the front seat).

Since the vertical and longitudinal shifting of the CG have been considered, it would be unfair not to at least mention lateral movement of the center of gravity.

If fuel is improperly managed and is consumed unevenly from wing or tip tanks, it is possible to notice a lateral shift of the CG by the tendency of one wing to fly lower than the other.

Can this affect performance? Yes, because having to continuously deflect the ailerons (with or without trim) creates unnecessary drag. In extreme cases, so much aileron might be required to hold up a heavy wing that insufficient roll control may be left to counter a strong crosswind during landing.

While it might be nit-picking to consider the weight of a housefly or the effect of doves hovering in the cockpit, an improperly located center of gravity could have serious consequences.

Chapter 6 **Flying Behind the Power Curve**

The unsuspecting hero of this tale was on final approach to a critically short mountain strip. Since this pilot had had recent experience with power-on, drag-'em-in, short-field landings, he wasn't particularly concerned about the successful outcome of this one.

The airspeed was a steady 65 knots, comfortably above the 51-knot stall speed. A half mile from the approach end of the runway, the pilot sensed he was a mite low and raised the nose gingerly. But alas, the sink rate increased, and the airspeed slipped to 60. Power was added. More back pressure, but the sink rate increased and the airspeed fell further. More power. 56 knots! Desperately, the pilot shoved the throttle to the firewall, but not in time.

The aircraft thudded to earth just short of the runway, resulting in a damaged left main landing-gear assembly and a blown right tire. A perplexed pilot stumbled out of his crippled craft wondering what mystical force had pulled him from the sky.

The insidious culprit responsible for this type of accident is not well understood by many general aviation pilots, as I learned while teaching at a flight instructor revalidation clinic. More often than not, when a pilot "falls" from flight on the back side of the power curve, he attributes the experience to a nonexistent downdraft or an inadvertent stall entry, neither of which is responsible.

Before the "back side of the power curve" can be easily understood, the two types of aerodynamic drag should be reviewed. The first, parasite drag, is familiar to all pilots and is simply the air resistance created by an object as it moves through the air. Parasite drag is the force that tries to break your arm when extended through the open window of a speeding automobile. The greater the speed, the more forceful the drag. Actually, parasite drag increases in proportion to the square of airspeed—that is, if airspeed doubles, parasite drag quadruples.

Figure 16 shows the relationship of parasite drag and airspeed. At relatively low speeds parasite drag is nominal; at higher speeds, it becomes increasingly influential. To maintain a constant airspeed in level flight, thrust must equal drag. It should be obvious, therefore, that doubling aircraft speed quadruples parasite drag and requires not twice as much thrust, but rather, about four times the thrust required at the lower cruising speed.

Parasite drag, however, is a relatively unimportant character in this story. The plot thickens when induced drag sneaks into the act. Unfortunately, induced drag is either ignored or scantily explained in many basic textbooks, yet it plays a leading role in slow flight.

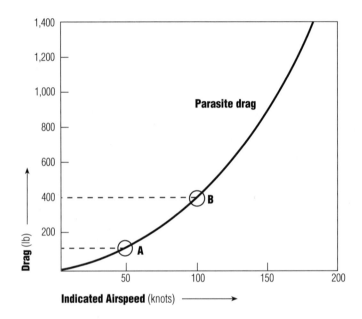

Figure 16. Indicated airspeed vs. parasite drag

Figure 17 shows a wing flying (mushing) at a large angle of attack and relatively low airspeed. As the free air stream approaches from in front of the wing, it deflects downward somewhat. Consequently, the average relative wind "felt" by the wing results in a smaller angle of attack than might otherwise be imagined. Since lift always acts 90 degrees to the average relative wind and not the remote free air stream, it is easily seen that the total lift generated by the wing acts slightly rearward. The vertical or effective component of lift supports aircraft weight. The horizontal component of lift acts rearward and retards forward progress. This rearward force is induced drag, an unavoidable byproduct of lift.

Induced drag is most influential at large angles of attack and low airspeeds; it is minimal in high-speed flight. Figure 18 illustrates how induced drag varies with airspeed at a constant altitude. Notice that induced drag is at a maximum when parasite drag is at a minimum, and vice versa.

Induced drag varies inversely with the square of airspeed. When airspeed is halved, induced drag quadruples; when airspeed doubles, all but one-fourth of induced drag disappears. This behavior is opposite to that of parasite drag. It is worth remembering that induced drag predominates in slow flight and parasite drag predominates in cruise.

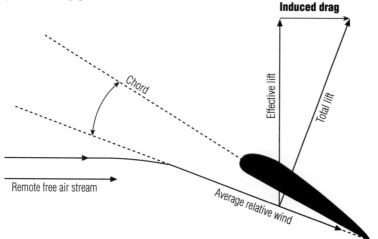

Figure 17. Induced drag resulting from a high angle of attack and low airspeed

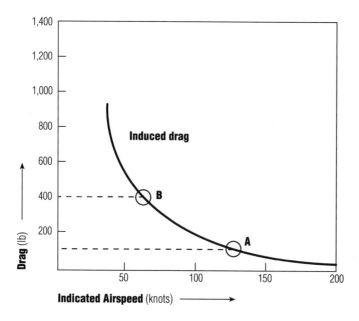

Figure 18. Indicated airspeed vs. induced drag

It is the combination of parasite and induced drag that determines the total drag acting on an airplane at any given indicated airspeed and the amount of thrust required to overcome it.

The heavily curved line of Figure 19 represents the combined effect of induced and parasite drag for a fictitious general aviation aircraft at a given gross weight. This "total drag" curve is obtained by geometrically adding the parasite and induced drag curves.

Notice that considerable drag exists during slow flight. This is the effect of induced drag. At high speeds, parasite drag predominates. In Figure 19, the bottom of the curve (point A) is the speed (80 knots) at which total drag is at a minimum. It is interesting to note that minimum drag occurs at the speed where induced and parasite drag are equal. The total drag at this speed is 500 pounds. Since thrust must equal drag in level flight, the required thrust at 80 knots is also 500 pounds. At lower speeds, additional thrust is required to offset the increased induced drag. Extra thrust is required to maintain altitude during slow flight. Above 80 knots, thrust requirements again increase because additional thrust is required to overcome the rapidly increasing effect of parasite drag.

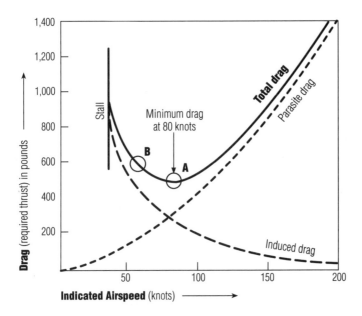

Figure 19. Indicated airspeed vs. total drag

The minimum-drag speed is of more than esoteric interest. It is at this indicated airspeed that an airplane flies most efficiently; this is the speed—the only speed—at which the lift/drag ratio of the airplane is at a maximum. Gliding at this speed, for example, results in the flattest or most efficient glide. In other words, this is the airspeed at which an airplane glides the farthest for every foot of altitude lost. To glide at any other airspeed—faster or slower—results in a steeper descent profile. Cruising at the minimum-drag speed may be a time-consuming affair, but this is the way to achieve maximum range and get the most mileage from every gallon of fuel. In other words, a pilot running low on fuel can increase the likelihood of reaching an airport by cruising at an indicated airspeed that is approximately the same as the optimum glide speed, a nifty rule of thumb to keep handy.

Technically, the minimum-drag speed varies slightly with gross weight, but for most light aircraft this variation can be ignored.

A drag curve offers other vital information. The speed at which induced drag is three times as great as parasite drag is the speed to use when a pilot is not anxious to get anywhere and simply desires to remain aloft as long as possible.

Referring again to Figure 19, for example, it can be seen that at point B (60 knots), induced drag is three times as great as parasite drag (75 percent of the total drag). This point usually occurs at a speed equal to approximately 75 percent of the minimum-drag speed. By cruising at this relatively low indicated airspeed, a pilot can remain airborne for the longest period of time. This is called "endurance flying" and should be performed at as low an altitude as is practicable. This is the optimum speed to use when a pilot is assigned to the rigors of a holding pattern, or whenever he wishes to remain aloft over a given area and is not concerned about getting anywhere. Hourly fuel consumption is at a minimum.

Power off, this same speed results in a minimum-sink glide (that is, the rate of descent is at a minimum), a maneuver used when a pilot needs to descend as slowly as possible and is not concerned about "stretching" his glide.

If a pilot knows only the optimum gliding speed for an airplane, then he also knows a good deal more. An airplane with a 90-knot glide speed, for instance, should be flown at approximately the same indicated airspeed to achieve maximum range. For maximum endurance or minimum sink, the aircraft should be flown at approximately 75 percent of the glide speed, which in this case is an indicated airspeed of 68 knots.

A drag curve can be called a thrust curve because drag and thrust are equal while a constant airspeed and altitude are maintained.

Once the drag curve is understood, it becomes easier to comprehend the significance of a power curve. Although drag (thrust) and power curves seem identical, they are not. A fallacy arises when thrust and power are equated; they are not the same. Thrust is simply a force created by the propeller and is used to overcome drag. On the other hand, power is a measure of work performed by an engine. Simply stated, an engine works by turning a propeller, which in turn exerts a force by accelerating air rearward.

The power curve in Figure 20 shows the amount of power (not thrust) needed to maintain any indicated airspeed at a constant altitude. Notice that for flying on the front side of the power curve (in the "region of normal command"), increased speed requires increased power. Nothing unusual about that. But notice what happens on the back side of the power curve (in the "region of reversed command"). Increased power is required to maintain altitude at progressively lower speeds. At first blush, it seems illogical to suggest that it takes increased power to fly more slowly, but it does. Such is the effect of induced drag, and this explains why STOL (short takeoff and landing) aircraft need so much power—to fly slowly.

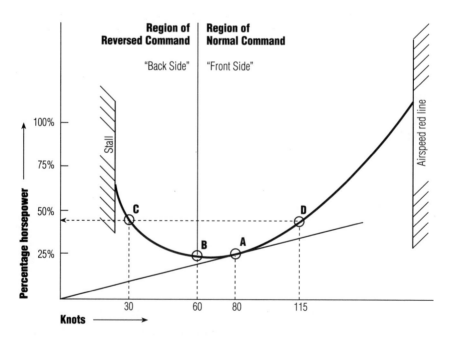

Figure 20. Indicated airspeed vs. power

Additionally, notice that as much power is required to fly at 30 knots (point C) as to maintain 115 knots (point D). For each speed on the back side of the power curve, there is a corresponding speed on the front side that requires just as much power.

Point B (the speed for maximum endurance and minimum sink) and point A (speed for optimum glide and maximum range) correspond to points B and A on the drag curve in Figure 19. Point B is always the low point on a power curve and represents the speed at which power and hourly fuel consumption are at a minimum. Point A is located by drawing a line from the origin (the zero-zero point on the chart) so that it is tangent to (barely touches) the power curve. Notice that flying at 80 knots requires slightly more power than flying at 60 knots, but the speed increase (20 knots) is considerable when compared with the slight additional power required. This explains why point A represents the speed for maximum range. At this speed, an airplane flies farther per gallon than at any other indicated airspeed.

It is important to recognize the differences in aircraft behavior when flying on one side of the power curve and the other. Only a proper understanding of these differences can help to prevent the anxiety and the resulting accident described at the beginning of this story.

Figure 21 is a typical power curve. Assume the airplane is flying at a constant altitude and is trimmed to maintain 120 knots (point M). The engine is turning at 2,200 rpm. The pilot momentarily applies slight forward pressure on the wheel, and the airspeed increases temporarily to 130 knots (point N). To maintain this higher airspeed without sacrificing altitude, power must be increased. Otherwise, the aircraft will decelerate—on its own—to 120 knots, the original trimmed airspeed.

Conversely, if the pilot raises the nose while at the trimmed airspeed, the aircraft will decelerate to 110 knots (point P). This lower speed requires less power, but since the throttle hasn't been touched, the aircraft will accelerate—on its own—to the original 120 knots.

When flying on the front side of the power curve, an aircraft has "speed stability." When airspeed fluctuates, an airplane tends to return to its original trimmed airspeed as long as the power setting remains unchanged.

But aircraft behavior changes somewhat when the plane flies in the region of reversed command.

Assume the aircraft is mushing on the back side of the power curve at 70 knots (point X in Figure 21). The throttle is set to the required power setting (2,100 rpm), and the aircraft is trimmed for hands-off flight.

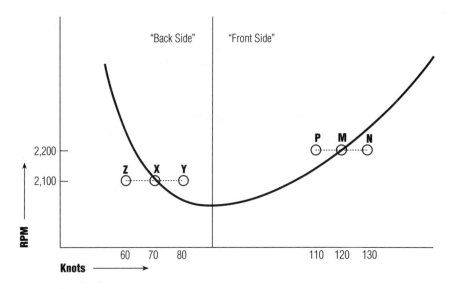

Figure 21. Flying in the regions of reverse and normal command

Now assume the nose dips temporarily, and the airspeed increases to 80 knots (point Y). To maintain this higher airspeed, less power is required. Unless the throttle is retarded, the airplane will be flown with a slight excess of power. The result of excess power is a climb.

It may seem confusing that lowering the nose causes an airplane to climb, but that is the way things work on the back side of the power curve. There is nothing serious about this. No one objects to a bit of extra altitude. But suppose the opposite were to occur.

A pilot is on a flat approach to a short field. The airplane is hanging on the prop with an airspeed of 70 knots (point X), requiring 2,100 rpm. During the approach, the pilot senses he is a bit low on altitude and raises the nose slightly to arrest the sink rate. The airspeed slips to 60 knots (point Z). Because of additional induced drag at this lower airspeed, additional power is required. Otherwise, at 60 knots, the airplane is flying with a power deficiency. Instead of decreasing the sink rate, the hapless pilot has unwittingly increased the sink rate by raising the nose. Further back pressure only aggravates the problem and causes a steeper descent. The only solution is to add power and, if necessary, lower the nose to increase airspeed and reduce the sink rate.

It seems paradoxical that raising the nose causes a descent and lowering the nose produces a climb, but such is aircraft behavior when flying behind the power curve. At higher speed, altitude can be controlled by varying pitch, but not at slow speeds. This points out and reemphasizes the importance of controlling altitude with power and airspeed with pitch, especially during a landing approach.

To fully appreciate the idiosyncrasies of flying in the region of reversed command, the interested pilot should fly there in his own airplane at a reasonably safe altitude. If he desires, he can also construct a power curve for his aircraft and determine the significant airspeeds discussed earlier.

While in cruise flight at constant altitude, jot down the observed airspeed and power setting. Then reduce airspeed in increments of 10 knots and record the power setting required to maintain each lower speed.

Finally a point is reached where increases of power are required to maintain altitude at progressively lower airspeeds. The speed at which minimum power is required is the entrance to the region of reversed command. At lower speeds, notice how power requirements increase.

After the data has been recorded, choose a speed halfway between stall and minimum power. While maintaining altitude, trim the ship to establish and hold this speed. Give the wheel a gentle backward nudge and let go. As the airspeed begins to fall, watch the sink rate develop. (A nose-up gust can produce the same results.) Next, nudge the nose down and observe the sink rate flatten. Repeat this procedure, varying power to prevent climbs and descents. This exercise provides excellent insight into aircraft behavior when flying behind the power curve.

Next, lower gear and flaps and plot another power chart while maintaining a constant altitude. This chart is useful in determining "backside" characteristics in the approach configuration.

Familiarity with the region of reversed command and a review of basic flying techniques can help to prevent a pilot from landing on his back side—of the power curve. And that can be a real drag.

Section 2

Proficiency and Technique

The goal of every pilot should be to develop proficiency far beyond that required by the FAA and knowledge far beyond that found in conventional textbooks. These nine chapters delve deeply into important subject areas that usually are not covered during flight training and can enhance the safety of any flight.

Chapter 7 **Everything You Need to Know About Climbing Flight**

For unscrupulous characters, it's not how you climb to the top that's important... as long as you get there.

For scrupulous pilots, however, it is precisely how you make the climb that is so important.

Often, climbing is regarded as a necessary evil, a slow-flight maneuver to be tolerated until the euphoria of cruise flight is attained. Usually, a pilot simply pulls back on the yoke and patiently awaits the top of climb. He rarely considers the available techniques and knowledge that not only can increase the efficiency of flight, but also the longevity of engine and pilot.

There are various climb techniques, each satisfying a specific need. But before these can be explored, it would be helpful to understand some underlying principles.

Figure 22 shows the relationship between the climb rate and airspeed of a typical lightplane being flown at maximum power. Notice that at 180 knots, the aircraft is neither climbing nor descending. This is the maximum possible cruise speed (for a given altitude) and requires all available power. When flying faster than 180 knots, the aircraft is in a dive and the climb rate is negative.

Similarly, at 40 knots the aircraft is maintaining a constant altitude. The angle of attack is so large and results in so much drag that—even with full power—the aircraft is unable to climb. Below 40 knots, the aircraft may actually descend prior to stalling.

Flight between 40 and 180 knots, in this case, results in a positive climb rate. This is because more power is available than is required to maintain any of these intermediate airspeeds while at a constant altitude. The excess horsepower, of course, produces a climb.

Inspection of the climb curve reveals that the maximum-possible climb rate of 1,000 fpm occurs at only one airspeed—100 knots. This is known as the best-rate-of-climb airspeed or, more simply, V_Y. It is at this indicated airspeed that minimum power is required to maintain altitude; a maximum excess of horsepower, therefore, is available to produce the maximum rate of climb.

It is important to note that a climb at any other airspeed results in a reduced climb rate. Pulling the nose higher and decelerating to less than V_Y

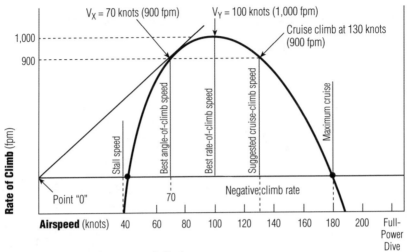

Figure 22. Airspeed vs. rate of climb

may result in temporary "ballooning," but the long-term result is diminished climb performance brought about by the increased drag at the larger angle of attack. Conversely, an increase in airspeed to above V_Y increases drag and decreases climb rate.

The climb curve also provides the best-angle-of-climb airspeed, or V_X. This is found by plotting a straight line from the origin of the graph (point 0) so that it barely touches (or is tangent to) the climb curve. This point of tangency with the curve reveals V_X, which, in this case, is 70 knots. When climbing at V_X, the climb angle is at a maximum, even though the rate of climb is only 900 fpm. This is an often confusing aspect of climb performance that is clarified in Figure 23.

Notice that when Aircraft A is climbing at V_Y (100 knots), it gains 1,000 feet in one minute. Simultaneously, it flies 1.67 nautical miles forward. In other words, the airplane gains 599 feet of altitude during each mile of flight. (The actual climb angle is 5.6 degrees.)

Aircraft B, however, is climbing at V_X, or 70 knots, and has a reduced climb rate of only 900 fpm. At the end of one minute, this aircraft has gained 900 feet while covering a horizontal distance of only 1.17 nautical miles. This is equivalent to an altitude gain of 771 feet per nautical mile of forward flight. In other words, this aircraft is climbing more steeply (at an angle of 7.2 degrees) even though its rate of climb is less.

The best-angle-of-climb airspeed (V_X) is used when trying to overfly an obstacle, when it is necessary to gain the maximum altitude in the minimum distance.

The best-rate-of-climb airspeed (V_Y) is used when it is desirable to gain the maximum altitude in the minimum time.

Fortunately, V_X and V_Y are usually specified in the pilot's operating handbook. However, these critical airspeeds vary with gross weight and altitude, factors that often are not taken into consideration, especially in older handbooks.

For example, consider a Cessna 310R. At maximum gross weight and while flying at sea level, V_Y is 107 knots. Elevate the aircraft to 20,000 feet and V_Y decreases to 91 knots. Reduce the gross weight by 800 pounds and V_Y drops another 6 knots to 85 knots. This represents a substantial 22-knot difference between one V_Y and the other. Unless indicated airspeed is appropriately adjusted for variations in weight and altitude, climb performance can suffer dramatically.

Fortunately, there are some reliable rules of thumb that can be used to approximately determine V_Y at various gross weights and attitudes. Even when the variability of V_Y is presented in operating handbooks, the following rules often are easier to use and more immediately accessible.

With respect to weight corrections only, V_Y and V_X each decrease about one knot for each 100 pounds less than maximum-allowable gross weight. An aircraft that grosses at 3,800 pounds with a best-rate-of-climb airspeed of 91 knots, for example, has an adjusted V_Y of 86 knots when loaded to only 3,300 pounds (500 pounds represents a 5-knot V_Y correction).

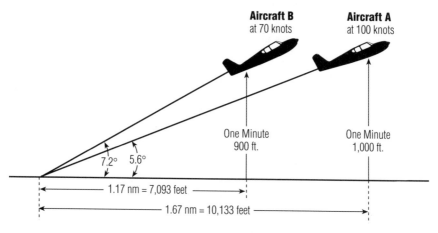

Figure 23. Climb performance using V_X and V_Y

The second rule: Reduce V_Y (but not V_X) by 1 percent for each 1,000-foot increase in density altitude. Consider the 3,300-pound aircraft mentioned above. Its revised V_Y (because of reduced gross weight) is 86 knots at sea level. At 10,000 feet, V_Y for this aircraft would be only 77 knots (86 knots minus 10 percent).

In actual practice, reduce V_Y by one knot during each thousand feet of climb, and this will result in very nearly the most expeditious ascent possible. These rules are valid, however, only for lightplanes with naturally aspirated, reciprocating engines.

Now for V_X, the best-angle-of-climb airspeed. Believe it or not, this performance figure often is unavailable. Oh, yes, operating manuals do specify V_X, for the flaps-down configuration, but rarely is V_X specified for a steep, flaps-up climb.

V_X (flaps up) is the speed to use when a steep climb gradient is required to overfly an enroute obstacle (such as a cloud or mountain) or to reach an IFR crossing altitude in the minimum forward distance. Why flaps up for a maximum climb angle? Simple. Airplanes generally climb most efficiently with flaps retracted.

Flaps usually are recommended only to overfly an obstacle at the departure end of a runway. This is because flaps help to increase the net climb angle, as measured from the takeoff end of the runway to the impending obstacle. With flaps extended, the takeoff roll is reduced, and the aircraft can begin its climb sooner. Also, valuable distance is not wasted while accelerating to the faster V_X (with flaps up).

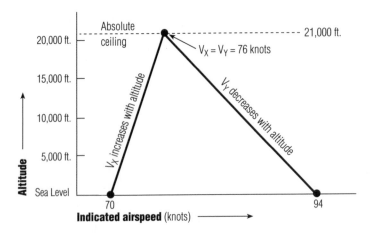

Figure 24. At the absolute ceiling, V_X and V_Y are identical

In other words, flaps do augment steep climb angles only when considering takeoff obstacles. Otherwise, the steepest climb angle usually results when flaps are retracted.

Figure 24 shows the relationship of V_Y to V_X (clean) for a P-model Beech Bonanza. Notice that V_Y decreases from 94 knots at sea level to 76 knots at the aircraft's absolute ceiling of 21,000 feet (a decrease of nearly 1 knot/1,000 feet). The chart also shows that, at the absolute ceiling, V_Y (best rate) and V_X (best angle) are identical.

This destroys a myth about high-altitude flying. Most pilots believe that upon reaching the absolute ceiling, the aircraft is just about ready to stall. Not so. To reach the absolute ceiling, the aircraft must climb at V_Y; otherwise, it could not get there in the first place. At this airspeed (which is 26 knots above the Bonanza's stall speed of 50 knots), all available power is required simply to maintain the absolute ceiling. No excess power (or thrust) is available. If the nose were raised or lowered—even slightly—the resultant drag rise would cause a sink rate to develop. There simply is not enough power available to maintain the absolute ceiling at speeds slower or faster than V_Y. Therefore, when at its absolute ceiling, an aircraft is not in danger of stalling unless handled improperly.

From Figure 24, notice that V_X varies differently than V_Y. Instead of decreasing 1 percent per 1,000 feet, V_X (flaps up) increases almost 0.5 percent per 1,000 feet. For the P-model Bonanza, V_X increases from 70 knots at sea level to 76 knots at 21,000 feet.

The industrious reader can utilize the example in Figure 25 (in combination with the rules of thumb offered previously) to construct a geometrically similar climb-speed chart for his own aircraft. All that is needed are V_Y and V_X (flaps up) at sea level and the aircraft's absolute ceiling (the service ceiling will suffice).

Figure 25 is a typical example of how climb rate varies with altitude. Notice that the decrease in climb rate is linear. In other words, the rate of climb decreases by a constant amount during each 1,000 feet of climb. This is true of all lightplanes (sans turbochargers) being flown at maximum power and at the proper V_Y.

If such a chart is unavailable for your aircraft, don't fret; it's a simple matter to construct one. All that is needed is the maximum rate of climb at sea level and the aircraft's service ceiling, data available in all operating handbooks and sales brochures.

Simply plot the sea-level rate of climb on the horizontal line, as shown in Figure 25 (point A). Since an airplane's service ceiling (by definition) is

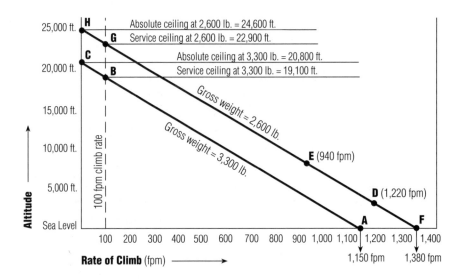

Figure 25. Rate of climb vs. altitude

the highest altitude at which a 100-fpm climb can be achieved, this point on the graph is located at the intersection of the appropriate altitude and the vertical line representing a 100-fpm climb rate (point B in Figure 25, for example). Then simply connect points A and B with a straight line. Next, extend this line until it terminates at the left side of the graph. The termination point of this line indicates the aircraft's absolute ceiling (point C in Figure 25).

With such a chart, a pilot has a very accurate method of predicting maximum climb performance at any given density altitude when the aircraft is fully loaded.

Reductions in gross weight, however, dramatically increase climb performance. Unfortunately, there are no valid rules of thumb for easily and accurately computing these improved climb rates. But one short flight in your own airplane can provide the basis for a cornucopia of climb data.

After determining the gross weight of your aircraft (when less than fully-loaded), enter a full-power climb while maintaining the appropriate V_Y. Then determine the rates of climb at any two altitudes at least 5,000 feet apart. (A stopwatch yields more accurate results than a vertical-speed indicator.)

Assume that the rates of climb at 3,000 and 8,000 feet are 1,220 and 940 fpm, respectively. Simply plot these points (D and E) as shown in Figure 25. Then connect these points with an extended straight line that should very closely parallel the original line AC. This new line (defined by the points D and E) will provide reasonably accurate predictions of the maximum climb rate at sea level (point F), the revised service ceiling (point G), the revised absolute ceiling (point H) and all intermediate climb rates for the reduced-weight configuration.

This climb performance, however, is predicated on the use of maximum-available power, something most pilots use only for takeoff and initial climb. This raises an interesting point. Unless otherwise required by the engine manufacturer, why reduce power prior to reaching cruise altitude? Factually, there is not much of a reason to retard the throttle after takeoff. Most of us do it because of habit or "to save the engine," neither of which is a valid reason.

If the throttle is left untouched after takeoff, climb performance can be downright startling. Besides, during each 1,000 feet of climb, the free-breathing engine naturally loses about an inch of manifold pressure, a form of automatic power reduction.

Leaving the throttle wide open during climb is not injurious to the engine (unless specified in the operating handbook), increases low altitude climb rates dramatically, and usually results in less fuel burn and time to reach a given altitude (when the airspeed is held at V_Y).

Consider also the widely held (and possibly erroneous) belief that the most likely time for engine failure is during the first power reduction after takeoff. So why be in a hurry to retard the throttle? If the power is available, use it. (Full-power departures are discouraged when the airport is surrounded by a noise-sensitive area. Once the airport neighbors are left behind, however, there is no reason why a maximum-power climb could not be resumed.)

Climbing at V_Y does result in the most rapid climb to altitude, but might not be the most efficient way to get from one place to another. For this, a cruise climb usually is required. One rule of thumb suggests that a reasonably efficient enroute climb is obtained by using a speed that is as much above V_Y as V_Y is above V_X.

A good example is found in Figure 22. Notice that V_X is 70 knots and V_Y is 100 knots—a difference of 30 knots. Now add this difference to V_Y to obtain a reasonably efficient cruise-climb speed of 130 knots ($V_Y + 30$).

When climbing at 130 knots, in this case, the airspeed is 30 percent greater than V_Y, while the climb rate is decreased by only 10 percent from 1,000 to 900 fpm, an advantageous compromise. The "cruise-climb" speed should be reduced 1 percent after each 1,000 feet of climb.

For those in a hurry and who do not need to reach altitude quickly, climb at full power and the shallowest climb rate consistent with safety.

The most efficient cross-country climb in terms of saving fuel results from selecting a fairly high climb speed, a shallow climb rate, and a reduced power setting that allows the mixture to be leaned during climb.

Irrespective of the climb technique used, always maintain a sharp eye on engine-operating temperatures. If the oil or the cylinder heads become excessively warm, increase airspeed and/or reduce power to cool the engine.

Upon reaching cruise altitude, do not be in a hurry to reduce power. Otherwise, the airplane will take forever to pull itself out of the mushing attitude and accelerate to cruise speed. Instead, leave the throttle alone. Use climb power to accelerate to a few knots faster than cruise, and then reduce power. The aircraft will decelerate and more easily stabilize at the target airspeed.

One final note of caution. Be constantly aware that any climb—especially a steep one—reduces forward visibility from the cockpit. While climbing, occasionally execute shallow S-turns or dip the nose gently to see what or who might lie ahead. A midair collision seriously erodes climb performance.

Chapter 8 **The Mysteries of Gliding Flight**

The sectional chart is not normally regarded as a lethal weapon. But to those of us who learned to fly in tandem-seat trainers, the sectional was something to fear.

The instructor sat behind the student in many of those ragcovered taildraggers. And since soundproofing had seemingly yet to be invented, cockpit communications varied between limited and impossible. Rather than yell and scream over the engine and air noises, the instructor often found it more convenient to indicate his displeasure with a student's performance by simply beaning him from behind with a rolled-up sectional. The student worked hard to please his mentor, if for no other reason than to stave off this dreaded assault.

According to my first instructor, Mike Walters, a chart would last for six to eight hours of dual instruction before losing its rigidity. But on October 3, 1954, I proved that the 25-cent charts simply weren't as good as they used to be. On that memorable day, Mike lost his cool and "totaled" a brand new chart with unmerciful blows to my cranium.

He was giving me post-solo dual in 180-degree, power-off approaches. My airspeed varied from less than 45 knots (when I was low) to more than 80 knots (when I was high). But despite and because of these sloppy efforts, I never came closer than 500 feet to the elusive touchdown target. Consequently, I was earning about four whacks per approach, which did little to bolster my confidence. Once, when I turned to ask him a question, I caught a blow on the nose and learned not to argue with Mike.

During the last circuit of the day, he screamed a dialogue that can not be repeated here. Every other sentence, however, contained the term "normal glide," but I was too busy nursing my wounds to pay attention.

The postflight briefing was short and to the point. "Look, Barry," began Mike's abbreviated tirade, "one of these days that little 'four-banger' under the cowling is going to quit. Your cork will unplug and down you'll go. And unless you learn something about glidepath control, you can forget about being able to glide safely into a small landing area."

Totally embarrassed, I paid for the lesson and lowered my head in shame, hoping that Mike would notice the welts on the back of my neck and offer a rare word of kindness. No such luck. He turned away disgustedly, walked to the filing cabinet, and withdrew a new sectional chart in preparation for his next victim.

As my log books began to pile up in the closet corner, I learned to appreciate Mike's exhortation (its bluntness notwithstanding). It took me a long time to fully understand gliding flight, but since misery loves company, I was delighted to discover that I was not alone. There are numerous misconceptions about optimum glide performance that prevail in even the most sophisticated quarters. Perhaps even more misunderstood are some of the techniques required to achieve it.

The normal, optimum, or maximum-range glide, is simply a power-off descent during which the airplane flies a maximum distance forward from any given altitude. The ability of an airplane to do this is indicated by its glide ratio, a number that simply specifies how many feet forward an aircraft can glide for every foot of altitude lost.

For example, one of the world's highest-performance sailplanes, the German Schleicher AS-W 12, has a glide ratio of 47 to 1; it can glide 47 feet forward during each foot of descent. To put it another way, from an altitude of 1 nautical mile (6,080 feet), this exotic craft can glide 47 nautical miles. Powered airplanes are not quite that efficient.

To determine the glide ratio of a Cessna 150, for example, it is necessary only to divide the (air) distance flown in one minute by the altitude lost during the same time period. The Cessna 150 has an optimum glide speed of 61 knots, which is equivalent to 6,181 feet per minute. Its sea-level rate of descent at this airspeed is 725 fpm. Dividing 6,181 by 725 results in the 150's glide ratio of 8.5 to 1.

If the pilot of a 150 were faced with an engine failure while flying one nautical mile (6,080 feet) above the ground level (AGL), he could glide 8.5 nautical miles in any direction, giving him a choice of landing sites anywhere within a 227 square-mile circle. But from twice the altitude (two nautical miles or 12,160 feet), the choice of landing areas is not doubled, it is quadrupled. From this altitude, the 150 has a 17-nautical-mile glide range and can touch down anywhere within a 908 square-mile circle. This certainly proves the adage that altitude is like money in the bank.

The optimum glide speed usually is found in the pilot's operating handbook and has much more significance than is generally appreciated. This is the only speed resulting in the optimum, or maximum-range glide.

Uninformed pilots, however, refute this. They claim that if an aircraft is low while on final approach, the glide can be "stretched" by raising the nose and reducing the sink rate. True, the rate of descent decreases, but so does the airspeed. It takes longer for the plane to get to the runway and more time is available for it to lose altitude. Glide performance suffers.

An example of this is shown in Figure 26. By reducing the airspeed of, say, a Cessna 150 to 50 knots, the rate of descent reduces to 640 fpm. The glide ratio at this airspeed, therefore, is 5,067 fpm (forward speed), divided by 640 fpm (downward), or 7.9, somewhat less than the 150's ability to glide at 8.5 to 1.

Other pilots insist that glide range can be extended by increasing airspeed, the theory being that this gets you to the runway sooner and the aircraft has less time to lose altitude. Not so.

If the 150 is flown at 70 knots (1⅙ nautical miles per minute, or 7,093 fpm), its rate of descent is 950 fpm. The glide ratio at this faster airspeed is, therefore, 7,093 divided by 950, or 7.5 to 1, a 12-percent reduction in glide performance.

It must be recognized that if flight at the optimum glide speed does not enable an aircraft to reach the runway, no amount of airspeed variation can help. There is no recourse other than to add power (if available) or select a closer landing site.

Another hazard of attempting to stretch a glide at reduced airspeed is that this may place the aircraft dangerously close to a stall; low altitude maneuvering is risky, and less reserve airspeed is available to counter an unexpected wind shear. Also, there may be insufficient airspeed with which

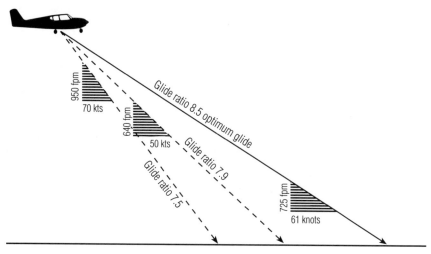

Figure 26. Effect of airspeed on glide range

to flare. Consequently, the aircraft could simply mush into the ground at a high sink rate, a maneuver known to decrease the longevity of both landing gear and spinal column.

The urgent need to maintain a safe and efficient gliding airspeed, especially after engine failure, cannot be overemphasized. It is much preferable to glide into the trees while under control than to allow the aircraft to choose its own method of crash landing.

There is one glide-stretching technique that can be used as a last resort. If the engine is dead, really dead, with absolutely no hope of a restart (such as after fuel exhaustion), raise the nose and reduce airspeed (but only at safe altitude) until the propeller comes to a halt. A propeller at rest creates considerably less drag than one that is windmilling and improves glide performance.

During tests conducted by the Cessna Aircraft Company, it was determined that stopping the propeller of a Cessna 172 increased the glide ratio by 20 percent. A similar increase occurs in the Cessna 150 (and most other light aircraft), which boosts the glide ratio from 8.5 to 10.2 and adds gliding distance that could convert a potential disaster into a safe landing.

Once the prop is stopped, however, lower the nose and accelerate to the normal glide speed.

When power-off approaches are practiced using the optimum glide speed, a pilot learns to visualize the glide path of his aircraft. With experience, he can predict just where on the runway (or off of it) the aircraft will touch down. The astute pilot can vary the airspeed while on a long final approach, to learn just how these changes affect the glide path. Also, he can learn that reducing airspeed slightly decreases glide range, a useful technique to lose surplus altitude.

Assume now that two identical aircraft are cruising side by side at 10,000 feet. One is loaded heavily, but the other is loaded lightly. Simultaneously, both pilots reduce power and begin gliding. Which aircraft will glide the farthest, the light one or the heavy one? Surprisingly, both aircraft will glide the same distance.

The gliding characteristics of an airplane are determined strictly by its lift and drag characteristics (Figure 27). Since neither of these is affected by aircraft loading, weight has no effect on glide range or ratio.

Weight, however, does have an effect on the airspeed that must be used to achieve the maximum glide. The Cessna 150's optimum glide airspeed of 61 knots, for example, is valid only when the aircraft is loaded to its maximum-allowable gross weight of 1,600 pounds. A gross weight decrease requires a corresponding airspeed reduction to maintain the 8.5: 1 glide ratio.

At 1,400 pounds, the 150 should be glided at 57 knots; at 1,200 pounds, the best glide speed is 53 knots. As a rule of thumb for most light aircraft, reduce glide speed 5 percent for each 10 percent decrease in gross weight.

The graph below shows how the lift and drag of a typical lightplane increase with angle of attack. The *ratio* of lift to drag (L/D) for any given angle of attack is shown by the heavily curved line. It is this characteristic of an airplane (or sailplane) that defines glide performance. As a matter of fact, the lift/drag ratio and the glide ratio of an aircraft are equal at any given angle of attack. Therefore, an airplane glides most efficiently when flown at that angle of attack where "L over D" is at a maximum which, in this case, is 5°. If the aircraft is glided at an angle of attack that is either smaller (faster airspeed) or larger (slower airspeed), both the L/D and glide ratio are reduced accordingly. This is why an airplane has only one optimum glide speed. When gross weight is either increased or decreased, the optimum glide still occurs at the same angle of attack (where L/D is at a maximum), but the airspeed required to achieve this will vary.

Does altitude have an effect on glide performance? Absolutely none. The same indicated glide speed should be used at all density altitudes. This

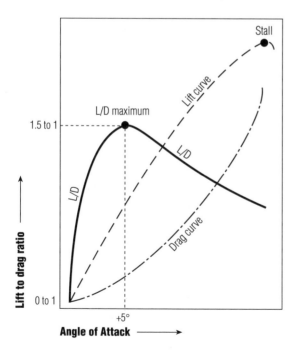

Figure 27. Angle of attack vs. lift-to-drag ratio

may sound a bit incredible, because at 12,000 feet, for example, the Cessna 150 has a more rapid, 870-fpm sink rate while being glided at 61 knots. But consider that this is an indicated airspeed (IAS), not a true airspeed (TAS). At 12,000 feet, a 61-knot IAS is equivalent to a true airspeed of 73 knots. Both the true airspeed and sink rate, therefore, are 20 percent greater than at sea level. Since these figures increase proportionately, the glide ratio remains the same.

Does wind affect glide performance? Absolutely. Gliding with a tailwind obviously extends glide range; a headwind shortens it. To maximize the effect of a tailwind, an airplane should be glided somewhat slower than usual. This has the effect of reducing the rate of descent and allows the aircraft to remain in the air longer. This increases the time during which the tailwind can be used to advantage.

When gliding into a headwind, airspeed should be increased somewhat. Although the rate of descent also increases, the extra airspeed is necessary to maximize forward progress against the headwind. An extreme example is flying into a headwind equal in strength to the airspeed; the aircraft is motionless over the ground, yet it descends vertically at its normal sink rate. The glide ratio is zero. But if the airspeed is increased, at least some forward progress can be realized. When gliding with a 10-, 20-, or 30-knot tailwind, a reasonably valid rule of thumb suggests decreasing airspeed by 4, 6, or 8 knots, respectively. Against a headwind, increase airspeed by 50 percent of the headwind component. (Figure 28 is a more accurate example of how various winds affect the glide ratio of a Cessna 150.)

Wind Condition	Best Glide Speed (IAS)	Glide Ratio	Rate of Descent
30 knot tailwind	55 knots	13.4	680 fpm
20 knot tailwind	56 knots	11.7	700 fpm
10 knot tailwind	58 knots	9.9	740 fpm
Calm	61 knots	8.5	780 fpm
10 knot headwind	64 knots	7.1	850 fpm
20 knot headwind	69 knots	6.1	900 fpm
30 knot headwind	75 knots	5.2	990 fpm

Figure 28. Effect of wind on the glide ratio of a Cessna 150 at 5,000 feet MSL

The effect of wind raises an interesting point. If a pilot is faced with an engine failure and a choice of two landing sites, he should favor gliding to the one downwind of his position (everything else being equal). Remember, tailwinds increase glide range; headwinds destroy it.

Although the normal glide is the most familiar, there is another type that can be equally important: the minimum-sink glide. This is used when glide range is not important, such as when directly over the landing area. At such a time, a pilot needs time more than anything else, time to attempt an engine restart or to simply gather his wits. By reducing to slightly above the minimum-controllable airspeed, sink rate is substantially decreased. Contact with the ground is postponed. But be careful. When 1,000 feet AGL (or higher), resume the optimum glide speed to increase maneuverability and to fly a reasonably normal glide path to touchdown.

The Cessna 150, for example, has a 725 fpm sink rate when flown at the normal glide speed of 61 knots. From an altitude of 10,000 feet, such a descent would last fourteen minutes. But when airspeed is reduced to near 43 knots, the rate of descent is only 600 fpm. Such a glide from 10,000 feet would take 17 minutes. This increases glide endurance by three minutes. And three minutes to a pilot in distress can be of considerable value.

It is true that whatever goes up must come down, but how an airplane comes down is of prime importance to those inside. If it is without power, there are only two ways: accurately and with a plan of action, or sloppily and with a surprise ending.

Chapter 9 **Slipping to a Landing**

There was a time when the intentional slip was a necessary part of every pilot's repertoire. This was when airplanes equipped with wing flaps were the exception rather than the rule. Slips were the only way to steepen a landing approach without diving and building excessive airspeed.

Since the vast majority of modern airplanes are equipped with flaps, the intentional slip has become somewhat of an anachronism. Consequently, slip training has been de-emphasized and the practice is becoming a lost art. This is unfortunate, because the slip can be a lifesaving maneuver.

Consider the Air Canada Boeing 767 that was cruising north of Winnipeg, Manitoba, at Flight Level 410 (41,000 feet) on July 23, 1983. Without warning, both engines flamed out because of fuel exhaustion. The captain established the powerless jetliner in a normal glide and headed toward 60-mile-distant Gimli, Manitoba, a former air force base now used for auto racing. While on final approach to the 8,000 foot runway, the captain recognized that the wide-body Boeing was too high. Drawing upon his general aviation experience, he lowered a wing, applied opposite rudder, and deftly slipped off the excess altitude to prevent an overshoot.

Slips not only can be invaluable during an approach to a forced landing (because wing flaps occasionally are not as effective as pilots need them to be), they also have other emergency applications. For instance, a slip can be used as an emergency means of speed reduction, to compensate partially for inoperative flaps, to assist closing a door that pops open, and to divert smoke and flames from an engine fire away from the cockpit.

More commonly, slips can be used during a conventional landing approach to bleed off excess altitude and airspeed or to adjust aircraft track during a crosswind. The steepness of the maneuver can be modulated easily to achieve any reasonable descent profile without changing airspeed, power, or aircraft configuration.

Before discussing slip technique, it is important to understand the principles involved and how a slip differs from its counterpart—the skid.

A slip occurs when the bank angle of an airplane is too steep for the existing rate of turn. It usually is the result of insufficient rudder when entering or recovering from a turn, inadvertently holding top rudder while turning, or not keeping the wings level while maintaining heading. The airplane flies sideways, and those inside tend to lean toward the low wing (as does the ball of the slip/skid indicator).

A skid, on the other hand, is the result of excessive rudder application. A skidding airplane also flies somewhat sideways, and those inside tend to lean opposite to the yaw (as does the slip/skid ball).

Slips and skids most often are the result of turbulence or improper (uncoordinated) rudder/aileron application. Although they usually are little more than annoying and are easily corrected, they do erode performance, especially if the airplane is held in a prolonged slip or skid. This is because an airplane flying sideways or askew creates excessive drag. Consequently, climb, glide, and cruise performance suffer whenever an airplane slips or skids.

The most significant difference between a slip and a skid becomes apparent when the airplane is made to stall while skidding. The excessive rudder being applied may cause the aircraft to spin in the direction of yaw. No difference exists between an intentional spin and one that results from an inadvertent skid. The necessary pro-spin force is the same in each case.

Unfortunately, the inadvertent, skid-induced spin most frequently occurs in the traffic pattern. The pilot turning from base leg might notice, for example, that he is overshooting final approach. Instead of steepening the bank angle (perhaps because of what psychologists refer to as ground shyness) or executing a go-around, the pilot subconsciously adds bottom rudder to increase the turn rate. This also causes the nose to drop and the bank angle to increase. He counters this with opposite aileron and nose-up elevator. The pilot is in a skidding turn at low airspeed. If the skidding turn becomes sufficiently aggravated, it may lead to a low-altitude spin from which recovery may be impossible.

A slip poses no such hazard, especially when performed during a power-off or low-power approach. If an airplane in a slip is made to stall, it displays very little tendency to yaw one way or the other. The aircraft may tend to roll into a wings-level attitude, but that is about it. In some aircraft, stall characteristics are improved.

An intentional slip is a cross-controlled maneuver that consists of banking in one direction while applying just enough opposite rudder to prevent turning. The airplane, however, no longer flies straight ahead. Instead, the horizontal component of wing lift seen in Figure 29 forces the aircraft also to move somewhat sideways (toward the low wing). Moving an airplane through the air in this manner obviously increases drag and explains why an aircraft in a slip can descend rapidly without picking up airspeed. The effect is the same as deploying drag-producing devices such as speed brakes or spoilers.

Other factors that contribute to increasing the sink rate while slipping include a reduced vertical component of wing lift, the drag produced by deflected control surfaces, and some loss of effective wing area.

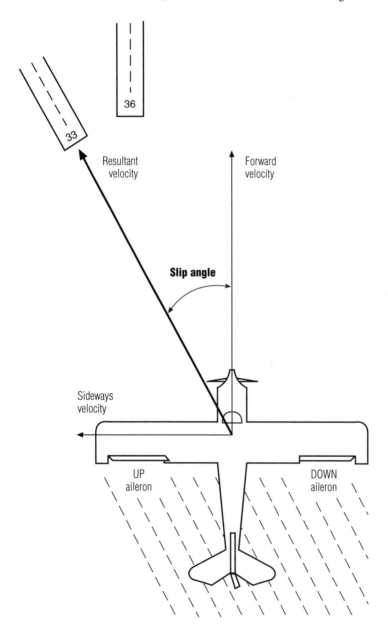

Figure 29. Intentional slip and horizontal component of wing lift

Four types of slips are discussed in this chapter, but the two most common are really one and the same. The difference between a forward slip and a sideslip simply is a matter of perspective, not aerodynamics. Notice in the figure that the airplane is heading north but is slipping along a track of 330 degrees (the slip angle is 30 degrees). If the pilot intends to land the airplane on Runway 33, he is executing a forward slip. Such a maneuver is used to descend while tracking along the runway's extended centerline, even though the nose is pointed elsewhere.

If the pilot intends to land on Runway 36, however, then the same maneuver is called a sideslip. This is because the aircraft is approaching the runway centerline from the side.

Even though a pilot may not realize it, he executes a sideslip during conventional, properly executed crosswind landings. The aircraft is banked into the wind so that the sideslip velocity is equal and opposite to the crosswind velocity (zero drift). Opposite rudder is used to keep the airplane pointed down the runway.

A shallow sideslip (sometimes called a sideslide) often is used during formation flying to close in on another aircraft without having to turn.

A forward or sideslip also is useful during a landing approach when a pilot cannot see easily over the nose (such as when flying from the rear seat of a North American T-6 or the front seat of a Pitts biplane) or cannot see through a windshield coated with ice or engine oil. When slipping, the pilot can view the runway through the side of the windshield or the side window without having to look over the nose. Since the purpose of such a slip is not to steepen the descent, power can be applied to prevent what might otherwise be an unacceptably high sink rate.

A third variety of slip is the slipping turn, which is a maneuver used to increase the descent profile when turning from downwind leg to base or from base to final.

During aviation's friskier, pioneering era, pilots used a fourth technique to dissipate airspeed and altitude—fishtailing. A pilot would alternately yaw the nose (using full rudder) one way and then the other while applying opposite aileron to keep the wings as level as possible. Also called the flat sideslip, this maneuver requites extraordinary coordination (or lack of it!) and has the potential to create more of a problem than it solves. It is, however, a challenging exercise to practice at altitude.

Conventional slipping is much tamer than fishtailing but should not be performed arbitrarily in all aircraft. The Cessna 172, for example, contains a placard stating that "slips should be avoided with flaps extended." This is not a prohibition, however. If it were, a pilot would not be allowed to make conventional crosswind landings with flaps extended. The advisory is posted because airflow across the tail may be disturbed during a flaps-down slip and result in some pitch oscillation. A few other aircraft are affected in this way.

Pilots also should avoid slipping (and skidding) with a low fuel supply, because the maneuver could result in unporting a fuel pump or fuel line, thereby starving an engine of fuel.

It also is advisable to warn passengers prior to executing a slip (or other unusual maneuvers) so they can anticipate the sensation of leaning and not have cause for alarm.

The modern airplane abhors a slip almost as much as nature abhors a vacuum. When rolled into a bank, the horizontal component of wing lift immediately tries to move the airplane sideways at a constant heading. But as the aircraft begins to move sideways, the relative wind changes direction and pushes against the side of the fuselage and vertical fin. This forces the aircraft to yaw in the direction of the low wing. Such a reaction to slipping is known as positive static directional stability (or "weather vane" stability) and explains why an airplane turns. In other words, an airplane in a turn is in a continuous process of entering and recovering from minute slips. (Some antique airplanes had neutral static stability. Yaw the nose or dip a wing and such a machine would continue to fly askew even after the controls were released.)

Since a modern aircraft recovers from a slip more or less automatically, an intentional slip requires cross-controlling ailerons and rudder throughout the maneuver. It is not necessary to be abrupt, however; just roll the aircraft into the desired bank and apply whatever opposite rudder is required to maintain the desired heading. The amount of slip—and, therefore, the sink rate—is determined by bank angle; the steeper the bank, the steeper the descent. As bank angle is increased, however, additional opposite rudder is required to prevent turning.

In most light planes, a slip is rudder-limited. That is, a pilot may reach a point where full rudder is required to maintain heading even though the ailerons are capable of further steepening the bank angle. This is the practical slip limit, because any additional bank would cause the airplane to turn toward the low wing, even though full opposite rudder is being applied.

If there is a need to descend more rapidly while performing a maximum-effort slip, simply lower the nose. Diving not only increases sink rate but results in additional airspeed. This makes the rudder more effective and permits a steeper slip. Such a technique can result in very impressive sink rates. Conversely, when the nose is raised, rudder effectiveness wanes and bank angle should be reduced.

When slipping, attitude is the key, not airspeed. Since the relative wind does not come from straight ahead while slipping, the airspeed indicator may be unreliable (especially in aircraft that have a single static source on one side of the fuselage). Instead of concentrating on a possibly erroneous airspeed indication, maintain approximately the same pitch attitude used during a normal glide. This usually requires forward pressure on the control wheel to counter the nose-up tendency created by holding top rudder.

Once the plane is stabilized in a slip, the pilot may need to vary heading slightly to maintain the desired track. The easiest way to do this is to adjust the bank angle while holding a fixed amount of rudder. In other words, steepening bank angle causes a turn toward the low wing, while decreasing bank slightly produces a turn in the opposite direction.

Most pilots prefer a left slip (left wing down) because it offers the best view of the runway. The direction of a forward slip, however, often is dictated by wind direction. If landing with a crosswind, it normally is best to slip into the wind so that it does not become necessary to change the direction of slip prior to touchdown. Also, do not allow anyone to lean heavily against a door while slipping, unless you have supreme faith in the latch. It is unlikely that anyone could fall out, but the shock of an open door could be disconcerting nonetheless.

The mechanics of a sideslip are the same as a forward slip. As mentioned, the difference between the two is one of perspective. During a forward slip, however, slip steepness determines only sink rate. But when executing a sideslip, bank angle also determines how rapidly the airplane moves laterally toward the extended runway centerline.

Although it is not necessary, a sideslip usually is performed while maintaining a heading that parallels the runway. If the aircraft tends to turn toward the runway, add additional opposite rudder, or decrease bank angle. A turn away from the runway is arrested by decreasing rudder pressure or increasing bank angle.

Pilots unaccustomed to slipping should recover from the maneuver (by simultaneously rolling into a wings-level attitude and releasing rudder pressure) no lower than 200 to 300 feet AGL to avoid high sink rates near the ground. With experience, a pilot can slip safely to within inches of the runway, flare and recover from the maneuver immediately before touchdown.

Forward slips and side slips usually are performed while maintaining a given heading. But there are times when a slipping turn might come in handy.

The easiest way to enter a slipping turn is first to enter a conventional turn. Then, after neutralizing the ailerons and rudder, simultaneously apply aileron pressure in the direction of the turn and opposite rudder. The amount of slipping is determined by the amount of cross-controlling. Rate of turn is increased by further steepening the bank angle or decreasing pressure on the rudder pedal, and vice versa. To recover from the slip, simply neutralize ailerons and rudder.

Pilots should consider that the turn rate of a slipping turn is not as great as would be expected from such a bank angle. This is because the application of top rudder inhibits turn rate. As a result, allow for larger-radius turns.

Although pilots of modern aircraft seldom need to slip, they should have the confidence and skill to call upon the maneuver when needed. Slipping safely is preferable to slipping up.

Chapter 10 **Another Way to Make a Crosswind Landing**

Perhaps I'm a sadist. One of my favorite spectator sports is watching inexperienced pilots enter into combat with a blustery crosswind. Their performances are like excerpts from a Laurel and Hardy movie. A dancing windsock plays the background accompaniment, and tire crunching lends an occasional percussion effect. The end of a particularly dramatic sequence is punctuated by the nasty sound of scraping metal.

The most entertaining scenes include either a wheelbarrow ballet, a grouplooping pirouette, or the more unusual love sequence that concludes when the tires softy kiss the concrete.

Developing the skill necessary to make consistently good crosswind landings is not easy. One reason is that we are infrequently confronted with the challenge; the opportunity to practice is rare. And then there are pilots who avoid crosswind landings whenever possible. While this may seem like an example of safe flight planning, it is not. Such misguided wisdom can backfire. Eventually, such a pilot is confronted with having to land in a strong crosswind at a single-runway airport. Lacking proficiency, how could he then muster the skill necessary to handle a 20-knot crosswind?

There are two other reasons why many pilots are inept at crosswind landings. One is that they fly aircraft considerably different from the one in which they received their initial training. Making a cross-controlled landing in a Piper Saratoga, for example, is not quite the same as in a Cessna 152.

Also, many pilots get their certificates without ever having made a difficult crosswind landing. A reason for this might be that a crosswind never presented itself during the course of a pilot's training It is entirely possible for a pilot to encounter his first stiff crosswind with a hundred hours under his belt and a planeload of nervous passengers buckled under theirs. Such a situation is not uncommon. Amuse yourself at the airport on a windy day, and you will see the consequences: an endless parade of rock-'n'-roll landings. And if you happen to be an aircraft sheet-metal worker, you might even pick up some business while there.

The solution to the crosswind landing problem is painfully simple, obvious to the point of being ignored. Wait for one of those days when the windsock points across the runway, hire a proficient instructor, and spend an hour or more honing crosswind skills. And what a thrill it will be to have the traffic pattern to yourself; everyone else will be on the ground, avoiding the crosswind as if it were carrying a dose of swine flu.

Once a pilot learns to touch down without drifting and with the airplane lined up with the runway, he might be ready to learn another way to make crosswind landings. Yes, there is another, perhaps better way than slipping to touchdown. But before a pilot is introduced to this somewhat unorthodox method, he should be reasonably proficient in the conventional, time-honored technique. And he should know his airplane well. So, if you don't meet these qualifications, perhaps you should stop reading and save this for another day. But if you are sharp, read on. To keep my conscience clear, may I suggest that you do not practice what you are about to read without the assistance of a competent instructor. Once this "new" technique is mastered, you may find it superior to conventional crosswind methods.

A conventional crosswind landing requires that, at the instant of touchdown on the upwind tire, the aircraft must be heading parallel to its direction of motion. Drift is prevented by banking into the wind, a maneuver that requires cross-controlling the aircraft. For example, a left crosswind is countered by applying left aileron to keep the left wing down and right rudder to prevent yawing toward the lowered wing. Technically, this maneuver is a sideslip. Were it not for the drifting effect of the crosswind, the aircraft would slip toward the left side of the runway while maintaining a heading parallel to the runway.

This sideslip configuration is usually established a few hundred feet above the ground, presumably so the pilot has sufficient time to establish just the amount of slip necessary to offset the drifting effect of the crosswind component. Too much slip and the plane drifts into the wind; not enough, and the aircraft drifts downwind.

The only thing wrong with this preparatory philosophy is that wind velocity often is quite variable at altitudes near the ground on a windy day. In addition to the effects of ground friction on wind, the influence of large hangars and buildings causes gross variations in local conditions. This was dramatically illustrated by a classic photograph published years ago in an FAA training publication. It showed three windsocks equally spaced along the edge of a long runway. The middle sock was almost limp. The other two stood out like howitzers but were pointed in opposite directions.

Since the degree of slip required to offset drift frequently must be varied with a change in altitude, the argument in favor of establishing the slip at 200 to 300 feet AGL is weakened.

Two additional major disadvantages of the slipping descent deal with a loss of roll control, which can result in a damaged wingtip — or worse. Consider a low-wing plane being slipped a few feet above the runway. The upwind wing is being held down to prevent drift. The pilot is about to begin the landing flare when the upwind (lowered) wing suddenly is assaulted by a strong, downward gust. This increases the bank angle farther and involuntarily. If a correction is not made quickly enough, both the wingtip and the pilot's pride are vulnerable to damage.

On the other hand, consider a gust that tends to right the aircraft. The pilot may have insufficient aileron control remaining to hold the upwind wing down because he is already using considerable aileron pressure in that direction just to maintain the slip.

Also consider that a slipping descent results in a slight loss of the vertical lift component produced by the wing. To compensate for this loss, a slightly faster approach speed may be required. This is in addition to the extra speed needed to compensate for gusts. (To protect against losses of airspeed caused by gust-induced wind shear, it is recommended practice to add one-half of the reported gust value to the normal approach speed. For example, if the wind is reported at 20 with gusts to 34 knots, then at least half the gust value — or 7 knots — should be added to the normal approach speed.)

But there is another way to combat the crosswind. It is a method used by the airlines because of the difficulty of slipping a Boeing 747 to a landing.

A close look at a jetliner with low-slung, pylon-mounted engines reveals why this is so: the engine pods hang too close to the ground. Landing in a bank to prevent drift has caused more than one embarrassed airline captain to write a letter explaining how he managed to drag an engine pod along the concrete. Also, the jetliner's swept wings cause the wingtips to be relatively far aft. When the nose is raised to the takeoff or landing attitude, the wingtips (which are well behind the main landing gear) move down toward the ground. Banking the aircraft at such a time jeopardizes the wingtips and could even scrape the inboard-flap sections.

The jetliner's geometry insists that conventional crosswind landing techniques be abandoned in favor of a better method, one developed for early jet bombers. This method not only eliminates the need to slip down the glideslope, but also enables a pilot to more precisely land on the touchdown target.

A modified version of the airline method is adaptable for use in light aircraft and, when proficiency in it is developed, offers improved safety, controllability, and passenger comfort during crosswind landings. Additionally, this technique allows a pilot to increase his personal crosswind limit. Parenthetically, and because of the technique about to be described, the Boeing 747 has a direct crosswind limitation of 30 knots, which is a monstrous wind for an aircraft of that size.

Now that you are sitting on the edge of your seat in breathless anticipation, the time has come to relieve the suspense. The "better" way to make a crosswind landing is called the "kickout" method, for reasons that soon will become obvious.

The landing scenario goes like this. While on final approach, offset the effects of wind drift by crabbing into the wind. Vary the crab angle as necessary during the descent according to variations in the crosswind component that occur during the approach.

As the aircraft nears the runway, retain the necessary crab angle. Do not transition to a slip. Maintain the crab angle with wings level until the flare has begun and the aircraft is only inches above the runway at a near-zero sink rate. Immediately prior to touchdown—and here is where some skill comes in handy—lower the upwind wing and push the upwind tire onto the pavement so as to make a firm, positive touchdown on that wheel. The idea is to plant the upwind gear on the ground, eliminating the need to enter a steep bank angle to prevent drift. Ground contact, in combination with the resulting bank angle, prevents the aircraft from drifting askew.

Simultaneous with the application of aileron, it is necessary to kick the aircraft out of the crab with firm application of opposite—or downwind—rudder. This straightens the aircraft so it is aligned with the runway at the instant of touchdown.

Once the upwind tire is on the ground, increase aileron pressure to keep it there. Continue to apply rudder as necessary to maintain runway heading.

The next step is familiar. Allow the other main landing gear tire to touch down, followed by the nosewheel or tailwheel.

The kickout method is surprisingly similar in execution to a conventional crosswind landing, the difference being that slip entry is delayed until an instant before touchdown. Banking the aircraft, however, is the manner in which touchdown is accomplished. The pilot doesn't have to sit and wait for the aircraft to plop down while he hovers above the runway with one wingtip dangling ungracefully and dangerously close to the ground. By lowering the upwind wing while the aircraft is only inches above the runway, the upwind tire is forced to descend and make firm contact with the ground.

It is a simple matter to determine when the aircraft has been banked sufficiently; just listen or feel for ground contact. Simply stated, the kickout method is a slip entry interrupted by a landing.

I experimented with this technique in a Piper Cherokee 140 one day while the wind was gusting across Santa Monica's Runway 3 at 30 knots. The conventional method of landing failed because I could not lower the upwind wing sufficiently to offset the drift. After three unsuccessful landing attempts, I altered my technique and tried the kickout method for the first time in a light airplane.

On final, I maintained a tremendous crab angle to the left and concluded how fortunate it is that there is no limit to the crab angle that can be maintained by an airplane in flight. There is, of course, a very definite limit to the degree of slip that can be maintained in any given airplane (depending upon the effectiveness of its controls). And since I did not have to cross-control and force myself against the cockpit sidewall, I felt relatively comfortable and at ease.

I held the crab to a point only inches above the runway and checked the rate of descent with a touch of back pressure on the control wheel. When the tires were only a second or two from scrubbing sideways against the surface, I simultaneously lowered the left wing and added right rudder; the left tire plunked cooperatively onto the concrete. The simple act of banking forced the aircraft to land. Because of the brutality of this particular wind, I simply pushed the aircraft over onto all three legs and braked to stop.

To confirm that this landing was not just a fluke, I made two more landings, much to the chagrin of the tower controllers, who thought they had a runaway lunatic in the pattern. The other two landings were equally successful. I was able to land in a crosswind that was almost insurmountable using conventional methods.

There are two mistakes common to the kickout technique. One is to begin slip entry at too high an altitude, negating the purpose of the maneuver. In such a case, however, the pilot is no worse off than had he elected to make a normal crosswind landing in the first place. He can opt to continue the landing conventionally or execute a go-around and try again.

The second and more serious error is to allow the aircraft to touch down while crabbing. Such neglect would punish the landing gear unmercifully. But this is where skill is required. Beginners should not attempt such a landing.

The kickout method is somewhat unorthodox, and no one should adopt this technique without first practicing it during relatively mild crosswind conditions. Stronger winds can be challenged as skill increases. During the progress to these more difficult conditions, a pilot should keep track of the crosswind components encountered and mastered so he will know how proficient he's becoming. (*See* Figure 30.) Remember, it is the crosswind component, not the total wind speed, that determines the drifting effect of the wind. The accompanying table provides the crosswind component during all wind conditions.

Perhaps equally helpful is a rule of thumb used to accurately determine the crosswind component at any point along final approach (or in cruise). This rule is especially convenient when landing at uncontrolled airports where wind velocity reports are unavailable. It is based on the "one-in-sixty" angular relationship used in off-course navigation.

When flying at 60 knots TAS, each degree of crab necessary to maintain a given course indicates the presence of a 1-knot crosswind. Similarly, at 120 knots, each degree of crab represents 2 knots of direct crosswind, and so on.

If an airplane has an approach speed of 90 knots, for example, each degree of drift correction offsets 1½ knots of crosswind. A 12-degree crab, therefore, would indicate the presence of an 18-knot crosswind component.

Angle Between Runway and Wind Direction

	10°	20°	30°	40°	50°	60°	70°	80°	90°
5	1	2	3	3	4	4	5	5	5
10	2	3	5	6	8	9	9	10	10
15	3	5	8	10	11	13	14	15	15
20	4	7	10	13	15	17	19	20	20
25	4	9	13	16	19	22	24	25	25
30	5	10	15	19	23	26	28	30	30
35	6	12	18	22	27	30	33	34	35
40	7	14	20	26	31	35	38	39	40
45	8	15	23	29	34	39	42	44	45
50	9	17	25	32	38	43	47	49	50
60	10	20	30	38	46	52	56	59	60
70	12	24	35	45	54	61	66	69	70

Total wind speed (MPH or knots) — (left axis label for rows)

Figure 30. Using wind speed and direction to determine crosswind component

Chapter 11 **Operating From Uphill and Downhill Runways**

Few pilots would disagree that it is usually better to take off downhill and into the wind than uphill and with the wind. But, is it safer to take off downhill and downwind, or uphill and upwind? Popular opinion suggests that a downhill, downwind departure usually is best; nevertheless, some highly respected sources claim otherwise.

Despite the good intentions behind such advice, there can be no correct answer without first analyzing the variables. If runway gradient is steep, a downhill run usually is best; but if the wind is strong, a takeoff into the wind usually is recommended. The problem becomes thornier when runway slope and wind component appear to have approximately equal significance.

A pilot might be faced with a similar problem when approaching a sloped runway. Should he land uphill and downwind, or downhill and upwind?

Some airports are labeled as one-way airports, which eliminates the need to decide which way to take off or land. The runways are sloped so steeply or have such tall obstacles (usually at the uphill end) that landings are made uphill and takeoffs are made downhill irrespective of wind speed and direction. Pilots who insist on taking off or landing in the wrong direction invariably litter the terrain with scrap metal.

One-way airports, however, usually are designated in various airport guides and pose a problem only to those who ignore the obvious. Perhaps more dangerous are those runways that are not sloped as steeply. Depending on the wind, the takeoff and landing direction might not be obvious, and those who opt to go the wrong way may be in store for a few anxious moments (or worse).

Whenever planning to fly into an airport where takeoff or landing performance might be of concern, call a fixed-base operator (FBO) on that airport and seek advice from those who routinely fly there. If the runway is sloped or has obstacles, local pilots often can provide suggested approach techniques and considerations. If the airport does not have an FBO, call one at a nearby airport. He probably will be familiar with your destination and can offer advice that more than justifies the cost of the call.

Numerous landing overrun accidents occur on sloped runways because pilots often do not recognize they are about to land downhill. Depending on the nature of the surrounding terrain, runway gradient can be difficult to appraise. Compounding the problem is the optical illusion created by a sloped runway. When approaching a downhill slope, pilots tend to fly a steeper-than-usual descent profile; when approaching an uphill runway, they tend to make flat approaches.

As a result, a pilot often can determine runway slope by monitoring sink rate and power. If the sink rate is high and the power low, he might be approaching a downhill runway; if sink rate is low and power high, he might be approaching an uphill runway.

If wind is not a factor, it obviously is best to land uphill (obstacles permitting). This is because a component of aircraft weight helps deceleration after touchdown. But how much tailwind is acceptable to gain the advantage of an uphill landing?

The answer is provided in Figure 31, which shows the approximate effect of the wind on takeoff and landing distances. Notice that a given headwind or tailwind component affects takeoff and landing distances equally. The chart can be used once the true airspeed at touchdown has been calculated. Simply divide the headwind or tailwind component by TAS to determine the windspeed-to-airspeed ratio. Assume, for instance, that an aircraft touches down at 80 KTAS with a 16-knot tailwind. The ratio of wind to airspeed is 0.2 and would increase the normal landing distance by 44 percent. If this increase can be tolerated, then such a downwind landing is safe. The landing distance actually required would be less because of the beneficial effect of landing uphill. Since this factor is not considered in the calculation, it provides a built-in safety factor.

When approaching to land with a tailwind, groundspeed on final is much greater than a pilot might be accustomed to. If he perceives this as an abundance of airspeed, he might tend to reduce airspeed unnecessarily. Such an instinctive reaction is best avoided by referring to the airspeed indicator before making what could be hazardous power and attitude changes.

When landing uphill, consider that the terrain rises ahead of the aircraft and frequently demands a more aggressive flare, which can result in a more rapid loss of airspeed and significantly less float. One hazard in landing uphill is that making a go-around can be more difficult, especially if terrain beyond the runway outclimbs the airplane. For this reason, it obviously is safer to drag a sloped runway by flying from the high end to the low end.

Assume that the wind is such that an uphill/downwind landing is inadvisable. The distance required to land downhill and into the wind also can be approximated. The first step is to consult the table to determine how much effect the headwind component has in reducing the required landing dis-

Ratio of headwind/tailwind component to takeoff/landing speed (TAS)	Percent decrease in takeoff/landing distance caused by headwind component	Percent increase in takeoff/landing distance caused by tailwind component
.025	5%	5%
.050	10%	10%
.075	15%	16%
.100	19%	21%
.125	24%	27%
.150	28%	32%
.175	32%	38%
.200	36%	44%
.225	40%	50%
.250	44%	56%
.275	48%	63%
.300	51%	69%

Figure 31. Approximate effect of headwind/tailwind components on takeoff and landing distances

tance. Then add 10 percent more distance for each 1 percent of downhill grade. This is tricky because runway slope is difficult to estimate. To be conservative, overestimate the amount of downhill grade. (Some airport guides provide the gradient of sloped runways.)

If these computations make it appear that a downhill landing can be made within the available runway length, do not think you have it made until you analyze some potential problems.

As the aircraft passes over the threshold, the pilot should be prepared for the runway to drop away. This can result in a prolonged flare and consume a considerable chunk of runway. In some cases, the runway falls off so rapidly that little or no flare is required to land. Unless touchdown occurs near the beginning of the runway, the pilot should be prepared for an immediate go-around. (The only good thing about landing downhill is that the terrain drops away even if the pilot just maintains altitude during the go-around attempt.)

Consider also that braking effectiveness is reduced when landing downhill, a problem that is worsened if the tires skip over the bumps of an unimproved surface.

Since landing downhill offers the least margin for error, pilots must be particularly careful not to cross the runway threshold with excessive airspeed or altitude.

Unless wind velocity substantially outweighs the adverse effects of a downhill slope, it usually is best to land uphill and downwind. Accident statistics seem to validate this, because there are many more overruns caused by downhill/upwind landings than by uphill/downwind landings. If neither alternative is appealing, then it probably is best to land elsewhere. Consider, too, that under some conditions it is possible to land but impossible to take off.

When preparing to depart on a sloped runway, it usually and obviously is best to take off downhill and upwind. Uphill/downwind takeoffs usually should be avoided. But what should a pilot do when confronted with a choice between taking off uphill and upwind, or downhill and downwind? The problem is similar to that of choosing between uphill and downhill landings. A pilot is best advised first to consider pointing the airplane downhill. He then should consult Figure 31 to determine if enough runway is available to tolerate departing with a tailwind component. If the runway is long enough, the operation is safe, because the calculation does not include the snappier acceleration made possible by the downhill gradient.

Unless the airport is equipped with an anemometer to measure wind speed, a pilot needs to be adept at estimating wind velocity, which explains why some mountain and bush pilots carry hand-held anemometers.

If conditions for takeoff appear to be safe but leave little margin for error, then be certain to use all of the available runway. Be sure also that the tires are inflated properly (because underinflated tires increase rolling friction), that the engine is developing maximum permissible power prior to brake release, and that the fuel/air mixture is adjusted properly (when appropriate). A rearward center of gravity (within limits) also enhances takeoff performance because it reduces stall speed, which decreases takeoff distance.

Since a downhill, downwind takeoff results in spunky acceleration and an unusually fast rolling speed—particularly at high density altitudes—do not allow the sensation of a seemingly excessive groundspeed to tempt a premature liftoff. Do not rotate until reaching a safe indicated airspeed.

The merits of a downhill takeoff become obvious immediately after liftoff. With the terrain falling away, a climb is not required—at least temporarily—to gain height above the ground. One problem associated with a downhill, downwind run, however, is the difficulty a pilot might have aborting a takeoff. Taking off downwind also increases the likelihood of climbing into an increasing-tailwind type of wind gradient (or shear), which could reduce climb performance below 2,000 feet AGL. On balance, however, the downhill takeoff most often is safest.

If the combination of downhill slope and tailwind component are unacceptable, a pilot might then consider an uphill takeoff, which can result in losing an uphill battle against gravity. To determine if such a departure is prudent, use the table to calculate the beneficial effect of the headwind component. Then add 10 percent of the required takeoff distance for each percent of runway gradient. If the result is favorable, do not rush to crank up and leave. There are several discouraging factors to consider.

First, remember that—once airborne—the uphill runway will be climbing, too. As a rule of thumb, do not take off unless the aircraft can climb at least twice as rapidly as the terrain, performance that might be difficult to achieve. When heavily loaded at high density altitudes, there are many aircraft that cannot climb as steeply as is required to make a safe, upslope departure.

Assume that a pilot taxis to both ends of a 3,000-foot-long, sloped runway and determines that the difference in elevation between them is 100 feet. Runway slope is determined by dividing 100 by 3,000, which is 3.3 percent. The pilot then uses Figure 32 to determine the climb gradient of his aircraft. If the best angle-of-climb airspeed converts—under existing conditions—to a groundspeed of 90 knots, for instance, and the anticipated climb rate is 400 fpm, the resultant climb gradient is only 4.4 percent. Since this climb gradient is not twice that of the runway, a takeoff is not recommended. (When heavily loaded at particularly high density altitudes, some underpowered aircraft cannot get off the ground at all.)

Some might wonder why an aircraft needs to climb twice as steeply as the runway. This is a safety buffer that compensates for the fact that an airplane does not assume the necessary climb angle and rate immediately after liftoff. Some time and distance are needed to make the transition from takeoff to climb. In other words, the effective climb angle usually is less than anticipated.

Since most sloped runways are situated in hilly or mountainous terrain, an uphill takeoff might necessitate having to climb over obstacles or steeply rising terrain adjacent to and beyond the runway. If a pilot can estimate the distance between the anticipated lift-off point and the top of the obstacle as well as the altitude needed to clear the obstacle, he can approximate the minimum slope required for climb. If the data from Figure 32 do not indicate that the aircraft can exceed such a climb gradient by a healthy margin, the notion of such a takeoff should be discarded.

| | **Rate of Climb** | | | | |
	200 fpm	**400 fpm**	**600 fpm**	**800 fpm**	**1,000 fpm**
60 kts	3.3%	6.6%	9.9%	13.2%	16.4%
65 kts	3.0%	6.1%	9.1%	12.1%	15.2%
70 kts	2.8%	5.6%	8.5%	11.3%	14.1%
75 kts	2.6%	5.3%	7.9%	10.5%	13.2%
80 kts	2.5%	4.9%	7.4%	9.9%	12.3%
85 kts	2.3%	4.6%	7.0%	9.3%	11.6%
90 kts	2.2%	4.4%	6.6%	8.8%	11.0%
95 kts	2.1%	4.2%	6.2%	8.3%	10.4%
100 kts	2.0%	3.9%	5.9%	7.9%	9.9%
105 kts	1.9%	3.8%	5.6%	7.5%	9.4%
110 kts	1.8%	3.6%	5.4%	7.2%	9.0%

Groundspeed During Climb (row labels)

Figure 32. Determining climb gradient/slope from groundspeed and climb rate

(A clever way to estimate the required climb angle between liftoff and the top of an obstacle requires only a standard plotter, a piece of string, and a small weight. Secure one end of the string to the hole at the center of the plotter and attach the weight to the other end. Then, sight the obstacle along the long edge of the plotter, allowing the string—or plumb bob—to dangle alongside the angle scale of the plotter. The required angle of climb can be read directly from the scale. Each degree represents a grade of about 1.7 percent. A plotter and plumb bob also can be used as a crude sextant in a survival situation.)

Even when it seems that an aircraft can hurtle the obstacle safely, a pilot should consider that an uphill/upwind takeoff is made toward the lee side of rising terrain. Therefore, he can anticipate flying into downdrafts that reduce climb performance.

There is not much to say in favor of an uphill takeoff during marginal conditions. An uphill grind, however, does make for an easier abort, and climbing into an increasing-headwind type of wind gradient may improve climb performance when below 2,000 feet AGL.

Calculations thus far have assumed taking off from a smooth, hard-surface runway. Unfortunately, many sloped runways—especially those in mountainous regions—are not paved, and it is necessary to consider the effects of these unimproved surfaces. Hard turf, for instance, increases pro-jected takeoff distances by approximately 7 percent, short grass by 10 per-cent, tall grass by 25 percent and soft ground by anywhere from 20 to 50 percent or more. Some runways can be so soggy, slushy, or snow-covered that takeoff can be impossible no matter how long the runway. (When land-ing, consider that wet grass, snow, ice, or standing water can double or even triple anticipated landing distances.)

Even after a pilot determines that a particular takeoff or landing can be made safely, he might simply look at the runway, review the potential haz-ards, and shake his head apprehensively. Numbers crunching indicates that he should be able to depart safely, but he feels something in his gut that says otherwise. Perhaps he knows that calculated performance data often are unreliable. (The takeoff and landing data for high density altitudes in some pilot operating handbooks are unrealistically optimistic.) Perhaps he realizes that his engine does not perform like new and that the nicks in his prop and the dents in his wing prevent his aircraft from performing the way it once did. Perhaps his short-field technique is rusty. Perhaps he has a strong sur-vival instinct.

Pay attention to apprehension, because a lingering doubt often is the most reliable computer available. After all, why not wait for the temperature to drop or the wind to shift? Why not off-load some fuel and reduce takeoff weight? Can any departure be so imperative as to place human lives in jeop-ardy? Of course not, but some pilots—because of carelessness, ignorance, or overconfidence—attempt to fly where more prudent pilots fear to tread.

Chapter 12 **Operating on Contaminated Runways**

Several years ago, a Japan Air Lines' captain taxied his passenger-filled 747 onto an ice-covered taxiway at Anchorage International Airport. While trundling carefully in a 20-knot crosswind (with gusts to 33 knots), he encountered considerable braking and steering difficulties. Unable to control the aircraft to his satisfaction, he stopped the 747, shut down the engines, and called for a tug to tow the Boeing off the icy surface.

While the crew waited for the tractor to arrive, the mammoth 747 began to behave like a giant weather vane and yielded to the crosswind. After yawing 70 degrees into the wind with the parking brakes still engaged, the 747 was blown backward off the taxiway and slid tail first down a shallow embankment. The aircraft came to an ignominious rest 250 feet later at the bottom of a ravine.

This is but one example of how a pilot can become a passenger in his own airplane. When airport surfaces are contaminated with ice, slush, snow, or water, the normally simple task of bringing an aircraft to a halt within the confines of a runway can be nightmarishly difficult or even impossible.

Braking on ice-covered runways can be reduced to nil, and landing-roll distances can be increased by 40 to 300 percent. Landing on ice in a crosswind can result in the wildest, most uncontrollable ride imaginable.

Despite the spectacular threat posed by icy runways, water-soaked runways actually claim the most victims.

Three types of hydroplaning (or aquaplaning) can render an airplane partially or totally uncontrollable during the landing roll. The most familiar type, dynamic hydroplaning, is similar to water skiing and is a relatively high-speed phenomenon. It can occur whenever a runway is contaminated with slush (a mixture of ice and water), standing water, or wet snow that is at least 1/10 inch deep.

As an aircraft begins to accelerate on such a runway, the tires simply push the water out of the way. But as speed increases, the water cannot escape fast enough, and a wedge of water pressure builds under and in front of the tires. At some speed, called the total hydroplaning speed (V_p), the water pressure equals the weight of the aircraft. The tires lose contact with the runway and ride—like water skis—on a film of water. Since traction is lost, the tires may spin down, stop, or even rotate slowly backward, despite the relatively high groundspeed.

Dynamic hydroplaning during takeoff, however, rarely is a problem; directional control is maintained easily by using rudder to keep the thrust vector pointed in the desired direction.

During a landing, the hydroplaning process works in reverse. If touch-down occurs above V_P, the airplane might immediately begin water skiing, which can render the brakes completely ineffective. Directional control—especially in a crosswind—may be impossible because the tires have almost no adhesion, which is a tire's resistance to sideways motion. Since the front tire is affected in the same way, nosewheel steering may be unavailable. An unfortunate aspect of hydroplaning is that, once it begins, it can persist until the aircraft slows to a speed well below V_P.

Considerable research (most of it by NASA), has determined that dynamic hydroplaning is related to tire inflation pressure. V_P normally is between seven and nine times the square root of the tire pressure, as shown in Figure 33. The main-gear tires of a Cessna 310R, for instance, normally are inflated to 60 pounds per square inch (psi). This means that these tires can be expected to hydroplane at any speed above a point between 54 and 70 knots. The 310R's nosewheel tire, however, might begin hydroplaning at any speed above a point between 44 and 57 knots, because it is normally inflated to only 40 psi.

Figure 33, which applies also to automobiles, is valid only when water or slush depth is equal to or greater than the tread depth of the tires. If the water is not that deep, V_P increases. This means also that worn tires with shallow treads tend to hydroplane in shallower water depths. Although tires should be inflated properly to prevent reducing V_P, do not overinflate the tires in an attempt to prevent hydroplaning because this reduces braking coefficients on dry runways.

The second hydroplaning threat is reverted-rubber (or steam) hydroplaning. It occurs when wheels lock and tires skid during heavy braking. Not much water is required; a thin film will do.

A skidding tire generates so much heat that the rubber in contact with the runway reverts to its original, uncured (gummy) state. This rubber shreds off the tire and accumulates around the aft perimeter of the tire footprint, trapping water under the tire. This water is then superheated to more than 250 degrees C and becomes steam. The steam pressure lifts the tires from the pavement, resulting in a loss of traction.

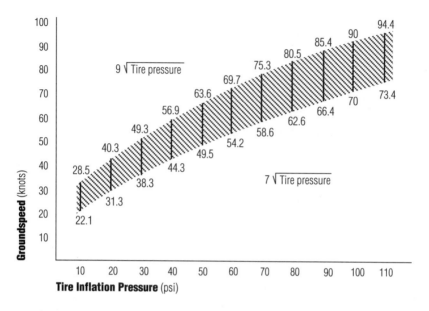

Figure 33. Effect of tire pressure on hydroplaning speed

This type of hydroplaning commonly follows an encounter with dynamic hydroplaning when the pilot might have the brakes locked in a futile attempt to slow down. Eventually, the aircraft does lose speed. The tires contact the runway surface and immediately begin skidding. The insidious aspect of reverted-rubber hydroplaning is that a pilot might not know when it begins. If he did, he would need only to release the brakes, allow the wheels to spin up and then apply moderate braking.

Reverted-rubber hydroplaning can persist to very low speeds (20 knots or less) and usually leaves white skid marks on the runway. It also can be verified, after parking, by a patch of gummy, unvulcanized rubber on each of the affected tires.

Viscous hydroplaning is the third member of the trio and is not hydroplaning in the true sense of the word. It does have the same effect, however, and requires as little as a thousandth of an inch of moisture (less than the thickness of morning dew) on a smooth surface such as asphalt or a touchdown area coated with the accumulated rubber of past landings. Such a surface can be extraordinarily slick and have the same coefficient of friction as wet ice. Viscous hydroplaning most frequently occurs when a pilot starts to turn off the runway. But instead of turning, the airplane just yaws while tracking (albeit, slightly askew) along the runway (and possibly off the end). It occurs also on slick taxiways and ramp areas, which is one reason to taxi slowly on damp surfaces.

Although dynamic, reverted-rubber, and viscous hydroplaning are independent phenomena, it is possible—under the right conditions to encounter all three during a single landing.

In hydroplaning conditions, it is best to land on a grooved runway (if available). This is because the spanwise grooves not only allow water to drain away, but they also provide escape channels for water being pressured by approaching tires. This keeps the tire footprints relatively dry and prevents hydroplaning under all but the most severe conditions.

Landing downwind on a runway that is not clean and dry can be disastrous unless its length is measured in miles instead of feet. This is because downwind touchdown speeds are significantly higher than when landing upwind, thereby increasing the likelihood and duration of hydroplaning.

For the same reason, touchdown speed should be as slow as practical. Also, do not execute a prolonged flare in an effort to make a smooth landing. It is more important to get the aircraft on the ground as soon as possible. Firm landings are best because they help the tires to penetrate the film of water and to make contact with the runway. Hydroplaning may develop soon anyway, but there is no sense in rushing things by skimming along the surface of the water while attempting to make a smooth landing.

Once on the ground, do not hold the nose high in an effort to take advantage of aerodynamic drag, because this reduces wheel-braking efficiency.

When a wing moves through the air—even after touchdown—it produces measurable lift. This lift is not sufficient to raise the airplane, of course, but it does prevent the wheels from supporting the entire weight of the aircraft. This decreases braking effectiveness because brakes perform in proportion to the amount of weight on the wheels. To maximize braking power, therefore, it is necessary to reduce lift by lowering the nose and reducing the wing's angle of attack. (Aerodynamic braking is an effective technique when brakes prove ineffective or to save brake linings and tire wear when runway length and hydroplaning are not critical factors.)

Additional wing lift can be destroyed by raising wing flaps immediately after touchdown. This further reduces the effective angle of attack and, in some cases, decreases wing area. The result is improved braking.

The FAA, however, cautions against flap retraction before exiting the runway because this increases the likelihood of inadvertently grabbing the wrong switch and retracting the landing gear instead. Although this certainly would preclude the possibility of hydroplaning and dramatically reduce the landing-roll distance, the technique can be painfully expensive.

Since it is desirable to put as much weight as possible on the mains (the braking wheels), very little aircraft weight should be supported by the nosewheel. But heavy braking creates a nose-down pitching moment that tends to plant the nosewheel firmly on the runway. Consistent with steering requirements, some or most of this weight should be taken off the nosewheel and transferred to the mains by applying up-elevator. (A raised elevator has the added benefit of increasing the aerodynamic download on the tail. This adds more weight to the main gear and further increases braking effectiveness.)

Moderate braking should be applied as soon as possible after touchdown to test the waters (no pun intended). If deceleration is not detected and hydroplaning is suspected on short runways, consider adding power, rejecting the landing, and proceeding elsewhere before it is too late. If the runway is adequately long, however, raise the nose and use aerodynamic drag to decelerate to a point where the brakes do become effective.

Proper braking requires more finesse than stomping on the binders. The brakes should be applied firmly until reaching a point just short of a skid. Heavier braking and the resultant skid can reduce braking effectiveness by as much as 50 percent (not to mention the possibility of tire failure and loss of directional control).

Many aircraft, particularly heavy ones, are equipped with antiskid systems that sense when a wheel is about to stop rotating. The antiskid system automatically releases just enough brake pressure to prevent a locked wheel and possible tire failure.

Since most light aircraft are not so equipped, the pilot needs to be more attentive during the landing roll. Should he sense a skid (or hear it), the pilot should release the brakes gradually until the skidding symptoms disappear. He should then increase brake pressure and try to approach a skid without actually encountering one. Modulating the brakes in this way results in the shortest possible landing roll. (Do not pump the brakes to keep them cool; the brakes of a light plane cannot be overheated during the time it takes to bring the aircraft to a halt.)

If the brakes seem ineffective due to hydroplaning at any time during the landing roll, release all break pressure. Then intermittently apply moderate braking to determine when hydroplaning has subsided. If the wheels are kept locked, it is possible to transition from dynamic hydroplaning to reverted-rubber hydroplaning to viscous hydroplaning without realizing it.

Once the brakes begin to take hold, consider that heavy braking can induce reverted-rubber hydroplaning. So, if the brakes seem to fade after initial application, release them (to allow the wheels to spin up) and reapply with moderation.

When landing on a contaminated runway with a strong crosswind, it might be a good idea to land on the upwind side of the runway. This maximizes the space available for recovery in case the aircraft begins to slide sideways on the slick surface. Do not touch down while drifting, and, in most cases, quickly get the nosewheel firmly on the ground (but do not slam it down) to maximize steering capability.

If the airplane begins hydroplaning, expect it to slide in an arc toward the downwind side of the runway, even though it probably will weathervane also (or yaw) toward the upwind side. If it threatens to slide off the runway (a common hydroplaning event), apply power to return to the runway centerline (commensurate with the remaining runway length). If the nosewheel is not also hydroplaning, avoid large, rapid movements of nosewheel steering. This is because a nosewheel tire develops maximum cornering forces and has maximum steering capability when it is only 5 to 10 degrees off center. If the nosewheel tire is hydroplaning, a pilot can expect little or no steering control.

When landing on an icy runway in a strong crosswind (not recommended) with pilot reports of "braking action nil," consider touching down in a wings-level, zero-drift crab.

Once things are under control, do not be in a hurry to get off the runway. Dissipate as much speed as possible before turning, even if this means using the full length of the runway. If dynamic or reverted-rubber hydroplaning fails to claim its victim, viscous hydroplaning might. Under such conditions, a pilot cannot be complacent until the wheels are chocked.

Although landing on contaminated runways usually poses the most critical problems, related takeoff problems must not be ignored. When taxiing on and taking off from wet surfaces in near-freezing temperatures, for instance, water that splashes onto landing-gear mechanisms and flap tracks might freeze shortly after takeoff and render these systems inoperative.

One technique used to avoid this problem on retractable-gear aircraft is to leave the gear extended for a period of time to allow the spinning wheels to throw off as much moisture as possible, then cycle the gear two or three times in succession to minimize freezing. Some aircraft should have some of the gear doors removed in the winter to minimize potential problems. Such advice is provided in the pilot's operating handbooks for affected aircraft.

Takeoff distance is increased substantially when the runway is covered with snow, slush, or standing water. One-half inch of slush or wet snow can double takeoff distance. One inch or more can prevent an aircraft from reaching liftoff speed no matter how long the runway. With respect to snow, consider that wet snow creates much more drag than dry snow. Also, the resistance to acceleration offered by a given thickness of dry snow increases as temperature decreases.

If a relatively short runway is covered by fresh snow, consider running a car up and down the runway a few times to clear a path. The same can be done in an airplane, but it takes longer and is more hazardous. Or, wait for someone else to take off and follow in his trail.

Interestingly, a takeoff on smooth ice improves acceleration because of reduced rolling friction. (The same is true of that portion of a takeoff roll characterized by dynamic hydroplaning.) But be cautious of crosswinds and consider that a safe abort might be impossible. This is particularly important for multi-engine pilots. Ice can dramatically increase the accelerate/stop distance. If the runway is sufficiently slick, the go/no-go speed (V_1) might be as little as 30 or 40 knots. Under these conditions it might be wise not to go at all.

Reversing propellers and reverse thrust are the most effective weapons against hydroplaning. They provide a dependable retarding force when all else fails. But if track and directional control become difficult when landing in a strong crosswind, the use of reverse thrust can compound the problem.

In Figure 34, an aircraft touches down at point A and immediately begins to hydroplane. Since the tires have negligible traction, the crosswind causes the aircraft to simultaneously weathervane into the wind and slide downwind (point B). The pilot applies reverse thrust. At point C, the aircraft is approaching the downwind edge of the runway as the pilot continues to apply reverse thrust. Notice that the reverse-thrust vector can be divided into two components. The braking component acts parallel to the runway and causes deceleration. The side component, however, acts in the same direction as the crosswind component and helps to force the aircraft off the runway. When such a runway excursion is about to occur, a pilot has little choice but to stop reversing. If the aircraft continues to drift laterally, forward thrust (commensurate with the amount of remaining runway) must be used to propel it toward the runway centerline. Once control has been restored, reverse thrust can be reapplied and the entire process repeated, if necessary.

Although waterskiing, ice skating, and bobsledding can be a lot of fun, doing the same on a set of aircraft tires can produce thrills a pilot is not likely to forget.

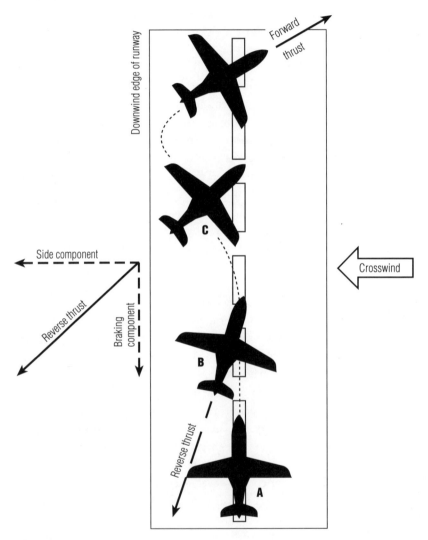

Figure 34. Side and braking components created when using reverse thrust in a crosswind

Chapter 13 **Using Soaring Techniques in an Airplane**

Charles Lindbergh was known to many for more than his historic flight to Paris. To some World War II navy pilots, he also was the maestro of long-range cruise control.

On several occasions, Lindbergh took off from an aircraft carrier and returned with considerably more fuel than others who had flown the identical mission. This happened often enough to rule out luck or a particularly efficient airplane.

One of Lindbergh's techniques recognized the advantages of flying through rising air and the penalties paid when flying through descending air. He skillfully used convective (vertical) currents to extract energy from the atmosphere, free power that can supplement lift, reduce fuel consumption, increase airspeed, or achieve exhilarating rates of climb.

None of this is particularly earthshaking to sailplane pilots. They began developing similar skills before the Wright Brothers had ever heard of Kitty Hawk. A few have accomplished some truly extraordinary feats. Consider Robert Harris, who soared to 49,009 feet above sea level in his Grob 102 sailplane, or Hans Grosse of West Germany, who flew his Schleicher AS-K 12 for a nonstop, straight-line distance of 789 nautical miles (908 statute miles).

No, there was nothing new about Lindbergh's ability to take advantage of rising air currents, but he was one of the first to successfully and dramatically demonstrate the feasibility of applying these techniques to powered flight. The lessons he taught to Navy pilots are even more valuable to those who fly general aviation airplanes.

There is a fascinating, enjoyable method by which soaring can be practiced in your own airplane (without shutting down the engine). But before the fun (described later), some time needs to be spent in the classroom.

Since the atmosphere is three-dimensional, a pilot needs more than a working knowledge of horizontal air motion (wind). Vertical currents also should be considered. It is important not only to know when and where to expect rising air, but also how to avoid sinking air, which can seriously erode performance.

For practical purposes, air rises only when it is heated from below (convection currents) or when it is lifted mechanically (orographically) by a mountain slope or other obstacle to the wind. (Although sailplane pilots also utilize mountain waves and frontal slopes, these sources of lift are not as useful during powered flight.)

Most pilots are aware of thermals, those columnar bubbles of relatively warm, rising air that usually produce a turbulent ride. When a thermal is sufficiently strong and contains sufficient water vapor, it results in a cumulus cloud, a visual signpost. The top of a cumulus cloud usually represents the thermal's uppermost limit. As every sailplane pilot knows, a rich column of lift usually can be found between the source of the thermal and the cloud base. But one cumulus cloud (or thermal) is normally not of value to a power pilot.

Fortunately, and because of Mother Nature's propensity for order and symmetry, cumulus clouds frequently occur in long, parallel rows (called "cloud streets") that extend for many miles. By flying along the street (below the clouds), a pilot can experience and take advantage of considerable lift for surprisingly long distances. To prevent gaining undesirable altitude, a power pilot simply lowers the nose and picks up additional airspeed. An increase of 5, 10, or 15 knots is not unusual. Or, if he desires, a pilot can reduce power, save fuel, and maintain normal cruise speed.

Power pilots tend to fly under the clear sky between cloud streets. But this is self-defeating and is like seeking out headwinds because the result is the same—reduced groundspeed. This is because air between cloud streets is generally sinking. Maintaining altitude here requires either additional power (and fuel), or an increased pitch angle and subsequent airspeed loss.

Lindbergh knew about the up- and downdraft activity in the vicinity of cumulus clouds and often altered his flight path to take advantage of the beneficial currents. Little wonder that he often returned with more fuel than did other pilots not so well informed.

The buoyant air feeding cumulus clouds does not always rise vertically, however. If there is a wind, a flight 2,000 or 3,000 feet below the cloud base might miss the rising current entirely.

Figure 35 demonstrates that when there is a wind, the flight path should be downwind of the thermal's source and upwind of the cloud base. When uncertain of wind direction (or speed), simply spend a moment observing the movement of the cloud's shadow. (None of this is meant to imply that pilots should fly under the base of a thunderstorm or even a massive and towering cumulus cloud; this discussion deals with fairweather cumulus.)

If thermals do not contain sufficient water vapor, the vertical currents can be used even though cumulus clouds do not develop to point the way.

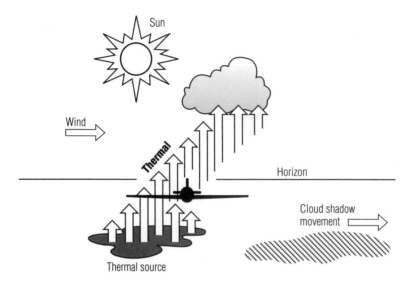

Figure 35. Identifying a thermal source

Instead, thermals must be located at their sources, such as small towns and factories that radiate considerable heat. In open country, look for contrasts in soil and fly over (or near) those areas that appear driest. Moist soil, areas of vegetation, and bodies of water usually do not generate significant thermal activity. Over mountainous or hilly terrain, the south-facing slopes exposed to the sun generally breed thermals better than north-facing slopes or valleys.

Sometimes, such as when overflying a desert or vast plain, it is impossible to tell where the thermals originate. It is simply a matter of flying from lift to sink to lift, and so on. At such times, improved performance (or reduced fuel burn) still can be achieved. When flying through updrafts, take advantage of them by accepting altitude gains and reducing airspeed slightly to remain longer in the surges of lift. When in a downdraft, resist the urge to raise the nose to avoid losing altitude. This prolongs travel through the sink. Instead, accept the altitude loss (and possibly increase airspeed) to get out of the area as soon as possible to minimize the negative effects. This technique also can be used when crossing cloud streets.

If the air is smooth and stable or the day is characterized by strong winds or stratiform clouds, forget about thermal assistance and wait for another day. Or try flying the ridges.

Lift can be found on the windward side of mountains and hills when the wind direction is within 30 to 40 degrees of a line perpendicular to the ridge (Figure 36). The wind speed required to generate sufficiently strong lift depends, of course, on the slope of the mountain or hill. The steeper the slope, the better.

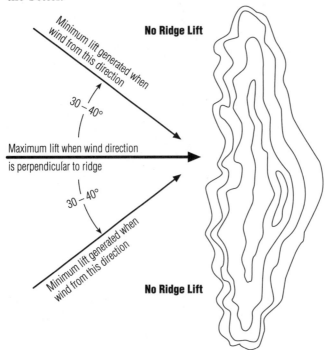

Figure 36. Lift on the windward side of a mountain

Conversely, flight in the lee of a ridge should be avoided. This is an area of steady downwash, which can erode performance substantially. The difference in airspeed between flying on the upwind and downwind sides of a ridge can be 10 to 30 knots, depending on wind velocity, slope steepness, and the proximity of the aircraft to the ridge.

To maximize the benefits, fly relatively close to the upwind side of the ridge at a position approximately 45 degrees above the ridge line (Figure 37). A pilot can experiment and find the area of maximum lift by slightly adjusting altitude and position relative to the ridge. Also, follow the ridge contour as closely as possible unless, of course, this requires unnecessarily large course changes. The additional time required to fly the longer distances may outweigh the advantages.

If any large breaks occur in the ridge, fly across these as rapidly as possible to avoid the sinking air often found there.

Soaring principles can be applied beneficially not only during cruise flight, but also after taking off in a heavily loaded or underpowered airplane at high density altitude. Instead of pointing the nose randomly and accepting a sickly climb rate, check the surroundings to ensure you are not in an area of sink. Then, fly toward sunlit slopes or other areas where convective lift can be expected. With respect to the wind, fly to and remain on the windward sides of any nearby slopes.

The intelligent pilot will decide on the most efficient departure route (with respect to help from rising air or hindrance from sinking air) prior to takeoff. A working knowledge of the atmosphere's third-dimensional movement can improve climb performance dramatically, to say nothing of avoiding excessive and potentially damaging engine temperatures.

Although mechanical and thermal lift can significantly increase flight performance, the benefits often are difficult to observe. This is due primarily to the camouflaging effect of engine power and the average pilot's inability to visualize the undulating currents of air. On a given day, for example, a pilot might say this about his airplane: "Wow, she's really spunky today." Is the airplane really feeling its oats, or is a gently rising air mass lending a helping hand? Often, it is the latter.

A sailplane pilot (don't ever call him a glider pilot), on the other hand, depends on outside sources of lift. Every nudge of air must be correctly interpreted. Otherwise, his flights are short-lived.

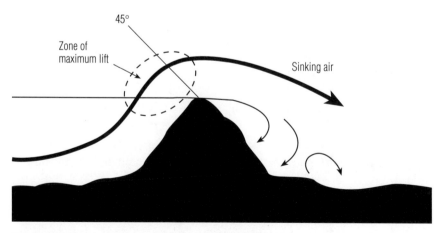

Figure 37. Benefit of flying near the windward side

His task is simplified, however, by flying his craft at relatively slow, aerodynamically efficient airspeeds. He knows the rate of descent to expect in still air. Any variation of this rate represents the presence of lift or sink.

But a sailplane is not needed to learn similar lessons; soaring can be practiced in an airplane without the risk of running out of lift and having to suffer the sailplane pilot's ultimate indignity, an enroute, off-airport landing.

Now for the rules of the game. On a smooth, stable day and while maintaining altitude, reduce airspeed to some arbitrarily chosen, slow, efficient airspeed. For the purpose of this exercise, it is satisfactory to use the airspeed recommended for optimum glide.

If this airspeed/power combination results in an uncomfortably nose-high attitude, extend the flaps no more than 20 percent (or to the first "notch"). Although additional power probably will be required to maintain the same airspeed, the aircraft body angle will be reduced (in most airplanes), which increases over-the-nose visibility.

Once the required power setting has been determined (flaps up or extended partially, your choice), either wait for a day of good thermal activity or proceed toward an area where ridge-induced lift can be expected.

The idea is to precisely maintain the best glide speed and a constant power setting while paying careful attention to the vertical-speed indicator (VSI), the altimeter, and the seat of your pants. If a climb is detected, you are soaring; if a descent is noticed, you are in sink. With practice and the proper conditions, you will find it possible to gain considerable altitude without varying airspeed or power. The goal, however, is not simply to taste the exhilaration of soaring, but to learn where and under what circumstances lift can be used to advantage and to confirm in a very realistic manner the workings of the atmosphere and its effect on flight.

Once a pilot has a feel for soaring, he then may desire to accept the ultimate challenge: trying to remain aloft or fly given distances without sufficient power to maintain altitude. This is, after all, the problem faced by every sailplane pilot. It is an exciting, safe, rewarding contest that pits plane and pilot against the elements.

The contest rules remain essentially unchanged. The same airspeed is to be used with or without partially extended flaps, as desired. But this time, a pilot needs to determine the power setting that results in a glide ratio (or descent angle) similar to that of a popular single-place sailplane such as the Schweizer 1-26. The 1-26 has a glide ratio of 23 to one, which means that the aircraft can glide 23 feet forward while losing only 1 foot of altitude. When flying an airplane at 60 knots, for example, this translates into a 260-fpm rate of descent. At airspeeds of 80 and 100 knots, use sink rates of 350 and 450 fpm, respectively.

Once an appropriate airspeed/power/sink-rate combination has been established, the glide performance of the airplane will very nearly simulate that of a true soaring machine.

Now head for an area of suspected lift and, once there, see just how long you can remain aloft or how far you can travel without changing the predetermined airspeed/power configuration. With practice and under the right conditions, this exercise can prove beyond a doubt the extent to which vertical currents can influence performance.

Any discussion of up- and downdrafts invariably leads to the question, "Can a strong downdraft force an airplane to the ground?" After polling many instructors about this, I found that most (including two FAA examiners) believed this to be impossible.

Their reasoning was, in essence, that as a descending column of air approaches the ground, it is forced to spread horizontally (Figure 38). In other words, the vertical component of the downdraft weakens rapidly near the ground and affords the airplane an opportunity to escape the grip of involuntary descent.

Sound logical? Of course. But is the answer correct? No. And the following helps to understand why.

An automobile is cruising along the highway. The relative wind is horizontally analogous to a strong downdraft. Enter a large bug. Does the unsuspecting insect follow the deflected airstream around the windshield to safety or does it go splat!

The bug is incapable of changing its direction so rapidly because the creature has inertia. An airplane also has inertia, which is why it can indeed be thrust into the ground by a sufficiently powerful downdraft.

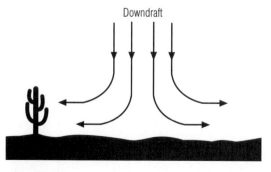

Figure 38. Descending air spreads horizontally near the ground

Chapter 14 **Scud Running**

Scud running is one of general aviation's most tempting and hazardous procedures. It claims numerous lives every year. Lacking formal definition, this technique generally is regarded as an attempt to maintain visual flight in marginal conditions, such as when the ceiling (or scud) is less than 1,000 feet and visibility is less than 3 miles.

Pilots criticized for scud running invariably defend themselves by pointing to regulations that effectively condone the procedure. They argue that VFR flight in Class G (uncontrolled) airspace during the day is allowed with a visibility of only one mile as long as the airplane is kept clear of clouds.

Though scud running may be legal, it can be extremely dangerous, and the danger increases as the performance capability of the aircraft increases. Also, consider that the weather conditions described above are less than the minimums required to complete many IFR (instrument) approaches.

Scud runners who get into difficulty usually do so by continuing into worsening conditions. Either disorientation or failure to see and avoid obstacles or terrain is typically the cause of a scud-running accident.

Since it can be suicidal to continue visual flight into such adverse conditions, it is logical to wonder why these pilots behave so irrationally. There appear to be two reasons for their determination to plunge toward disaster.

The first, and most obvious, combines a pilot's overestimation of his ability with his determination to succeed and his optimistic attitude regarding weather conditions ahead. In other words, he is guilty of poor judgment.

The second reason is much less understood and often is a major contributing factor in scud-running accidents.

When flying at low level in gradually worsening visibility, a pilot considering course reversal generally glances rearward first to appraise this escape option. Most pilots, after all, are not suicidal (despite occasional actions that seem to indicate otherwise). But when looking behind him, a scud runner sees his fleeting ground-reference points disappearing behind the veil of restricted visibility through which he had been flying. This creates an illusion that can lead him to believe that conditions behind are worsening or "closing up." Contributing to this deception is the feeling that conditions ahead are improving because forward motion of the airplane causes progressively more of the terrain ahead to come into view. The overall effect of this illusion increases with airspeed.

Consequently, pilots are reluctant to turn around while the opportunity still exists. In most cases, weather immediately behind an airplane does not deteriorate that rapidly. If it was safe to overfly the area a minute ago, it usually is equally safe to turn around and do it again. The same cannot be said for the conditions ahead. In addition to the obvious hazards, consider the complications of a mechanical difficulty. What normally would be regarded as little more than a nuisance or inconvenience can become a serious distraction with which scud-running pilots are unable to cope. When obstacles are probing for the belly, pilots need to devote almost all of their attention to controlling the airplane and maintaining visual flight.

In the case of power failure while scud running, the emergency must be treated as an engine failure after takeoff. If the pilot is flying a single-engine airplane, precious little time is available to select a landing site and prepare for touchdown.

Mechanical irregularities aside, scud running is uniquely hazardous because the pilot usually has had no training or preparation for this type of flying. Something as simple as navigation can be extremely difficult at 500 feet AGL with only a mile or so of visibility. Those who doubt this should challenge themselves with an hour-long, low-level flight in VFR conditions. It is surprising how few checkpoints can be seen from 500 feet. Then imagine complicating the problem with limited visibility and a low, ragged ceiling.

Experienced scud runners usually abide by a set of self-imposed rules. They seldom carry passengers because innocent bystanders should not be exposed to the risk. They rarely go themselves, unless an IFR option is available; this means that both the airplane and the pilot must be qualified and prepared to intentionally climb into the overcast as a means of emergency escape. Scud running at night or in mountainous terrain is too risky to consider. Anyone attempting such a stunt has only himself to blame for the predictable consequences.

Scud running obviously is dangerous. However, if a pilot elects to underfly weather, he first should make a thorough study of the terrain and become familiar with the nature of enroute checkpoints and obstacles. The most prominent of these should be highlighted on the chart. When possible, a scud runner should plan to follow highways, railroads, and other forms of reliable guidance. Consider, however, that these also can lead to tunnels, bridges, and other hazards.

Pilots also should not expect VHF communications or navigational assistance at low altitude except when in the immediate vicinity of a ground transmitter. (An ADF bearing might be the only available radio aid.)

A course through the area should be plotted in advance. The chart should then be folded open to avoid having to fumble with it and becoming distracted at critically low altitudes. Some experienced scud runners recommend placing the chart between the thumb of the left hand and the control wheel so that it can be seen with minimal eye movement and vertigo-inducing head twisting. It also is helpful to mark the course line with 5- or 10-mile ticks to help keep track of enroute position. When checkpoints are few and far between, the dock becomes an important ally; knowing how many miles are covered every two minutes, for example, provides a reasonably effective form of dead-reckoning navigation.

Excessive speed complicates scud running. At an airspeed of 180 knots, for example, it takes only 20 seconds to fly 1 mile, which often is the limit of forward visibility. Little time is available to see and avoid obstacles, which seem to appear from nowhere. At 60 knots, on the other hand, the pilot has a full minute—three times as much time—to appraise and react to approaching terrain.

Although reduced airspeed has advantages when scud running, a pilot must be careful not to go too far. Low-level flying provides a greater-than-usual impression of speed. This causes some to believe they are flying too fast. As a result, they subconsciously reduce airspeed (especially when turning) to a dangerously slow rate. Speed control, therefore, becomes a serious concern when scud running. It should be slow enough to avoid obstacles, but fast enough to provide stall protection while maneuvering.

If a pilot inadvertently enters an area of reduced visibility (less than one mile), he should consider partially deflecting the flaps. This not only provides added stall protection, but also places the airplane in more of a nose-down attitude, which improves over-the-nose visibility.

(Since helicopters have different capabilities than fixed-wing aircraft, regulations allow pilots of these aircraft, during certain conditions, to fly VFR with no minimum visibility as long as they can see other traffic or obstacles in time to avert a collision.)

Most scud runners give little thought to the threat of colliding with other aircraft. Flying in such limited airspace—limited by ceiling and visibility—a pilot feels very much alone. Some even report feelings of claustrophobia. But when following landmarks such as rivers, highways, and railroads through a patch of inclement weather, consider that it would be just as logical for a pilot heading in the opposite direction to use the same topographical guidance. And since a low ceiling compresses VFR traffic vertically, other airplanes are likely to be at approximately the same altitude. Common sense suggests that scud runners fly to the right of highways, rivers or whatever landmark they have chosen to follow. This also places the course line to the left of the airplane, making it easier for a pilot to see at all times. Also, every available exterior light should be turned on.

Most novice scud runners have a tendency to lose altitude. This is because an inexperienced pilot perceives the natural horizon to be lower on the windshield than it really is, an illusion created when low clouds and restricted visibility obscure the true horizon.

On the other hand, some pilots are ground-shy and tend to allow the aircraft to drift up toward the overcast. This partially explains why instrument flying skills are necessary even when flying in certain visual conditions.

Another illusion occurs when flying in a crosswind. At very low altitudes, drift is much more apparent, even distracting. This causes some pilots to perceive a slip or skid (especially in turns) even though the slip/skid ball is centered. Their actions to correct this sensation have led to numerous stall/spin accidents. This is why some pilots, prior to scud running, tape one end of a 6-inch length of yarn in the center of the windshield. Glider pilots routinely use such a yaw string as a form of head-up display to help detect and correct uncoordinated flight without having to refer to the gauges.

Another scud-running technique is to fly along the downwind side when in a narrow valley that limits maneuvering room. Should a 180-degree turn become necessary, this maximizes the space available. Turning into the wind makes the maneuver safer because this reduces turn radius; a turn away from the wind, of course, dangerously increases turn radius.

One problem associated with flying on the downwind side of a valley is that this places the airplane on the upwind (windward) side of the hills. A pilot unaware of this can be lifted into the cloud base by persistent updrafts.

Other scud-running hints: keep a hand on the throttle at all times in anticipation of a sudden need to maneuver; when an immediate climb is necessary to avoid ground contact, do so at the best-angle-of-climb airspeed (V_X); when practical, use climbing S-turns to maintain a forward view; it usually is best to maintain an altitude two-thirds of the way between the ground and the cloud base; exercise extreme caution when flying over snow-covered terrain that blends with a milky overcast to eliminate any visual horizon (a condition known as whiteout); similar caution is required when flying toward the sun in dense haze. And never fly beyond the point of no return.

When it appears that a pilot is sticking his neck out too far, he should exercise one of two options: swallow his pride and turn around (usually the simplest), or try to contact air traffic control and obtain an IFR clearance to climb into the overcast, leaving the hazards of scud running behind and below.

If neither of these options is possible or practical, consider a precautionary landing. Occasionally, it is better to risk this inconvenience and potential hazard than to continue into deteriorating weather with only a hope and a prayer that there is light at the end of the tunnel.

Pilots who collide with the ground while scud running usually do so because of some inexplicable compulsion to continue when conditions clearly dictate otherwise. Even fully qualified instrument pilots fly into frightful conditions while struggling to maintain visual contact with the ground. They are reluctant to give up until it is too late.

Although it is illegal to intentionally climb into IFR conditions without a clearance, such an option might be considerably safer than continuing in IFR conditions at low altitude.

If the situation is desperate, a spiraling climb to avoid surrounding higher terrain eventually places the airplane safely above all obstructions. Also, the availability of navigation and communications facilities increases with altitude. While ascending into controlled airspace (literally as pop-up, IFR traffic), the transponder should be squawking the emergency code (7700) to alert air traffic control of your presence. Once communications are established—on the emergency frequency, if necessary—and a clearance is obtained, the remainder of the flight becomes routine. Once you land, however, you might be called on to explain your violation.

If the pilot or the airplane is not IFR qualified or if icing conditions are forecast, a pilot probably should not yield to the temptation to scud run.

A cardinal sin is to pass up an enroute airport or reasonably attractive landing area when the situation becomes critical. At such a time, a pilot should take advantage of any opportunity to shift the odds in his favor.

If deteriorating weather encourages a pilot to land, he might have to fly the traffic pattern at an abnormally low altitude, which is not without hazard.

Figure 39 shows an airplane (A) on the downwind leg at a normal pattern altitude of 1,000 feet AGL. The pilot has become accustomed to viewing the runway from a 30-degree angle above and abeam. If he sights the runway along the same line while at a significantly lower altitude, the airplane (B) is positioned much closer to the runway.

Consequently, the pilot has less room to execute turns from the downwind leg to base, and from base to final. He invariably compensates by using abnormally steep turns (at relatively low altitudes).

A pilot aware of this problem intentionally flies farther from the runway than appears normal (airplane C in the figure). In other words, the pilot perceives being low for the simple reason that he is.

Another problem is that a pilot flying a low pattern altitude tends to begin descent prematurely (when downwind and abeam the approach end of the runway, for example). But since he is low to begin with, such a descent keeps the airplane well below the normal, visual glideslope. Descent should be delayed from a low pattern altitude until intercepting a normal slot.

When turning at very low altitudes, pilots have a greater-than-normal sensation of speed because of their close proximity to the ground. Often, they counter this by subconsciously reducing airspeed, an action that cannot be tolerated at a time when the airplane already may be turning sharply at low altitude (for reasons discussed previously). Airspeed management while scud running must be based solely on the instruments; seat-of-the-pants corrections can be lethal.

Although this discussion deals with the techniques of scud running, it must not be interpreted as any form of encouragement. The best way to deal with the problem is to avoid it in the first place.

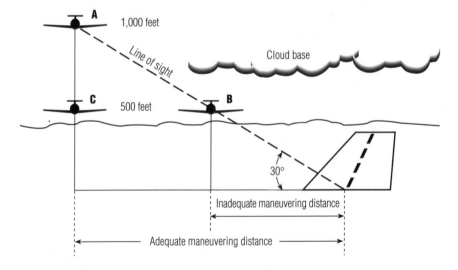

Figure 39. Deceiving effect of a low downwind leg

Chapter 15 **Flying a Taildragger**

Until the advent of jet propulsion, almost all military fighters were taildraggers. And for good reason. A raised nose was required to provide ground clearance for the huge propeller.

There were, of course, some notable exceptions such as the Bell P-39 Airacobra and Lockheed P-38 Lightning, but the taildragger reigned supreme.

General aviation really did not utilize the nosewheel until the late 1940s and early 1950s. Among the first to sprout tricycle "training wheels" was the Ercoupe (1946). It was followed by the classic Beech Model 35 Bonanza (1947), Piper's flying "milk stool," the Tri-Pacer (1951), and Cessna's venerable model 172 Skyhawk (1956). The nosewheel became extremely popular because it is an easier, more forgiving method of maneuvering an airplane on the ground. Cessna was so enthused that it referred to its 172 as having "Land-O-Matic" landing gear. Although that was an obvious exaggeration, even the stalwart champions of conventional gear (which has become a modern-day misnomer) had to admit with nostalgic regret that this claim contained a certain element of truth.

It was anticipated that the tailwheel would become as anachronistic as the horse and buggy, but to the surprise of most and the delight of others, the tailwheel survives. Taildraggers still are being manufactured because they are ideally suited for certain special purposes.

Bush pilots, for example, know that—in addition to offering greater propeller clearance—the tailwheel allows taxiing turns in tight quarters because the airplane can be pivoted on one main tire. (This normally should be avoided, however, because such abuse can wear flat spots on a tire.) Also, a tailwheel weighs less than a nosewheel, creates less drag, and is less expensive to manufacture, replace, and maintain. Some people even contend that a taildragger has better short-field performance than an identical airplane with a nosewheel. Although some might disagree with this, the claim is accurate.

Figure 40 shows a "trike" and a conventional aircraft being rotated for takeoff. Notice that the horizontal tail surfaces produce a downward force to raise the nosewheel. This "negative lift" effectively adds weight to the airplane and requires the wing to produce additional lift for takeoff.

But look at the taildragger. The horizontal tail surfaces produce an upward force (positive lift) to raise the tail. Since the tailfeathers support some

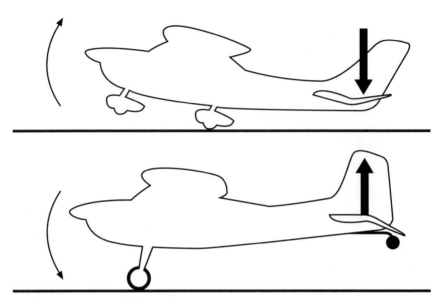

Figure 40. Lift forces of the tail surfaces in nosewheel vs. tailwheel aircraft

aircraft weight, the wing does not have to produce as much additional lift to get the airplane off the ground. In other words, the taildragger requires slightly less airspeed for takeoff than does a trike.

The taildragger also is best suited for unimproved and soft-field operations. This is because the tailwheel usually can be lifted quite early in the takeoff roll, and the wing can be set at the maximum lifting angle, poising the airplane for flight very early in the game.

The nosewheel, on the other hand, cannot be raised until the aircraft achieves a faster speed. As a result, the nosewheel follows the irregular terrain like a cartographer's pen. This causes the airplane to bobble along the ground and the wing's angle of attack to vary considerably during the takeoff roll. Consequently, acceleration is impeded.

A common mistake made by new taildragger pilots is raising the tail too high during takeoff. This can set the wing at a negative angle of attack and drive the main landing gear harder onto the ground. The increased tire friction created, along with the additional drag produced by such a tail-high attitude, retards acceleration considerably. Such an improper technique can even prevent some low-powered taildraggers at high-density altitude from ever reaching liftoff speed.

The nemesis of the neophyte taildragger pilot is directional control. There are two reasons for this. First, the taildragger is a marvelous weather vane, especially if equipped with a fully swiveling tailwheel. Seemingly with a mind of its own, the contrary airplane is like a hunting dog that always wants to nose into and sniff every zephyr (even when there isn't any). Consequently, considerable attention must be paid to the machine whenever in motion on the ground. Some instructors (of which there now are very few schooled in the fine art of taildragging) advise students to constantly and gingerly "walk" or "fan" the rudder pedals while taxiing. Presumably, this prevents the pilot's feet from falling asleep at the controls and allowing the aircraft to wander off track. Once airborne, of course, there is essentially no difference between taildraggers and trikes.

Since taildraggers head into a strong wind like a horse heading for the barn, such an intentional turn while taxiing is simple; let go and the airplane almost turns itself.

Turning the other way—downwind—can be very tricky (and even impossible) when the wind is blustery. The effort can require full rudder, hefty differential braking, and a heavy hand on the throttle (to blow air across the rudder and increase its effectiveness). Weathervaning is not a serious problem with other airplanes because a nosewheel resists being pushed to the side.

But weathervaning is only one reason why it can be difficult to keep a taildragger's nose pointed in the right direction. The second has to do with the location of the aircraft's center of gravity (CG) with respect to the main landing gear. Out of necessity, the CG is behind the main gear; if this were not so, the beleaguered taildragger would simply and ungracefully plop on its nose.

Figure 41 shows a taildragger taxiing in a straight line and then swerving somewhat to the left, intentionally or otherwise. Notice that the CG becomes positioned behind the right main wheel. Because of momentum (or inertia), the CG tends to continue moving along its original path, which is straight ahead. In other words, the CG (or the weight of the airplane itself) tends to continue the turn by pushing against the outside wheel. In this respect, the taildragger is unstable. Once a turn on the ground has begun— for any reason—the aircraft tends to continue turning...and turning...and turning. Only the attentive pilot can reverse the process before the airplane eventually runs out of steam and slows to a halt.

On a trike (Figure 42) this situation is reversed. To prevent the tail from striking the ground (as when the aft baggage compartment is overloaded), the CG must be forward of the main landing gear. This is convenient because it keeps the nosewheel on the ground where it belongs.

The stabilizing effects of this arrangement are that once the aircraft has begun to swerve, the momentum of the aircraft (acting through the CG) tends to pull forward on the inside wheel and straighten things out.

The difference between a taildragger and a trike is most easily understood by comparing these aircraft to the manipulation of a wheelbarrow. Steering a taildragger is like pushing a wheelbarrow; it always wants to veer to one side or the other. Maneuvering a trike, however, is like pulling a wheelbarrow, it goes exactly where you want it to. Little wonder that the nosewheel has become so popular.

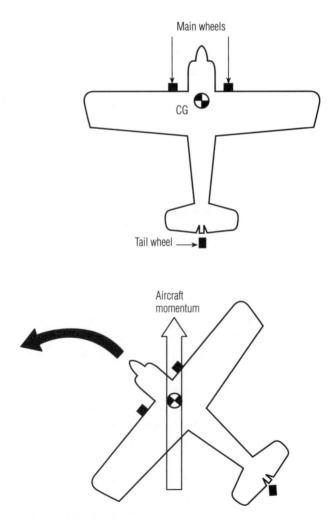

Figure 41. Directional instability of a taildragger

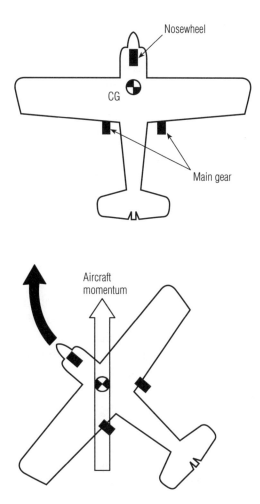

Figure 42. Directional stability of a nosewheel airplane

When the combined troublesome effects of weathervaning and CG location are considered, it is easy to understand why pilots have developed a
respect for taildraggers. Attention to directional control is critical. Otherwise
the taildragger will bite when least expected. This behavior can range from
having the nose swap ends with the tail to the infamous groundloop, a
usually involuntary maneuver where the pilot becomes his own passenger.
He becomes helpless to do anything but survey the horizon as it streams
rapidly across the windshield. Sound like an exaggeration? Believe me, it is
not. The groundloop can punctuate the end of a flight with blurring, embar-
rassing finality.

The scenario for a groundloop usually begins with an improperly executed crosswind landing or by an inattentive pilot taxiing sharply off the runway at high speed. The nose begins to swerve and, unless arrested, continues to yaw with a progressively shorter turning radius.

As the arc described by the aircraft begins to spiral inward, the rate of turn also increases. Physicists explain this phenomenon with a relatively fancy phrase: moment of inertia. Simply put, this means that as the radius of a revolving mass decreases, the rate of turn increases. A ballet dancer takes advantage of this by bringing her arms closer to her body (reducing the radius) to increase rotational velocity during a pirouette.

Pirouettes are lovely on dance floors and ice-skating arenas, but they are not graceful when performed by an airplane. Once the groundlooping process begins, turn radius continues to decrease, which quickens the rate of turn. Simultaneously, centrifugal force increases. Unless this whirling dervish is interrupted with some deft and timely handling of flight controls and throttle, the aircraft ultimately loses balance and topples toward the outside wing. Although rarely injurious to those inside, the cost of repairing a wingtip and possibly a folded main gear can be substantial.

Fortunately, groundloops usually are not that difficult to avoid. Directional instability is a problem only to those who are inattentive or lack respect for that cute little wheel on the tail. In some respects, however, it is worth considering that a taildragger landing really is not complete until the aircraft has been parked, the wheels are chocked, and the pilot is at home with a cold beer in hand.

Another problem pilots have with taildraggers is bouncing during a landing attempt, a taildragger mannerism usually and erroneously attributed to springlike landing gear. A bounce occurs because of improper landing technique; otherwise, pilots of Cessna 170s and early-model 172s, for example, would encounter similar bouncing difficulties because each has identical main landing-gear struts made of spring steel.

The bounce occurs in a taildragger primarily because of CG location and from not touching down in a three-point attitude. (Unfortunately, too many pilots have perfected three-point landings while flying nosewheel-equipped airplanes, a skill not worth bragging about.)

Notice that the upper aircraft in Figure 43 has been allowed to touch down prematurely; the tailwheel is still off the ground. If the touchdown occurs with any significant sink rate, the momentum of the CG (which is aft of the main gear) tends to push the tail farther down. But in the process, the nose rises, which increases the wing's angle of attack. As a result, additional lift is produced, causing an involuntary liftoff.

The opposite occurs during landing in a trike. When the main wheels punch the concrete, the nose-heaviness of the aircraft forces the nosewheel down. This is another reason why the trike is so much more tolerant of sloppy technique. Bounces do occur when flying a tricycle-gear aircraft, but these usually are caused when pilots apply excessive back pressure during a premature touchdown.

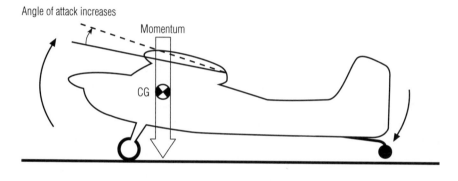

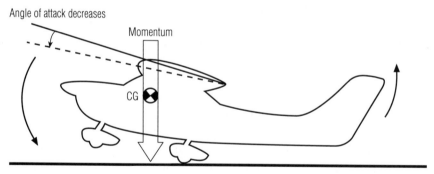

Figure 43. Effect of touchdown in a taildragger and nosewheel airplane

The key to a successful landing in a taildragger is to touch down without drifting (to preserve directional control) and in a three-point attitude (to prevent bouncing). If the tailwheel touches simultaneously with the main gear or slightly earlier, the angle of attack cannot be made to increase. Additionally, designers usually arrange for taildraggers to be virtually stalled when in the three-point attitude, a convenience that results in a minimal touchdown speed.

The "wheel landing" is another method of reconnecting a taildragger with the ground. Although the maneuver is strangely named (it is hoped that all landplanes land on wheels), it is more aesthetically pleasing to observe and somewhat more difficult to perform than conventional taildragger landings. The wheel landing is executed in a near-level attitude by literally flying the main wheels onto the runway. Although touchdown occurs at a faster airspeed than that of a three-point landing, the advantages include being able to land more precisely on a chosen spot and having better crosswind handling because of crisper control responses during touchdown at a higher speed.

There are two noteworthy forces at work during a wheel landing. The first is the tendency of a taildragger to bounce nose high, as previously discussed. The second is a nose-down pitching moment caused by the retarding frictional effects of the tires that occur at touchdown. The trick is to land in such a way as to balance these nose-up and nose-down forces—a delicate procedure. To ensure that the first is the only touchdown, it usually is necessary to add a bit of forward pressure on the control wheel (or stick). This is the difficult phase of a wheel landing for all new taildragger pilots (and some experienced ones). There is a fear of applying too much forward pressure and using the nose to dig a furrow in the runway. This anxiety generally is unfounded.

Although it is possible under certain extreme conditions to buzzsaw the runway with the propeller tips, this would require an extraordinary application of forward control pressure. In theory, it is impossible to actually nose over during touchdown. The force of the relative wind pushing against the top of the horizontal tall surfaces prevents the tail from being raised to such an exaggerated attitude. (But don't try it.) At slower speeds and when taxiing into the wind, it is possible to nose over, but this usually requires using full-forward elevator pressure, heavy breaking, and some power.

The only other problem that often plagues new taildragger pilots (especially short ones) is restricted over-the-nose visibility while taxiing. This handicap, however, is easily overcome by slowly S-turning along the taxiway to maintain a watchful vigil for other traffic.

It can be said that flying a taildragger is more difficult than flying a trike. It is more of a challenge in the sense that it demands to be handled properly at all times. To fly a trike properly also can be demanding, but such an aircraft is more tolerant of errors made along the way.

In the final analysis, taildragging disciplines a pilot to fly well and attentively at all times when near the ground—lessons all of us can use.

Section 3

Flightworthy Considerations

The following five chapters focus on safety issues that should be given serious thought before departing on any flight. The intention here is to create a mind-set that enables pilots to readily recognize certain insidious hazards and the potential consequences of failing to give them due consideration.

Chapter 16 **Responsibilities of the Pilot-in-Command**

The Federal Aviation Regulations contains this apparently simple mandate: "The pilot in command of an aircraft is directly responsible for, and is the final authority as to, the operation of that aircraft."

Although it is contained in the "General Operating and Flight Rules" (Part 91), the mandate applies as much to air-taxi and air-carrier pilots as it does to those who fly solely for recreation and personal transportation.

Unfortunately, some pilots do not regard this regulation with sufficient gravity. If they did, many accidents and fatalities might never occur.

Pilots spend considerable time critiquing aircraft designs, learning procedures, evaluating new equipment, studying new technology, and honing skills. Much of this is done in the name of safety. But many fail to pay sufficient attention to the single greatest threat to safety: the pilot (who frequently and colloquially is referred to as the nut behind the wheel or the first person to arrive at the scene of the accident). As most pilots will acknowledge, almost anyone can be taught to fly, but not everyone can be taught to fully comprehend and abide by the responsibilities of pilot-in-command.

A poster recently published by Trans World Airlines (TWA) for display in its dispatch offices puts it more succinctly. It reads, "The most important wings on a plane are [worn by] the pilot." The message is that a flight is no safer than its pilot. This applies as much to the captain of a Cessna 152 carrying one passenger as it does to the captain of a Boeing 747 carrying hundreds.

An airline pilot spends years of apprenticeship in the right seat as a first officer (co-pilot), learning the responsibilities of command through training, observation, and osmosis. A private pilot receives no such training formally. And yet, after only fifty to seventy hours of experience, he is in a position of similar responsibility. Presumably, he will exercise the necessary attitude and judgment. Too often, he does not.

Why is it, for example, that a pilot will strut like a cock because he was the last to "duck in" before the field closed? This often is less a reflection of skill than it is of poor judgment. A pilot, after all, does not have the right to risk lives unnecessarily, especially when his passengers are unable either to assess or to reject the risks to which they may be subjected. Most passengers place an inordinate amount of trust in their pilot. That trust is violated too often by pilots who do not consider the responsibility of their position.

It is said that the 180-degree turn is one of aviation's most effective lifesaving maneuvers. It also can be an unwelcome consideration because it may bruise a pilot's ego. He often is reluctant to abort or cancel a flight because of how he thinks others will perceive him. A responsible pilot takes pride in his ability to recognize when discretion is the better part of valor. Any pilot worthy of his certificate has a yellow stripe along his back that widens and intensifies with age and experience, and he is not afraid to show it. (Yes, a conservative pilot has guts, but he also wants to keep them intact.)

Pilots often are quick to complain that regulations are excessively restrictive, but in the case of a private pilot, the opposite may be true. This is because he is allowed more operational flexibility than a commercial pilot. The Federal Aviation Administration says indirectly that passengers who pay their way are entitled to greater regulatory protection than those who do not. But does this mean that private pilots—those governed by FAR Part 91—should expose their passengers to unwarranted risk? Of course not, but many do.

Many pilots have established or have been advised to set their own personal minimums—standards above and beyond those required by law. This not only reflects good judgment, but is the responsibility of every command pilot who recognizes that he may not always be able to cope with a circumstance simply because it is legal to do so. Unfortunately, this is as far as the advice goes; nothing concrete is offered.

A few instructors suggest that noncommercial pilots review and perhaps adopt some of the standards in FAR Part 135, which apply to air-taxi and commercial operators.

Charter pilots, for example, must use oxygen when above 10,000 feet in an unpressurized airplane for more than 30 minutes, must not allow a passenger to touch the controls, must carry a fire extinguisher on board, must not fly a single-engine aircraft above an overcast unless VFR conditions exist below the clouds, must not fly a single-engine aircraft beyond gliding distance of land, must have an instrument proficiency check every six months, must not fly more than eight hours in any 24-hour period, and so forth.

Many of these air-taxi regulations make sense for private operators. Although governed solely by Part 91, most corporate flight departments have incorporated Part 135 standards in their flight operations.

Interestingly, Part 135 defines specifically some of the responsibilities of the pilot-in-command that Part 91 only implies. For example, a charter pilot—who only may be carrying a passenger in a Cessna 152 on a 30-mile flight—is required to brief his passengers about all pertinent emergency procedures. Although this is not spelled out in Part 91, the following demonstrates that a private pilot is equally responsible for the well-being of his passengers.

The pilot of a privately operated amphibian was urged by his passengers—who also were his friends—to make an unscheduled landing on a nearby lake because the nearby destination was obscured by fog. During the landing, the aircraft struck a submerged object, which tore a hole in the hull. As the water began to gush in, one passenger jumped out the rear door of the still-moving aircraft and drowned.

During subsequent litigation, the court found the pilot negligent and responsible for the death of his friend, but not because of the accident itself. The pilot was hung out to dry because he failed to brief his passengers about emergency procedures and the use of available life jackets.

The lesson here is that every command pilot is expected to act appropriately for the safety of his or her passengers, even when these obligations are not detailed by regulation.

Since the pilot landed the amphibian on the lake at the insistence of his passengers, should this have reduced at least some of his liability? Not according to the court, because it was felt that only the pilot-in-command is qualified to assess the circumstances and arrive at a sound decision.

Every mode of travel involves some risk. When placed in perspective, therefore, the role of the command pilot is to assess continually the risks that occur during every flight and accept only those that allow him to reach his goal safely. Unfortunately, many pilots do not consider the risks that may develop because, if sufficient thought were devoted to them, a pilot might not take off in the first place, which is precisely the point.

Simply put, risk management is a critical element of flight, tempered by a continual series of judgments. Unfortunately, there is no way for the FAA to determine whether a pilot is capable of exercising such judgment. During a flight test, for example, almost every applicant exercises judicious care and conservatism. But once away from the watchful eye of an examiner, he may, and often does, behave differently. If every pilot were to perform as if his flight instructor were watching his every move, many accidents might never occur.

A pilot's ability to perceive risk depends, in part, on an intimate knowledge of his capabilities and limitations as well as those of the aircraft he flies. Many, however, do not recognize these limits, which points out a glaring weakness in training and personal discipline. Too much time and attention is devoted to what a pilot can do and not enough to make him appreciate what he cannot or should not do. (A pet peeve of mine is the aircraft salesman who tries to convince a low-time, prospective buyer how easy it is to fly a particularly complex airplane. Such an attitude may erode some of the limitations a pilot has learned to respect.)

It can be said that every flight is a calculated risk, a willingness to embark on a course of action that offers prospective rewards that outweigh the perceived hazards. But what if the end does not justify the means? Perhaps the option should be declined.

Pilots fly because of trust, trust that the wings will remain attached, trust that a fuel cell will not spring a leak, trust that the laws of aerodynamics will not fail. Such trust is acceptable because it has a sound foundation. Care must be taken, however, not to allow trust to erode into complacency—a hope (and sometimes a prayer) that the worn left tire will last for another landing, that the oil quantity is okay even though it was not checked before departure, that the weather will improve despite a forecast that indicates otherwise...

It generally is agreed that, when a pilot is making a decision, his assessment of the risk is dependent upon the perceived realities of the moment and upon his identical or related experiences. Unfortunately, many pilots do not perceive reality. They suffer from a normative philosophy, meaning that they anticipate what should or ought to be, not what really is. Also, many are blissfully ignorant of the risks because their years of uneventful flying create a false sense of security. In other words, they may be convinced that "it cannot happen to me." But as we know, "it" can happen to anyone, especially those who least expect it.

All of this makes the continual process of risk management a bit difficult to employ as a safety tool, since many are unaccustomed to thinking in these terms. Those who fail to assess the risks properly play a form of Russian roulette; they fly ever so closely to the brink. Occasionally, some fall off.

If this form of logic fails, then perhaps pilots should pay greater attention to their instincts when these suggest that something is awry. Such gut feelings should be pacified by eliminating the circumstances creating the anguish or discomfort. Since an accident often results from the cumulative effect of several errors, taking the steps necessary to eliminate the first link in this potentially lethal chain may prevent catastrophe.

Taking a positive action to eliminate the first indication of a threat is an attitude referred to by TWA as aggressive safety. In other words, safety does not just happen; flights have to be made that way.

A TWA safety instructor may have been guilty of oversimplification when he once said to his class of newly hired airline pilots, "Gentlemen, you must learn to deal with three major threats to your asses: gravity, inertia (or momentum), and inflammables. Each can be lethal, and no accident can occur without losing control of at least one of these elements." W. O. "Sailor" Davis is gone now, but those who have benefited from his advice are forever grateful.

Although pilots recognize the need for thorough pre-flight inspections, many fail to assess their personal airworthiness prior to departure, a factor in many accidents attributable to pilot error. For example, FAA studies have shown that pilots suffering from malnutrition (low blood sugar), fatigue, pain, dehydration, mild hypoxia, and so forth often cannot perform with the required proficiency.

Psychological stresses also make a pilot more vulnerable to error. These can be caused by such events as the death of a spouse, marital difficulties, a financial crisis, marriage, and even such seemingly mundane events as a petty argument at home or a change in eating, sleeping, or living habits.

It is the pilot's responsibility to determine when these factors might interfere with safety, and act accordingly.

It also is the command pilot's responsibility to recognize those human traits that predispose him toward the taking of unnecessary risks. Although the following list is not complete, it does point out most of the factors responsible for triggering that train of events that so often leads to tragedy.

Get-home-itis. Some pilots behave like horses heading for the barn and risk their lives getting there.

Distraction. This has caused a number of air-carrier accidents as well as numerous general aviation fatalities. The cardinal rule is to concentrate on flying the airplane first; everything else is secondary. Most distractions seem to be caused by mechanical irregularities, passengers, and air traffic control.

Intimidation. Pilots often pay more attention to passenger desire than to common sense. Never be so anxious to please that safety is jeopardized.

Systems management. Either the pilot fails to understand a given aircraft system or he fails to engage his brain before using it. There is no excuse in either event.

Egoism. The danger in allowing an aircraft to become an extension of a pilot's personality is that he may be unwilling to accept the machine's limitations because he may perceive this as a limitation of himself.

Commercial compunction. Is any appointment, meeting, or job really worth risking lives?

Peer pressure. Someone who may scoff at your failure to complete a flight because of safety considerations probably does not qualify as a peer in the first place; he is less of a pilot than you are, despite his experience or ratings. Never try to impress anyone who fails to respect sound judgment.

Stupidity. Ignorance may be excusable because a pilot may not know better. But stupidity, which is inexcusable, is when a pilot knows better but defiantly proceeds. A command pilot's never-ending responsibility is to overcome ignorance and recognize stupidity.

Someone once said that an aircraft is an assemblage of parts flying in tight formation. It is a pilot's legal and moral responsibility to keep it that way. Any behavior demonstrating a willingness to accept less must not be tolerated. Remember, it does happen only to the other person—until it happens to you.

Chapter 17 **Wind Shear: Mystery of the Vanishing Airspeed**

On June 24, 1975, an Eastern Airlines' Boeing 727 crashed on short final approach to New York's John F. Kennedy International Airport. More than 100 passengers perished, making this one of the worst air disasters in U.S. history.

According to the National Transportation Safety Board (NTSB), this tragedy resulted from an encounter with a strong wind shear.

Because of this accident's spectacular nature, considerable attention suddenly became focused on wind shear. It is shameful that a disaster of this magnitude was required to attract industry-wide attention to a phenomenon with which pilots have always had to cope.

Air-carrier aircraft, of course, are not the exclusive victims of this invisible hazard. General aviation aircraft also fall prey to this misunderstood, underestimated menace. Hundreds, if not thousands, of accidents presumably caused by pilot error may have been direct or indirect results of wind-shear encounters. It is imperative, therefore, that pilots be familiar with the potentially lethal effects of wind shear and the various conditions during which these effects are most likely to occur.

Simply stated, wind shear is a variation in wind velocity (speed and/or direction) that occurs over a relatively short distance. Airspeed is affected when an airplane is flown from one wind condition—through a wind shear—into another wind condition in less time than the aircraft can adjust to the new environment. The consequences can range from annoying power and attitude corrections to complete loss of control.

Wind shear is a unique hazard not only because it frequently is undetectable, but because some pilots do not acknowledge the threat. They consider it incredible that a change in wind velocity can alter airspeed; it is contrary to their earliest lessons of flight.

"Airspeed," they were taught, "is determined solely by variations in aircraft attitude, configuration, and power setting; wind affects only track and groundspeed." Unfortunately, this simplistic axiom is but the tip of another iceberg and applies only when the wind is constant or changes gradually. Unless a pilot examines what lies beneath the surface, he is liable to fly unwittingly into the jaws of what has come to be regarded as one of aviation's most insidious killers.

To understand wind shear is to recognize that an airplane has inertia. As a result, it resists a change in groundspeed. This is best stated by paraphrasing Sir Isaac Newton, the brilliant English physicist who developed the inescapable laws of motion: an aircraft in flight at a given groundspeed tends to remain at the same groundspeed unless acted upon by an exterior force.

For example, Figure 44 shows a temperature inversion overlying a coastal city from the ground to 2,000 feet. Within the inversion, the wind is westerly at 5 knots. Immediately above, the wind is easterly at 20 knots (not an unusual situation). The narrow band separating the two "air masses" is called a shear line.

An aircraft descending toward the shear has an airspeed of 120 knots; its groundspeed is obviously 100 knots. This groundspeed represents aircraft momentum with respect to the earth and, according to Newton's First Law of Motion, is the quantity resisting change.

As the aircraft penetrates the shear line and enters the inversion, groundspeed does increase, but not instantly. Because of aircraft inertia, groundspeed after crossing the narrow shear line is very nearly what it was earlier—100 knots.

But since the aircraft is now under the influence of a 5-knot tailwind, something has to give. That something, unfortunately, is airspeed, which reduces from 120 knots (above the shear line) to 95 knots (below the shear

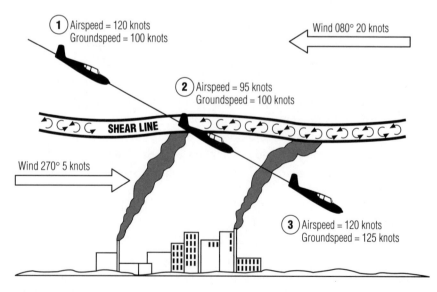

Figure 44. Wind shear caused by a temperature inversion

line), a net and rapid airspeed loss of 25 knots. Notice that the theoretical airspeed loss (25 knots) is equal to the difference between the headwind and tailwind components above and below the shear line.

The reduced airspeed, of course, results in reduced drag. Assuming neither attitude nor power is changed, the aircraft accelerates to its original trimmed airspeed (120 knots), at which time thrust and drag are again in balance. But because of inertia, this acceleration takes time; lost airspeed cannot be recaptured instantly.

Just how long it takes to recover lost airspeed was dramatized in a U.S. Air Force report by Major C. L. Hazeltine. He demonstrated that if a given aircraft, maintaining a constant altitude and power setting, encounters an abrupt 20-knot loss (due to wind shear), recovery of only 10 knots would require 78 seconds, and recovery of 16 knots would require 176 seconds. Adding power and/or sacrificing altitude reduces recovery time significantly. This points out the alarming need for pilots to be particularly alert for a low-level wind shear when on final approach or when climbing out at marginal airspeed. The problem of airspeed recovery is critical if the airspeed loss results in the drag rise associated with flight behind the power curve, when required power and altitude may not be available.

(In reality, the airspeed loss is not quite as large as shown in this example because some acceleration occurs while the aircraft crosses the shear line, depending on the line's width.)

Would the pilot have any warning about the impending airspeed loss? In this case, yes. When two opposing air currents rub shoulders, there is bound to be some frictional turbulence. The degree of turbulence increases in proportion to the change in wind velocity and decreases in proportion to the width of the shear line. For similar reasons, the air surrounding a jet stream is often turbulent, even though a smooth ride can be found within the core.

The aircraft in Figure 44 encountered a rapidly decreasing headwind, which has the same effect as an increasing tailwind: an airspeed loss. If the direction of the aircraft is reversed, so that it flies into an increasing headwind (or decreasing tailwind), airspeed will increase when the shear line is crossed. The theoretical gain would be 25 knots.

The effect of wind shear is similar to what happens to a hobo who jumps from a bridge to the top of an express train passing below. As the man leaves the bridge, his groundspeed (forward motion) is nil. The train, however is clipping along at 60 mph. When the hitchhiker first touches down, it should be obvious that he cannot remain on the roof at the point of initial contact. His inertia prevents him from being accelerated so rapidly, from zero to 60 mph. Instead, the hapless hobo will fall and roll backward with respect to the train. Eventually, the friction of the train acting on his body will accelerate him to 60 mph. Whether he will survive to realize this is questionable.

If the unfortunate chap were to misjudge and jump immediately in front of the train, the locomotive would force his body to adapt quite rapidly to the speed of the train. But the acceleration would exert such overwhelming and crushing G-loads that the hobo would instantly regret not having purchased a ticket and boarded the train under more comfortable circumstances.

For those who cannot correlate the hobo and the train with an aircraft in flight, consider this extreme, but illustrative, example. A Cessna 152 is cruising at an airspeed of 100 knots, directly into the teeth of a 100-knot headwind. The 152's groundspeed obviously is nil. Assume, also, that the headwind disappears, suddenly and without warning.

The pilot—just as suddenly—finds himself high and dry without any airspeed whatsoever. The beleaguered 152 pitches down rapidly and loses considerable altitude before the combined effect of diving and power can accelerate the aircraft from a standstill to an airspeed/groundspeed of 100 knots in the calm air.

Conversely, had the 100-knot airplane been flying with a 100-knot tailwind, the groundspeed would have been 200 knots. The sudden disappearance of this wind would cause a healthy increase in airspeed (theoretically to 200 knots), an immediate pitch-up, and a substantial gain in altitude.

In the foregoing examples, the pitching is a result of longitudinal stability, the design characteristic of an airplane by which it automatically seeks its original trimmed airspeed.

All pilots have encountered some form of wind shear without realizing it. Perhaps, after a period of smooth flight, a pilot runs into a patch of light chop, followed by more smooth air. A comparison of groundspeed and drift before and after the turbulence might reveal a wind velocity change. Airspeed fluctuations under these conditions are rarely perceptible, however. Such a shear line is usually wide, allowing ample time for groundspeed to adjust to the new wind condition.

Whenever an approach to landing is made on a gusty day, the pilot is actually encountering numerous wind shears. Every gust of air causes extremely localized shearing. Carefully monitor the indicated airspeed during such an approach and notice how the needle shifts rapidly above and below target airspeed. Some of this erratic needle movement is caused by gusts punching the pitot tube at oblique angles, but, for the most part, actual airspeed varies every time a gust is encountered or left behind.

Curiously, an approach or departure in gusty air is not normally as dangerous as flying through a strong, smooth shear. This is because gusts provide a seat-of-the-pants warning of possible hazards. A pilot is more alert to needed power and attitude corrections. Also, most pilots use slightly higher approach speeds in gusty air to maintain controllability. This also provides a hedge against higher, G-load-induced stall speeds and possible airspeed losses due to wind shear.

An excellent rule of thumb suggests adding at least half the gust factor to normal approach speeds. For example, if the surface wind is reported at 22 knots, gusting to 38 knots, the gust factor is 16 knots. Add at least eight knots (half the gust factor) to the normal approach speed.

This rule provides ample protection except when the turbulence is caused by thunderstorm activity. The only protection against this type of severity is to avoid any well-developed cell by at least 10 miles, especially when taking off or landing. A healthy gust in advance of an approaching thunderstorm can quickly steal 20 to 30 knots of airspeed (or more).

Pilots also should be on the alert for local obstacles, on or near the airport, which can disrupt the flow of a reportedly smooth, strong breeze. Figure 45 shows an aircraft about to touch down into a strong, quartering headwind. As the aircraft begins to flare downwind of the large hangar, the headwind component all but disappears, leaving the pilot insufficient airspeed to avoid the impending plop. Numerous hard landings (or worse) can be traced to similar circumstances.

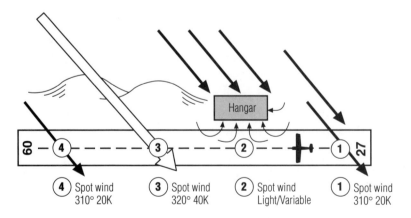

Figure 45. Landing into a strong quartering headwind

Two small hills are situated farther down the same runway and form a Venturi-like constriction. This can change normal wind flow into a jet of high-speed air squirting across the runway from between the hills. Entering such a localized condition could lead a departing pilot to believe he has sufficient airspeed to fly. But not for long. When this "river of air" has been crossed, the resultant shear causes a speed loss that could be sufficient to force the aircraft back to the runway.

When the wind is strong, local velocities are easily affected by topographical features. It is not unusual for windsocks at opposite ends of a runway to point in opposite directions and indicate different wind speeds. A wind shear lies obviously somewhere in between.

The type of wind shear that seems to catch most pilots off guard is the wind gradient, a condition where wind-velocity changes are somewhat more gradual. Although airspeed changes are not as abrupt as in the case of a narrow shear line, the final results have spectacular potential. Gradients are particularly hazardous because flight conditions can be deceptively smooth; pilots are lulled into complacency and frequently are unable to determine that something is amiss until it is too late.

Figure 46 depicts a wind pattern overlying relatively flat terrain. Near the surface, the wind is light, flowing directly from high to low pressure. But as altitude is gained, the frictional effects of the ground are reduced, and the influence of the earth's rotation (Coriolis force) increases. This causes wind speed to increase and wind direction to shift clockwise (in the Northern Hemisphere) so that above the ground the winds are considerably stronger than at the surface and flow approximately parallel to the isobars. Under the circumstances shown in the figure, a pilot climbing westbound would experience an increasing tailwind (from calm at the surface to 40 knots at 1,100 feet). Such a strong wind gradient would make it difficult to maintain a normal climb speed and would result in an anemic rate of climb.

Figure 47 illustrates the problems associated with windshear encounters when making ILS approaches from, say, the east and the west. Assume that in each case an approach speed of 100 knots is used, and wind velocity over each outer marker at the glideslope-intercept altitude is from the east at 40 knots.

When the aircraft is approaching from the east, groundspeed over the marker is 140 knots. Over the runway threshold, where the wind is essentially calm, groundspeed should be only 100 knots if the target airspeed has been maintained during the approach. During the approach, therefore, groundspeed must be reduced from 140 to 100 knots, a deceleration rate of 23 knots per minute.

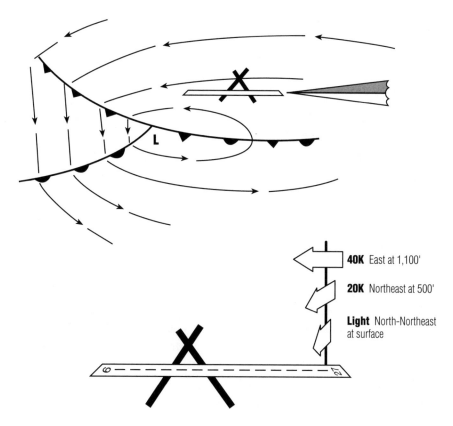

Figure 46. Wind gradient

But if the pilot is unaware of the strong tailwind over the OM he will not anticipate the need to decelerate. This is the crux of the problem. When a tailwind decreases faster than groundspeed is reduced, airspeed is forced to increase. The excess airspeed results in a tendency to rise above the glideslope (either visual or electronic) and, to compound the confusion, also might cause a nose-up pitch. Unless judicious control and power adjustments are made during the descent, the aircraft will wind up over the approach lights with excessive altitude and airspeed. This diminishing tailwind (or increasing head-wind) approach has been responsible for innumerable overshoot incidents.

This example utilizes a wind gradient of 40 knots per 1,100 feet, or 3.6 knots per 100 feet. During wind shear studies in Florida and Texas, this has been found to be an average gradient. Low-level wind shears with 10 times this magnitude (35 knots per 100 feet) have been observed. A gradient of 10 to 15 knots per 100 feet is not considered unusual.

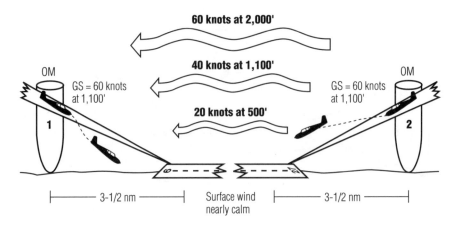

Figure 47. ILS approaches and wind shear

Curiously, this situation (descending into an increasing headwind) also can result in an undershoot. As the shear is encountered and the aircraft begins to rise above the glideslope, a pilot usually reduces power to remain in the approach slot. But once stabilized at the new, slower groundspeed, considerably more power is required to remain on the glideslope. And unless sufficient power is added in timely fashion, the aircraft could wind up sinking into the approach lights.

When the pilot is approaching the runway from the west, conditions are reversed. Groundspeed during the approach must be increased from 60 to 100 knots. If this is not done, airspeed will decay in proportion to the headwind loss that occurs during the descent.

To avoid sinking below the glideslope, losing critical airspeed, and encountering a possible pitch-down, considerable and seemingly excessive power must be applied during the descent. This poses another threat, since less reserve power is available for a possible missed approach. Such a loss of headwind requires considerable pilot attention and action to avoid the potential undershoot. During such conditions, aircraft have developed high sink rates and contacted the approach lights with all engines developing full power. Similarly, aircraft departing into an area of either an increasing tailwind or a decreasing headwind have settled into the ground with engines developing full power.

When a pilot finds himself nearing the ground while having difficulty maintaining a safe airspeed/sink-rate combination, he should execute a missed approach and either try again, wait for the wind shear to subside, or divert to another airport.

Anyone under the mistaken notion that wind gradients cannot affect him in this manner should be interested in what happened at JFK one day in April, 1971. Aircraft approaching the airport encountered a decrease in tailwind of 20 knots per 1,000 feet. And during a two-hour period, nine professional pilots executed missed approaches (some diverted to other airports) even though the surface wind was light and the ceiling was 700 feet with adequate visibly below.

Chapter 18 **Operating at High Density Altitudes**

The approach of summer signals the disappearance of freezing rain, low-level icing, and blizzards. But as every pilot knows, these wintry hazards are replaced by other weather elements that can be equally dangerous.

The most insidious summertime phenomenon is probably high density altitude because, unlike thunderstorms, the threat is less dynamic and not as easily recognized. Consequently, many pilots fail to consider its deleterious effects on aircraft performance, and contribute to the lengthy list of annual accidents attributable to operations at high density altitudes.

Although flight training always includes considerable study of the effects of air density, many pilots fail to make the connection between theory and the real world. Many cannot even define the phenomenon except to s ay, "Density altitude is pressure altitude corrected for temperature." This technical definition is accurate and may help to pass a written examination, but it fails to clarify the subject and leaves many in need of something more illuminating.

When pilots discuss the takeoff and climb performance of an airplane, they usually do so with respect to standard, sea-level conditions: absolutely dry air (no humidity), an atmospheric pressure of 29.92 inches of mercury (Hg)—which also is expressed as 1,013.2 millibars or Hectopascals—and an air temperature of 59 degrees F (15 degrees C). At such a time, the density of air is 0.076 pounds per cubic foot. In other words, 1,000 cubic feet of standard air at sea level weighs 76 pounds. The density of air provides the substance needed to create aerodynamic forces (lift, drag, and propeller thrust) and feed the air-breathing engine a sufficient diet of oxygen. Any reduction in the density, or substance, of the atmosphere results in a corresponding decrease in takeoff and climb performance.

Standard, sea-level conditions are rarely encountered. Similarly, the standard, three-dimensional atmosphere described in Figure 48 is even more of a rarity, but it does provide a basis for predicting aircraft performance at various altitudes. Most pilots recognize that, when climbing in the standard atmosphere, pressure and temperature decrease about 1 inch Hg and 3.5 degrees F (2 degrees C) per 1,000 feet. Note also that air density decreases a little more than 2 percent per 1,000 feet. At 10,000 feet, for example, standard density is only 0.056 pounds per cubic foot, 26 percent less than the density of air at sea level.

Standard Atmosphere				
Altitude (ft.)	**Standard Barometric Pressure** (in/Hg)	**Standard Temperature** (°F)	(°C)	**Density of Air** (lb/cu ft.)
msl	29.92	59.0	15.0	.076
1,000	28.86	55.4	13.0	.074
2,000	27.82	51.9	11.0	.072
3,000	26.82	48.3	9.1	.070
4,000	25.84	44.7	7.1	.068
5,000	24.90	41.2	5.1	.066
6,000	23.98	37.6	3.1	.064
7,000	23.09	34.0	1.1	.062
8,000	22.22	30.5	-0.8	.060
9,000	21.39	26.9	-2.8	.058
10,000	20.58	23.3	-4.8	.056
11,000	19.79	19.8	-6.8	.055
12,000	19.03	16.2	-8.8	.053
13,000	18.29	12.6	-10.8	.051
14,000	17.58	9.1	-12.7	.050
15,000	16.89	5.5	-14.7	.048
18,000	14.94	-5.2	-20.7	.044
20,000	13.75	-12.3	-24.6	.041

Figure 48

This decrease in air density is the reason that indicated and true airspeed differ by about 2 percent (2.5 percent would be more accurate) per 1,000 feet of altitude. Since air at altitude has less substance, the amount entering the pitot tube creates less ram pressure within the airspeed indicator.

Air density in the standard atmosphere decreases with altitude because of the decrease in atmospheric pressure. However, air density can be affected in other ways. When air is heated, for example, it expands and becomes less dense, losing some of its substance.

Assume, for example, that sea-level temperature rises to 92 degrees F. This would cause standard, sea-level air to expand, and the density of air would be only 0.072 pounds per cubic foot. In a standard atmosphere, such an air density is found at 2,000 feet MSL (see chart). So even though this heated air is at sea level, it can be said to have a density altitude of 2,000 feet MSL. An airplane flying in such a condition would perform as if it were at 2,000 feet on a standard day, even though the altimeter indicated zero. In other words, performance is determined by how high the airplane "thinks" it is (based on ambient air density), not how high it really is.

Unfortunately, many pilots use indicated altitude (or airport elevation) to predict required takeoff distance, rate of climb, and so forth. They often are surprised later to find the airplane considerably more lethargic than anticipated. It would be helpful if every airplane had two altimeters, one to indicate actual altitude and perhaps an even larger one to portray density altitude. This might help some pilots to recognize more readily that, in terms of available performance with respect to the standard atmosphere, the airplane may be much higher than they realize.

A rule of thumb worth remembering is that density altitude increases 60 feet for each increase of 1 degree F above standard. For example, consider a pilot about to depart an airport with an elevation of 5,000 feet MSL. According to the table, standard temperature at this elevation is 41 degrees F. But on this particular day, the mercury has shot up to 101 degrees F, which is 60 degrees F above standard. Using the rule of thumb, which is reasonably accurate, the density altitude is really 8,600 feet MSL—5,000 feet (the elevation) plus 3,600 feet (60 degrees F x 60 feet). In other words, the airplane will behave as if it were at 8,600 feet, even though the altimeter indicates only 5,000.

In addition to elevation and temperature, a third factor to consider is the variation in atmospheric pressure as indicated by the altimeter setting. When the setting is 29.92, atmospheric pressure is standard. But an altimeter setting that is less than standard also causes density altitude to rise. Generally, however, this does not cause a serious jump in density altitude. Each tenth of an inch below 29.92 represents an increase in density altitude of only 100 feet. However, if a pilot were to find himself in the eye of a hurricane where the altimeter setting might be 25.00 inches, for example, this alone would cause density altitude to increase by 4,900 feet. Conversely, when atmospheric pressure is high (the altimeter setting is more than 29.92), density altitude decreases 100 feet for each 1/10 inch above 29.92.

Even pilots who are conscientious about computing density altitude before departure usually ignore humidity—a factor that has far more significance than generally is realized.

When air is humid, it contains a certain amount of water vapor that weighs about one-third less than dry air. So it is obvious that humid air is lighter and therefore less dense than dry air. But how much lighter? Measurements taken at Tafaingata in Western Samoa—virtually an open-air sauna— reveal that this extremely humid air contained only 0.023 pounds of water vapor for each pound of air. In other words, even the most humid air imaginable is not that much lighter (or less dense) than dry air.

So why all the fuss about humidity? B-29 bomber crews operating in the South Pacific during World War II discovered that, although humidity may cause only a slight loss of aerodynamic efficiency, it also causes reciprocating engines to lose a considerable amount of power. For example, if the ambient temperature is 80 degrees F and the relative humidity is 90 percent, power loss due solely to the presence of water vapor is 6.5 percent. Higher temperatures or relative humidity can reduce power by as much as 10 percent. (Remember, every increase of 20 degrees F doubles the ability of air to absorb water vapor.)

Such a power loss can be significant anytime, but is especially hazardous during operations at high density altitude. Unfortunately, operating handbooks do not account for the adverse effects of humidity. So when the air is sultry, raise the calculated density altitude by 1,000 feet to compensate for the aerodynamic efficiency losses due solely to humidity. Then decrease calculated performance by a conservative fudge factor of 10 percent to compensate for the power-robbing effect of humidity.

Water vapor in the atmosphere reduces power in normally aspirated and turbocharged engines, because it displaces some of the air ingested by the engine, reducing the amount of oxygen available for combustion. Humidity also retards the speed at which the flame spreads within the cylinder, which has the same effect as retarding the ignition. Finally, water vapor enriches the mixture. (Turbine engines are not nearly as affected by high relative humidity.)

The most serious consequences of operating at high density altitudes are increased landing distances, dramatically increased takeoff distances, and anemic rates of climb.

Since the indicated stall speed of a light airplane does not vary with altitude, an approach to a high-density-altitude airport can and should be flown at the same indicated approach speed used at sea level (usually 1.3 times V_{S0}, which is the power-off stall speed in the landing configuration). But as density altitude increases, a given indicated airspeed translates into a higher true airspeed, explaining why a longer landing roll is required. For example, a Cessna R172K Hawk XP has a recommended approach speed of 63 knots. At a sea-level airport on a standard day, the airplane would cross a 50-foot obstacle with a groundspeed of 63 knots (assuming zero wind) and consume 1,270 feet of runway before stopping. But at an airport with an elevation of 6,000 feet and a temperature of 104 degrees F, the density altitude would be 10,050 feet (excluding the effects of humidity and a possibly low altimeter setting); the same approach speed of 63 knots would result in a true airspeed and groundspeed across the fence of 73 knots. The extra 10 knots would increase the landing distance to 1,595 feet, only 325 feet more than sea level.

Such a minimal increase in landing roll often is all that is necessary to set the stage for tragedy. An inexperienced pilot might say to himself, "Gee, landing at such a high density altitude is almost like landing at home [sea level]; what's the big deal?" With that, he has the fuel tanks topped, loads his passengers, and prepares to take off without even consulting a performance chart.

During the takeoff roll, he will have to accelerate the Hawk XP to a liftoff speed of 56 KIAS. But this equates to a true airspeed (or no-wind groundspeed) of 65 knots. That is, the engine must accelerate the airplane to a higher groundspeed than necessary at sea level. This explains why even turbocharged aircraft require a longer takeoff roll at altitude than at sea level.

An additional 9 knots may not seem like much, but every knot of additional acceleration requires more distance than the previous knot, especially when significantly less than sea-level power is available. This is why manufacturers of STOL aircraft work so hard to shave an additional knot or two from the lift-off speed. The effort pays handsome dividends in terms of reducing runway length requirements.

But the Hawk XP is not a STOL airplane, and its normally aspirated engine is short-winded at altitude. Consequently, acceleration is anemic; the airplane needs more than twice as much runway at a density altitude of 10,050 feet as would be required at sea level. If high humidity, low atmospheric pressure, improper leaning, low tire pressure, a slight uphill slope, a slight tailwind component, or an unimproved runway surface is thrown into the equation, the engine simply may not have enough power to get the airplane airborne before the end of the runway. In some cases it might be impossible to accelerate to lift-off speed with an infinitely long runway. There are a number of cases on record describing pilots who landed easily but had to wait for a strong wind (or winter) before a safe departure could be made. A fascinating and extreme example is La Paz, Bolivia, where the elevation is 13,000 feet MSL and density altitude in the summer can extend well above 17,000 feet.

Preparing for departure from a high-density-altitude airport should begin soon after landing. Resist refueling until confident that you can carry the load safely. If takeoff conditions are marginal, consider leaving with only a partial payload. Drop off the load at a nearby airport where more favorable conditions (lower density altitude or longer runway) exist, and then return to fetch the balance of the payload.

During the takeoff roll, expect poor acceleration and demonstrate the patience of Job as airspeed slowly builds. If it does not appear that rotation speed can be achieved in time to lift off within the confines of the airport and climb over existing obstacles, abort the takeoff while there is still sufficient runway available. It may be necessary to await more favorable conditions, such as cooler temperatures and stronger winds.

The most common mistake made by inexperienced pilots is to rotate the nose during takeoff before the airplane has accelerated to a safe lift-off speed. Although logic should preclude such foolishness, some pilots get the urge to lift the nose prematurely because they sense that the aircraft has sufficient speed even though the airspeed indicator insists otherwise. This occurs because the groundspeed, not the indicated airspeed, is faster than what they are accustomed to at sea level. The airplane confirms this by vibrating a bit more than usual. This, combined with the rapid approach of the end of the runway, compels many to disbelieve the airspeed indicator and attempt to take off anyway. Big mistake. In some cases, the added drag of a nose-high attitude not only prevents further acceleration but actually slows the aircraft. Or, the airplane might have enough speed to lift off but not to climb out of ground effect with the nose held high. Such accidents occur during the summer at Lake Tahoe (6,264 MSL) and Big Bear City (6,748 MSL) Airports in California. And these have fairly long, level, hard-surface runways—6,400 and 5,800 feet, respectively.

Once the takeoff has been negotiated safely, try not to overfly any towering obstacles that might be lurking near the end of the runway until first accelerating to the best-angle-of-climb speed. High density altitude significantly affects climb rate and angle. Also, if the outside-air temperature is much above standard, the service ceiling will be considerably lower than published. And the closer an airplane is to its service ceiling, the less tolerant its pilot can be of downdrafts, especially when attempting to cross high ridge lines.

Since climb rates and angles often are less than satisfactory at high density altitudes, it is important to be familiar with the airplane's go-around capability before committing to land at a warm and lofty airport. This is done by establishing the airplane in landing configuration (gear and flaps down) while on the downwind leg. Then establish a normal approach speed and sink rate, which is followed by a simulated go-around.

While the throttle is fully open, lean the mixture for maximum power, then enrich it very slightly because the go-around, if necessary, will occur at a slightly lower altitude. Unless this procedure is followed, the mixture control probably will be positioned incorrectly for a go-around. (This recommendation does not apply to engines equipped with turbochargers or automatic mixture controls.)

To further maximize go-around performance, do not extend the flaps fully until prepared to commit the airplane to a landing.

Many pilots find it difficult to appreciate and accept just how devastating high density altitude can be to airplane performance. Usually all that is necessary to convince them is to fly into a Rocky Mountain airport on a hot summer day. But this may not be practical for a pilot building time in Birmingham, Alabama, or Baton Rouge, Louisiana. But he can simulate a high-density-altitude departure, a truly eye-opening experience for lowlanders.

For example, the pilot of a Piper Comanche equipped with a 250-hp Lycoming O-540-A engine can simulate taking off from an airport with an elevation of 5,000 feet and an ambient temperature of 100 degrees F. He first must consult his engine-operating manual to determine how much power would be available at such a density altitude (8,620 feet). According to the manual, the O-540-A loses 39 horsepower when at a pressure altitude of 5,000 feet and an additional 13 horsepower due to the unusually high temperature. This represents a total loss of 52 horsepower. For the O-540-A to develop only 198 horsepower (250 – 52 = 198) at sea level, the manual suggests using maximum rpm (2,575) and a relatively meek 22.3 inches of manifold pressure instead of full throttle. (Similar computations can be used for other aircraft and combinations of pressure altitude and temperature.)

Next, fill the tanks and load the airplane with volunteer heavyweights. During the subsequent takeoff use no more than the reduced power setting to simulate the maximum power available at altitude. Also, do not attempt to lift off until the airspeed is 10 knots greater than normal, to simulate the higher groundspeed, to which an airplane must be accelerated at high density altitude.

The takeoff obviously will take forever, if you have not given in to the urge to shove the throttle home. The shallow climb angle will have the cows running for cover.

If this procedure is performed faithfully, under the watchful eye of a competent instructor and from an airport where safety or noise-abatement procedures are not compromised, the pilot will gain appreciation and respect for the hazards associated with high-density-altitude operations.

Chapter 19 **Hazardous In-Flight Illusions**

The world of flight can be strangely deceptive, offering many misleading clues that should not be believed even though they can be seen.

Take the classic example of the VFR pilot flying above an inclined cloud layer. Because he is not disciplined in the skills of instrument flying, the pilot perceives the sloped cloud layer as the natural horizon. Influenced by this illusion, he tends to fly askew unless able to rationalize the deceptive visual reference with the less conspicuous, contradictory display of the attitude instruments.

Many pilots have difficulty flying over desolate terrain on a moonless, VFR night. Even though there are no ground or celestial references, they attempt to fly visually in conditions clearly requiring instrument-flying techniques.

The situation is complicated by the introduction of a single light on the horizon, a target toward which a pilot can aim his craft. If the pilot stares at this beckoning beacon for any period of time, it may soon appear to move from side to side in wide, irregular arcs—a phenomenon known as autokinetic motion, or "stare vision."

In the absence of other outside references, a pilot's senses often interpret this apparent movement of light as a change in aircraft heading or attitude. As a result, the pilot—without realizing it—maneuvers the aircraft so as to keep the light positioned in his windshield. In the meantime, his senses provide the erroneous sensation that the aircraft is on an even keel. The instruments contradict this sensory illusion, but a confused pilot may choose to ignore them. A sufficiently bewildered pilot could encounter vertigo and possible loss of aircraft control.

Autokinetic motion can be duplicated by sitting in an otherwise dark room and staring at a pinpoint of light. After a short while, the light can be observed drifting in various directions—a most perplexing phenomenon.

The U.S. Air Force has blamed numerous night VFR accidents on autokinetic motion and teaches its pilots never to stare at a single light source in an otherwise dark flight environment, and to frequently glance at the more trustworthy message spelled out on the instrument panel.

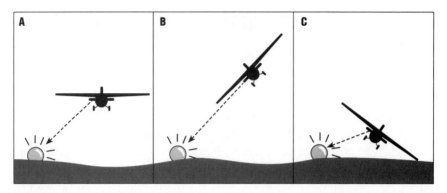

Figure 49. Flying VFR at night when natural horizon is not visible

In 1952, Capt. Prosper Cocquyt of Sabena Belgian World Airlines prepared an award-winning paper describing another dangerous illusion with respect to night flying and a light on the ground. Unfortunately, this profound information never reached general aviation, even though this sensory deception has been the probable cause of many night accidents.

The problem deals with VFR night flying at a relatively low altitude (such as when approaching or departing an airport) when the natural horizon is not visible.

Figure 49A shows a wings-level aircraft flying abeam a light on the ground. The pilot senses he is at a safe altitude because the light appears below the aircraft (as it should). But consider Figure 49B, a situation where the pilot inadvertently allows the aircraft to bank left. (Remember, the horizon is not visible.) By glancing at the light, which is sighted by looking parallel to the wing, the pilot perceives that the aircraft and the light are at the same altitude-ground level. This produces the erroneous sensation of an urgent need to climb. The illusion received when a pilot has inadvertently banked toward a light is considered a "safe-side" illusion because altitude is perceived to be less than actual and the pilot, by climbing, will err on the safe side.

The dangerous illusion is shown in Figure 49C, a situation where the aircraft is inadvertently allowed to bank away from the light. The pilot has no sensation of being too low because he thinks he is looking down at the light, when in fact, he is not. Unless the pilot sees the silent warning of the artificial horizon, he might be the victim of a fatal shock.

Inadvertent excursions in pitch also can have serious consequences. Figure 50A shows an aircraft approaching a light (or group of lights) on the ground. Since the aircraft is maintaining a constant altitude, the pilot must look down at an angle to see the approaching lights. If this angle is sufficiently large, the pilot sees that he is at a safe altitude. But suppose that he inadvertently allows the nose to rise slightly while at a dangerously low altitude, as shown in Figure 50B. The pilot senses being at a safe altitude because he appears to be looking down at a large angle, when, in reality, he is looking primarily forward.

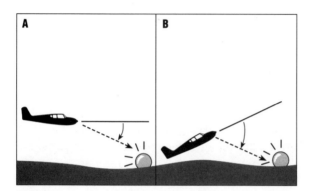

Figure 50. Pitching the aircraft at night

Such an illusion is most likely to occur during a nose-high departure at night toward gently rising terrain, especially when there are no visible landmarks between the aircraft and the light(s) toward which the aircraft is heading. A pilot can easily be deceived into believing he will clear an obstacle.

A night approach toward an airport can create an equally dangerous illusion if there are no visible landmarks between the aircraft and the airport. Under these conditions, a pilot can be totally unaware that he is being lured into the ground.

The departure problem can be prevented by climbing in the traffic pattern until a safe altitude is reached. Arrival difficulties are best resolved by avoiding straight-in approaches when the approach corridor is dark or by utilizing a steep descent path toward the airport.

An additional illusion often is encountered during a straight-in approach at night when visibility is unlimited, a condition frequently found in the desert and mountain areas of the West. Approach and runway lights appear brighter than usual at such times and cause a pilot to believe that he is closer to the airport than he really is. The result often is a premature descent toward intervening obstacles.

For this reason, experienced mountain pilots often delay a descent until safely within the confines of the traffic pattern. They use another interesting technique, which although quite logical, is something about which most pilots are unaware.

When descending toward a distant city, for example, keep a sharp eye on the lights at that edge of the city closest to the aircraft. Should any of these lights disappear, then something (such as a ridge) has risen to block the view and dictates an urgent need to arrest the descent and recapture altitude until the lights are once again visible. As long as these lights remain in sight, the aircraft is above all enroute obstacles.

Restricted visibility also can be deceptive because of the dimming effect it has on airport lights. When approaching an airport on a hazy night, for example, a pilot unknowingly interprets his altitude as being higher than it actually is. This phenomenon results in the common tendency of a pilot (when first sighting the runway during an ILS approach) to reduce power and drop below the glideslope—an extremely hazardous reaction.

During daylight hours, the effect is similar because visibility restrictions dilute shadows normally used as an aid to depth perception.

Moisture on the windshield can produce unpredictable illusory effects because of the irregular refraction of light caused by the droplets. Depending on the moisture pattern and the shape of the windshield, a pilot may perceive significant glideslope and/or localizer deviations, even though the ILS needles are centered.

Experienced pilots never completely abandon the cross-pointers during the final, visual phase of an ILS approach. Instead, they monitor the needles to confirm that outside clues are not leading them astray.

Variations in runway and approach lighting intensity also can be misleading. When these lights are set to maximum intensity, the airport appears closer than it is. Conversely, when the lights are dim, the airport appears farther away.

A few years ago, I was flying with an advanced student who I asked to approach an airport at night while maintaining 3,000 feet AGL. I instructed him not to descend until intercepting what appeared to be a normal, 3-degree, visual-approach slot. (The ILS needles were hidden from his view, and unknown to him, I had prearranged with the tower controller to vary the runway and approach lighting intensity during our approach.)

As we began the long, straight-in approach, the airport lights were set to minimum intensity and, predictably, the student was considerably above the glideslope before initiating descent; he sensed being farther out than he really was. I clicked the mike button twice, which signaled the controller to gradually increase the lights to maximum brilliance. As the lights "came up," I noticed a gradual increase in sink rate and power reduction until, finally, we were literally diving toward the airport.

Although well above the glideslope at the beginning of descent, we were now uncomfortably below it. This became more apparent as we neared the approach lights, causing the confused pilot to add considerable power and back pressure to prevent the impending undershoot.

Although a pilot is not likely to experience such gross variations in lighting intensity during any given approach, this experiment did verify (and exaggerate) the illusory effects that can be expected when airport lights are unusually dim or bright.

Although most illusions occur at night, daylight operations also offer some fascinating deceptions.

Figure 51A shows an aircraft in a normal, 3-degree, visual descent toward a level runway. The pilot can maintain this "3-degree slot" quite accurately because he has spent his entire flying career practicing approaches that "feel" comfortable. He approaches a runway so that the visual glideslope "seems" neither too shallow nor too steep.

A visual illusion develops when approaching a runway with a pronounced upslope (Figure 51B). If a pilot establishes a 3-degree approach slot relative to the horizontal, while approaching a runway with a 2-degree upslope, for example, he would sense that he is descending too steeply. This is because he would be aware of descending at a 5-degree angle with respect to the runway. As a result, the pilot automatically compensates by "dropping down" until the runway "looks right." In other words, he settles onto a 3-degree glide-path with respect to the runway, as he always does. Unfortunately, this re-sults in a dangerously low, flat approach.

One popular southern California resort airport, Catalina, is reputedly hazardous because the first half of the runway has considerable upslope. Unsuspecting pilots are affected by the illusion and approach this airport at dangerously shallow descent paths. Numerous aircraft have made impres-sions (literally) on the bluff at the approach end of Catalina's Runway 22, causing the FAA to install a set of visual approach-slope indicator (VASI) lights. When followed religiously, Catalina's VASI prevents the previously common undershoot accident, but pilots must resist the urge to fly below the red-and-white glidepath, which does appear steep but, in fact, is not.

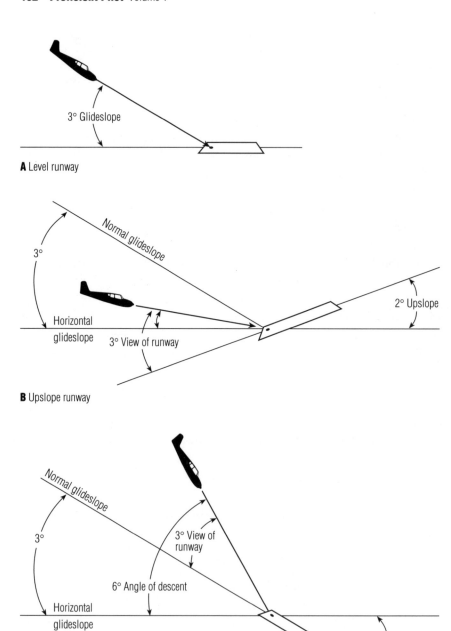

A Level runway

B Upslope runway

C Downslope runway

Figure 51. Effects of a sloped runway

The downslope runway (Figure 51C) leads to overshoots. The runway shown has an admittedly steep (3-degree) downslope, but illustrates the illusion associated with shallower slopes.

When in a 3-degree approach slot relative to the horizontal, pilots can only see the approach edge of the runway, leading them to believe they are extremely low. As a result, they level off until the runway can be viewed at a normal, 3-degree angle. This, of course, produces a steep, 6-degree descent path with respect to the ground and substantially increases the likelihood of an overshoot.

The terrain surrounding an airport often has a slope comparable to that of the runway, which makes it difficult to determine in advance whether a given runway is sloped or level. Often, the only clue afforded the observant pilot is the abnormal sink rate required to maintain what appears to be a normal slot.

When approaching a bowl-shaped runway with a pronounced dip in the middle, the proper procedure is to use only the first half (the downslope portion) of the runway to establish a visual glidepath. By maintaining what then appears to be a somewhat flat approach, you will be close to the proper slot.

Conversely, if the runway is convex (a hump in the middle), refer only to the first, uphill portion of the runway and establish what appears to be a slightly steep approach path.

Runway geometry also can be deceiving. Without realizing it, a pilot usually assesses the runway before him by comparing it with the runway to which he is most accustomed. Assume that a pilot is conditioned to landing on a 4,500 by 150-foot runway (which has a length-to-width ratio of 30 to one). From above and afar, a longer runway with the same proportions (6,000 by 200, for example) has an identical appearance. But because the runway is larger, the pilot is led to believe that he is closer and lower than he really is.

The more hazardous illusion occurs when approaching a shorter runway with those same, familiar proportions (2,250 by 75, for example). When on

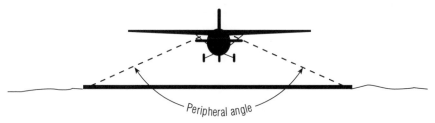

Figure 52. Runway width illusion

final to this smaller runway, the pilot perceives being farther from the runway and higher above the ground than he really is.

Runway width, irrespective of length, can adversely affect judgment during the landing flare. Whether or not he realizes it, a pilot uses peripheral vision to help determine when he is at the proper height above the runway to initiate the landing flare. He does this during the last several feet of descent by subconsciously waiting for the edges of the runway to spread laterally beneath the aircraft until reaching the angle (Figure 52) to which he is conditioned.

When descending toward an unusually wide runway, this peripheral angle forms while the plane is considerably higher above the ground than usual. By yielding to the subconscious suggestion that he initiate the flare at this time, a pilot may run out of airspeed while several feet in the air. Conversely, when descending toward a narrow runway, the lateral spread of the runway edges may not be sufficient for the peripheral clue to form and can result in the failure of a pilot to flare in time to avoid a hard landing.

The problems posed by wide and narrow runways are particularly acute at night, when it is more difficult to judge height above the ground. This is due to the lack of contrast between the runway and the surrounding terrain. All is in blackness, a condition that decreases depth perception. A similar loss of depth perception occurs during daylight hours when there is little or no contrast between the runway and the adjacent terrain, such as when the entire airport is snow- or water-covered, when landing on open areas of dirt or grass, and when approaching hard-surface runways surrounded by similarly colored sand. Visibility restrictions aggravate the problem by further reducing color contrast.

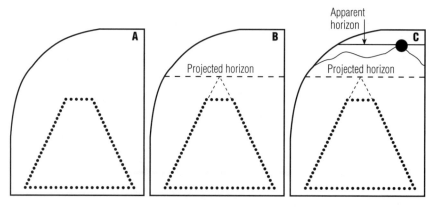

Figure 53. Flying a straight-in approach at night

During the late 1960s, The Boeing Company instituted a comprehensive research program to determine those factors adversely influencing a pilot during visual, straight-in approaches at night. The practical aspect of this program involved twelve senior jet instructors who were asked to execute several simulated approaches to an airport at the near edge of a sprawling matrix of city lights. Furthermore, each pilot was advised that the city (not the airport) had a pronounced upslope. Not only did most of the test pilots fly considerably below the normal glideslope, but many flew their simulators below the elevation of the airport.

One major problem of a straight-in approach at night is the frequent lack of a natural horizon. But by practicing the following technique, a pilot can learn to create an imaginary one.

Figure 53A displays the runway as seen from the cockpit on a night when the horizon is not visible. Since the parallel rows of runway lights, when extended, intersect at the horizon (Figure 53B), the pilot can project an imaginary horizon on his windshield.

This is a particularly useful technique when hilltop lights beyond the airport (Figure 53C) elevate the apparent horizon to a confusing height. When such a false horizon is used instead of the real one, a pilot is led to believe he is on a normal glidepath when he is actually far below.

When a pilot passes over the approach lights at night, the runway lights occupy a large portion of the windshield area (Figure 54A). But when sliding down the electronic banister to very poor visibilities (4,000 feet or less), an instrument pilot breaks out of the overcast and sees only the lights in the touchdown zone (Figure 54B). These appear in the lower portion of the windscreen and create the illusion of being too high. It is a natural tendency under these conditions for a pilot to tuck below the glideslope in a subcon-

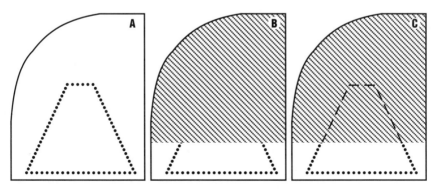

Figure 54. Flying a straight-in approach at night in instrument conditions

scious effort to fill more of the windshield area with lights, as is usually the case when visibility is good. To call this dangerous is an understatement. It is the direct cause of numerous undershoot accidents following ILS approaches.

If all runway lights are not visible when breaking out of an overcast, attempt to mentally extend those that are visible to create the image of a full-length runway (Figure 54C).

The National Transportation Safety Board is responsible for determining the probable causes of all fatal aviation accidents. In many cases, the epitaph at the end of a report often states, with obvious simplicity, that the pilot failed to maintain adequate altitude or airspeed.

What is not so obvious are the reasons why a pilot might have been misled in the first place. Often, he has been the victim of one or a combination of sensory illusions, which prove that seeing should not always be believing.

Chapter 20 **How to Interpret Engine Instruments**

In our increasingly complex society, many more people are breaking down under stress than ever before. Aircraft engines obviously are not subjected to psychological pressures, but they do have equally critical limits that must not be violated. Otherwise, they too, can fail.

Fortunately, engine-operating limits are defined precisely, usually displayed as green, red, and yellow instrument markings (not always, in older aircraft). But not all of these radials and arcs are understood. (And not all of the instruments are as accurate as they should be.)

Consider, for example, the green arc on the manifold pressure (MP) gauge. This represents the normal operating range. But what is the significance of the low end of the arc (usually about 15 inches of mercury)? When developing power "within the green," the engine powers the propeller. But when "below the green," it usually is the windmilling prop that drives the engine.

Prolonged operation below the green can be as detrimental to the engine as rough and rapid throttle action. This is because crankshaft counterweights (designed to dampen engine vibrations) may become erratic and detune the engine. The results are increased vibration and internal wear, which lead to reduced engine life, more expensive overhauls, and in some cases, powerplant failure.

For the same reason, a simulated engine failure should be induced by fully retarding the mixture control and leaving the throttle open. This allows manifold pressure to remain high and keeps the combustion chambers filled with a supply of shock-absorbing air. Prior to rekindling the engine, slowly retard the throttle. Then advance the mixture control and allow the engine to warm.

The upper limit of manifold pressure for normally aspirated (nonturbocharged) engines is 30 inches. But rarely can this much be achieved. That is because of induction losses from restrictions to the flow of intake air such as filters, bends in the plumbing, and the throttle valve itself. The typical engine at sea level can develop only 28.5 to 29.5 inches MP at full throttle. Readings much below these values may be indicative of trouble and should be investigated.

Exceeding the maximum allowable MP of a turbocharged engine is called overboosting and is destructive. But, according to Textron Lycoming, a momentary overboost can be tolerated as long as rated manifold pressure is not violated by more than 3 inches for no more than five seconds. Such an overboost may occur when applying takeoff power, as the turbocharger controller "overshoots the throttle." A 5-inch overboost for ten seconds or less suggests an engine inspection; up to 10 inches (for any period) warrants disassembling the engine. Exceeding 10 inches requires overhaul and crankshaft replacement. Teledyne Continental offers similar advice but in some cases imposes more conservative limits.

Pilots are taught to reduce power by first retarding the throttle and then reducing rpm. This is because a combination of high manifold pressure and low rpm can induce damaging detonation. But this does not mean that MP never can "exceed" rpm (28 inches and 2,600 rpm, for example). This does, after all, occur during every takeoff from a low-elevation airport. A rule of thumb for nonturbocharged engines is that detonation can be avoided by not allowing MP to exceed rpm by more than "four" (28 inches minus 2,400 rpm, for example, equals four).

Since high propeller rpm is responsible for most after-takeoff noise, there is nothing wrong with a slight rpm reduction prior to throttle retardation, as long as the rule of four is not violated. It is a handy technique to use when a pilot wants to soften his noise footprint but cannot justify a significant power reduction. This suggestion, of course, does not supersede advice to the contrary published in the airplane flight manual.

The red line on a tachometer indicates more than the maximum-allowable rpm; it also represents the rpm required to obtain the engine's rated horsepower. This illustrates a significant difference between constant-speed and fixed-pitch propellers. With a constant-speed prop, engine rpm can be increased to the red line while the airplane is motionless. In other words, the engine can develop rated horsepower without any airspeed whatsoever. But the maximum-obtainable static rpm of an engine with a fixed-pitch propeller may be as much as 400 rpm below the red line. In other words, such an engine cannot develop rated horsepower during a full-throttle runup. This explains why an airplane equipped with a constant-speed propeller has better takeoff performance than a similarly powered airplane equipped with a fixed-pitch propeller. (As the latter airplane accelerates along the runway, rpm and horsepower steadily build, because increasing airspeed aerodynamically unloads the propeller.)

During the pre-flight runup, pilots can do more than check the magnetos to determine engine health. When operating a constant-speed propeller, learn what manifold pressure to expect at runup rpm. Excessive MP at a given rpm, for example, could indicate a failed cylinder. A full-throttle runup of an engine with a fixed-pitch propeller is not a bad idea (unless pebbles are under the aircraft); this proves whether an engine is capable of developing the expected static (aircraft motionless) rpm. Something is wrong, for example, if the engine of a Cessna 152 cannot develop 2,280 static rpm (the red line is 2,550 rpm).

Exceeding the red line of the tachometer is called overspeeding and can accelerate the wear of stressed engine parts. If allowed to occur frequently, the engine or the propeller could fail. Some propellers have critical rpm limits very close to the red line. So, in some powerplant/propeller/airframe combinations, the propeller is more subject to failure than the engine.

Overspeeding a constant-speed propeller usually is caused by a malfunctioning propeller governor. But a momentary overspeed may occur when the throttle is advanced rapidly for takeoff. This is caused by the reaction time of the governor and usually is not serious if rated rpm is not exceeded by 10 percent for more than three seconds. If the overspeed lasts for more than three seconds, an engine inspection and possible maintenance may be warranted. An overspeed that exceeds 10 percent of rated rpm for any period of time probably justifies an engine overhaul. Tachometers, which often indicate excessively high or low, should be periodically checked for accuracy.

Overspeeding a fixed-pitch propeller is equally serious and is caused by an excessively open throttle at too high an airspeed. An overspeeding propeller also loses efficiency and therefore produces less thrust. This loss is caused by cavitation, compression of air at transonic tip speeds, and other factors.

Pilots should avoid continuous operation within the yellow band of a tachometer, a restriction imposed on a few aircraft (the Mooney M20F, for example). This caution range is not a characteristic of the engine, but of the engine/airframe. While flight testing a new airplane, the manufacturer may detect a harmonic or resonant vibration within a usually narrow range of rpm. This not only is uncomfortable, but could induce metal fatigue (and possibly failure) of a structural member, if allowed to continue for long periods of time.

The first instrument to be given serious attention after engine start is the oil-pressure gauge. Everyone knows that insufficient pressure after 30 seconds of engine operation mandates an immediate shutdown because of possible damage resulting from insufficient lubrication.

A problem not often considered is excessive oil pressure, a condition that may develop after starting an engine with very cold oil. The pressure should decrease to normal, however, as the oil warms. If it does not, the problem might be caused by an improperly set pressure-relief valve (easily adjusted by a mechanic) or oil of the wrong viscosity. In either case, takeoff should be postponed until the difficulty is resolved. Excessive oil pressure can strain the weakest link (sometimes the oil cooler and its hoses) to the point of rupture, at which time the oil simply gushes overboard.

For similar reasons, power should be kept at a minimum after engine start until the oil is warm. Otherwise, powerful oil-pressure surges within the engine can cause damage. An excessive in-flight oil pressure indication probably is caused by an instrument malfunction. But the problem could be caused by an oil restriction in the engine. The pilot should try to decrease the pressure by operating at a reduced power setting.

One of the most traumatic in-flight indications is the total loss of oil pressure. Although this could be caused by a failed gauge or an obstruction in the pressure-relief valve, experts agree that it usually is caused by an insufficient supply of oil. They advise that, although engine instruments are not very accurate, they rarely fail. So if the pressure drops to zero when flying a single, believe the indication and quickly find a place to land. When flying a twin, shut down the ailing engine before it self-destructs. (Most engines develop oil pressure with as little as two or three quarts.)

Some textbooks claim that an engine malfunction, such as a loss of oil pressure, can be confirmed by an abnormal indication of another instrument. But this is not necessarily true.

If an engine loses oil gradually, there might be a slight increase in oil temperature. But if the loss occurs rapidly, such as when an oil line ruptures, there may be insufficient time for an oil-temperature rise to register prior to engine failure. When all oil pressure is lost, there actually may be a decrease in oil temperature, as oil ceases to flow past the temperature-sensing probe in the engine.

Similarly, cylinder-head temperatures (CHTs) may rise slightly in response to a rising oil temperature as oil quantity slowly dips below a marginal level. But if oil is lost rapidly, there probably will not be a noticeable rise in CHT.

A pilot should not rely on other indicators to confirm the total loss of oil pressure. Nor will he have much time to ponder the problem. An engine operating at cruise power and without oil probably will seize (due to extreme friction) in about 30 seconds. Although the prop will come to an abrupt standstill, the shock poses no threat to the engine mounts or the airframe. But do plan on buying a new engine.

Noticing a loss of oil pressure, a pilot should reduce power as much as practical to prolong engine operation. At idle, for example, the engine might continue to run for 5 to 15 minutes, depending on engine condition. This gives the pilot of a single some time to find a landing site and possibly have a few seconds of reserve power available for emergency use.

Does a fluctuating oil-pressure needle signify an imminent loss of pressure? Probably not. This usually indicates either a malfunctioning gauge or an improperly seated, thermostatic-bypass valve, an easily corrected problem.

In addition to lubricating an engine, oil also is used to carry heat away from the cylinders and to help keep an engine relatively cool. But if oil temperature is allowed to become excessive, the oil loses much of its cooling ability. This allows cylinder-head temperatures to rise and increases internal wear. Excessive oil temperature sometimes can be confirmed by a slight reduction of oil pressure.

Hot oil and cylinder-head temperatures do not always occur simultaneously, however. The early-model Cessna Cardinal, for example, had an unsatisfactory oil cooler but a very effective cowling and baffle system. Consequently, it was not unusual to notice a high oil temperature and only a moderate CHT.

Excessive oil temperature during a climb is best countered by reducing power and leveling off, increasing airspeed. After the oil cools, resume the climb until the temperature again nears unacceptable limits, and repeat this procedure as necessary. This is known as step climbing.

Cold oil, of course, is incapable of providing sufficient lubrication and can generate destructive pressure surges that do not register on the oil-pressure gauge. This is why an engine should not be allowed to develop significant power before the oil has had an opportunity to warm. Common knowledge? Of course. Then why do so many pilots allow cold engines to start with a roar and apply breakaway power to jump a tiedown cable before the oil-temperature needle has been given a chance to move from its place of rest? Such mistreatment accelerates wear and increases the likelihood of failure.

To discourage this kind of abuse, some airframe manufacturers offer more precise advice. Beech Aircraft, for example, warns not to allow the engine of a V35B Bonanza to exceed 1,200 rpm until the oil temperature rises to 75 degrees F.

Oil temperature, of course, should be "in the green" prior to takeoff. But what if the indicated temperature fails to rise after a normal runup period? Unless the oil is cold-soaked because of frigid outside air temperatures, the gauge probably is at fault. At such a time, a takeoff is permissible as long as the engine does not balk at full throttle and the airframe or engine manufacturer does not prohibit it.

High power settings also should be avoided until cylinder-head temperatures have warmed sufficiently. Otherwise, a takeoff could scuff and damage rings, pistons, and cylinder walls.

Excessive head temperatures must be avoided because they are the most likely cause of detonation and preignition. Although a high CHT often is accompanied by correspondingly high oil temperature, do not count on seeing such a verification. Broken or missing baffles can cause high head temperatures without affecting oil temperature.

Excessive cylinder-head temperatures often are caused by a slow-speed climb on a hot day. When this occurs, rising temperatures can be held in check by patiently step-climbing to altitude.

An increasingly common cause of high CHTs is excessive leaning—a probable result of high fuel prices. Fuel may be expensive, but replacement pistons are more so.

The CHT gauge measures the temperature of what is considered to be the "hottest" cylinder, determined by the airframe manufacturer during the flight testing of a new aircraft. Theoretically, therefore, other cylinders are cooler than is indicated by the gauge. But it does not always work this way in practice.

Uneven fuel distribution (in carbureted and fuel-injected engines) can cause any of the cylinders to be the hottest at any given time. So while the CHT gauge indicates something less than the maximum-allowable temperature, another cylinder could be overheating and detonating without the pilot knowing it.

To combat this problem, be very conservative about head temperatures. A better solution is to install a multiprobe, cylinder-head or exhaust-gas temperature gauge. With such instrumentation, the pilot can determine the hottest cylinder at any given time.

Speaking of cylinder-head temperatures, consider applying this suggestion when a faulty magneto is discovered during runup: turn off the good magneto and operate the engine only on the other for several minutes while returning to the parking area. Immediately after shutting down the engine, open the cowling and feel each cylinder head (carefully!) with the palm of the hand. If the magneto problem is caused by a faulty spark plug, one relatively cool cylinder will be felt. This quickly identifies the faulty plug and saves having to remove and inspect the others.

There is nothing particularly serious about excessive fuel pressure or fuel flow, but this could cause a rough-running engine. Resolve this problem by leaning until the roughness is eliminated.

Low fuel pressure usually is caused by a failing pump or vapor lock. In either case, turn on the auxiliary fuel pump.

Fortunately, modern aircraft engines are remarkably tolerant of abuse and neglect. But their reliability is dependent upon our respect for their limitations. Otherwise, like us mortals, they too can yield to the stress and fail.

Section 4

Getting There

In an era of increasing reliance on satellite navigation, pilots are tending to become complacent about the elements of basic navigation. But a failed microchip or dead batteries can necessitate immediate reversion to compass-and-clock navigation. The following chapters are intended to bolster the fundamentals and can be applied to radio and GPS navigation.

Chapter 21 **Dead Reckoning Navigation is Alive and Well**

It generally is agreed that the compass is a pilot's primary navigation tool. But when it comes to specifying the second most valuable such device in the cockpit, there often is some difference of opinion.

New pilots generally favor the VOR or GPS receiver. But those with more experience vote for the clock. After all, when a fuse blows or the left/right needle behaves like a metronome gone berserk, a pilot must resort to basics. The reliable compass and clock become his primary weapons in a battle of wits against the elements. The compass indicates where he's going, and the clock tells him how far. Without either of these allies, a pilot can get very lost very fast, especially when above clouds or when over terrain where checkpoints are confusingly few and far apart.

Compass-and-clock, or dead-reckoning navigation, however, is slowly becoming a lost art as increasingly more reliance is placed on electronic guidance. Although no one can deny that radio and satellite navigation has simplified cockpit workload, pilots must avoid becoming too complacent.

Some, for example, do not keep track of their forward progress while navigating along a radial. They simply wait for the to/from flag to drop, which may provide the first positive fix since passing the previous station. But shouldn't a pilot always know his position relative to the nearest airport?

Dead-reckoning, or DR navigation, is a relatively painless procedure that can and should be combined with electronic navigation so that a pilot is aware of his approximate position at all times.

According to popular definition, dead reckoning is short for "deduced reckoning" or, as the old-timers like to say, "you're dead if you don't reckon right." In truth, however, the term originated with maritime navigation and refers to "reckoning or reasoning (one's position) relative to something stationary or dead in the water." Simply stated, DR navigation is a method of predicting progress enroute based on the direction of flight and the estimated groundspeed since the last known position.

Unfortunately, the mere mention of DR often makes a pilot uncomfortable with memories of FAA written examinations, wind triangles, and E6-B "confusers."

But DR does not have to be laborious.

Consider, for example, Jack Chrysler, a friend who flies his airplane all over North and South America. Chrysler so simplified his dead-reckoning procedures that he considers them not only fun to use, but they frequently result in reduced flight time because he is not confined to the dog-legged dictates of Victor airways. Also, he claims to be more relaxed holding a constant heading than reacting to the semaphorelike movements of a VOR needle.

Prior to a VFR flight, Chrysler simply uses a yardstick and a planning chart to plot a direct course between the departure and destination airports (assuming that intervening terrain and other restrictions do not interfere).

He then uses forecasted winds aloft, together with Figures 55 and 56, to determine true heading and groundspeed. Assume, for example, that the measured true course is 040 degrees and the winds aloft are expected to be from 010 degrees at 40 knots. In other words, the wind will be blowing from 30 degrees to the left of the nose. Using Figure 55, he determines that this is equivalent to a 35-knot headwind component and a 20-knot left crosswind component.

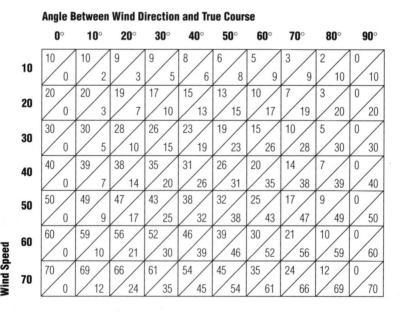

Angle Between Wind Direction and True Course

Wind Speed	0°	10°	20°	30°	40°	50°	60°	70°	80°	90°
10	10 / 0	10 / 2	9 / 3	9 / 5	8 / 6	6 / 8	5 / 9	3 / 9	2 / 10	0 / 10
20	20 / 0	20 / 3	19 / 7	17 / 10	15 / 13	13 / 15	10 / 17	7 / 19	3 / 20	0 / 20
30	30 / 0	30 / 5	28 / 10	26 / 15	23 / 19	19 / 23	15 / 26	10 / 28	5 / 30	0 / 30
40	40 / 0	39 / 7	38 / 14	35 / 20	31 / 26	26 / 31	20 / 35	14 / 38	7 / 39	0 / 40
50	50 / 0	49 / 9	47 / 17	43 / 25	38 / 32	32 / 38	25 / 43	17 / 47	9 / 49	0 / 50
60	60 / 0	59 / 10	56 / 21	52 / 30	46 / 39	39 / 46	30 / 52	21 / 56	10 / 59	0 / 60
70	70 / 0	69 / 12	66 / 24	61 / 35	54 / 45	45 / 54	35 / 61	24 / 66	12 / 69	0 / 70

Figure 55. Headwind/tailwind and crosswind components for various wind velocities. The upper-left figure in each square represents a headwind or tailwind component depending on whether the wind is coming from ahead or behind. The lower-right figure represents a left or right crosswind component (depending also on wind direction).

True Airspeed

	80	100	120	140	160	180	200	220	240
5	4°	3°	2°	2°	2°	2°	1°	1°	1°
10	7°	6°	5°	4°	4°	3°	3°	3°	2°
15	11°	9°	7°	6°	5°	5°	4°	4°	4°
20	14°	12°	10°	8°	7°	6°	6°	5°	5°
25	18°	14°	12°	10°	9°	8°	7°	7°	6°
30	22°	17°	14°	12°	11°	10°	9°	8°	7°
35	26°	20°	17°	14°	13°	11°	10°	9°	8°
40	30°	24°	19°	17°	15°	13°	12°	10°	10°
45	34°	27°	22°	19°	16°	14°	13°	12°	11°
50	39°	30°	25°	21°	18°	16°	14°	13°	12°

Crosswind Component (left side label)

Figure 56. Crab angle necessary to compensate for a given crosswind component when flying at a given true airspeed; valid for knots or mph. **Caution:** Crabbing or turning into the wind results in some loss of groundspeed but this loss is not significant when the crab angle is less than 10°.

Since the planned true airspeed is 220 knots, he expects the enroute groundspeed to be 185 knots (220 - 35 = 185).

Next he consults Figure 56 to determine that a 20-knot, left crosswind combines with 220 knots of airspeed to require a 5-degree (left) wind correction angle. The true heading for the proposed flight, therefore, is 040 degrees less 5 degrees, or 035 degrees. End of problem—without a wind triangle.

If more than one wind condition is to be encountered en route, they may be arithmetically averaged with reasonable accuracy if wind directions don't vary by more than 90 degrees and wind speeds are within 15 knots of each other. For example, assume that the winds aloft for each of three flight segments along the direct route are forecast to be 080 degrees/15 knots, 100 degrees/30 knots and 150 degrees/30 knots. The average wind direction is (080 degrees + 100 degrees + 150 degrees) divided by 3 = 110 degrees. Similarly, the average wind speed is 25 knots. This technique should not be used, however, when maximum accuracy is required (such as on a long, over-water flight).

En route, Chrysler keeps track of his progress visually or uses elapsed time and estimated groundspeed to plot a "DR position." He often does not turn on the GPS or dual VOR receivers until within range of the destination—if at all. (When necessary, he applies a midcourse correction to compensate for an errant wind forecast.)

Dead reckoning works, and it's reasonably accurate. Ask the man who pioneered the 2,000-mile, Newfoundland-to-Ireland route in 1927 as well as the thousands of pilots who have flown in his wake...with little more than a compass and a clock.

(Lindbergh was luckier than is generally realized, however. According to John P. V. Heinmuller, one of the official observers for the New York-to-Paris flight, a freak wind condition existed over the North Atlantic on May 20-22. The pressure patterns were arranged in such a way that the net drift acting upon the Spirit of St. Louis was zero, the first time this had ever been recorded by weather experts.)

If an aircraft maintains its predicted groundspeed and track, then a positive fix obtained at any time during the flight will agree with the aircraft position as determined by DR methods. More likely, however, an actual fix (using radio or pilotage or both) will disagree with the DR position. Usually, this is because one or more variables have been appraised incorrectly. In other words, there is an element of uncertainty surrounding every position determined purely by dead reckoning.

A rule of thumb states that 90 percent of the time, the maximum dead-reckoning error (per hour of flight) is 20 miles plus 1 percent of the estimated distance flown during that hour.

Figure 57, for example, shows where the pilot of a 150-knot aircraft has computed his position to be at the end of one hour. The radius of the circle of uncertainty is equal, therefore, to 20 nautical miles plus 1 percent of 150, which equals 21.5 nautical miles. In other words, there is a 90 percent probability that the pilot is actually within 21.5 nautical miles of where he thinks he is.

It also can be shown that 50 percent of the time, the aircraft is located within a circle with only one-third the radius of the larger circle. In this

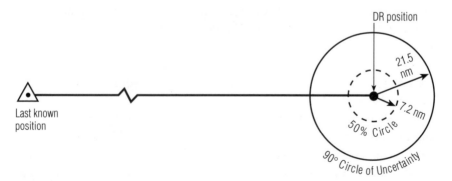

Figure 57. Determining reliability of a fix using the circle of uncertainty

case, the pilot has a fifty-fifty chance of being within 7.2 nautical miles of the DR position.

One way to reduce the size of dead-reckoning errors is to ensure that the compass-deviation card is reasonably accurate. The FAA does not require a periodic compass swing, but pilots would be wise to perform this check at least annually. Deviation errors can change significantly over a period of time.

Also, make it a habit to glance at the compass whenever lining up on a runway of known magnetic direction. Remember, however, that the runway number usually represents the magnetic direction rounded off to the nearest 10 degrees. Some runway numbers disagree by more than 10 degrees with the actual magnetic directions. Tucson's Runway 11L, for example, has a magnetic direction of 122 degrees.

None of this should be interpreted as an argument against radio navigation in favor of DR. But it is nice to know that there is an alternate, reliable way to get from one place to another when GPS, VOR, or LORAN is unavailable and pilotage is difficult. All that is required is some common sense. The idea is to be aware of the wind and its effects and to maintain a running score of flight progress either on a flight log or by making marks on the chart and labeling each position (estimated or actual) with the time of passage.

Not only can DR be used to compute progress along a radial, for example, it also can be used in conjunction with VOR to arrive at a "running fix."

Consider the pilot flying from A to B in Figure 58. He is not necessarily lost, but it has been a while since the last positive fix. He also is having difficulty correlating contour lines on the chart with those on the ground.

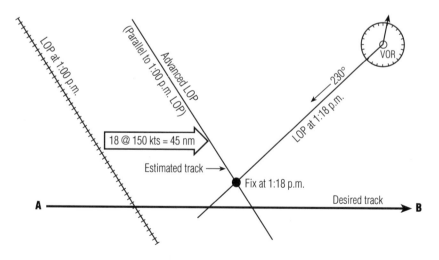

Figure 58. Determining position using an advanced LOP

At 1300 UTC (Zulu time), the aircraft crosses a railroad track, an excellent line of position (LOP). But one LOP does not establish a fix. Eighteen minutes later, the pilot is within range of a VOR station and determines that he is on the 230-degree radial. Again, the pilot has a single LOP, not enough to establish position. Or is it?

A fix can be obtained by advancing the 1300 LOP (the railroad tracks) toward the second LOP (the radial). This is accomplished by first estimating the distance flown since crossing the first LOP.

Assume, for example, that the estimated groundspeed of the aircraft in Figure 58 is 150 knots. In eighteen minutes, therefore, the distance flown is about 45 nautical miles. The first LOP is then advanced (parallel to itself) 45 nautical miles in the direction of the estimated track being flown. The point where the advanced LOP intersects the VOR radial (the second LOP) is the fix for 1318 UTC and shows the aircraft to be north of course.

A running fix can be obtained using any two LOPs as long as they cross at a reasonably oblique angle. They may be highways, rivers, or even a pair of radials crossed at different times.

Another combination of DR and VOR navigation is called the "single-line approach." This technique can be lifesaving and is illustrated in Figure 59.

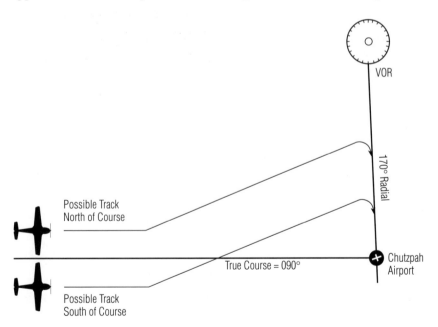

Figure 59. Determining position using single-line approach

A pilot is endeavoring to fly a true course of 090 degrees toward the Chutzpah Airport, which is on the 170-degree radial of a VORTAC (far to the north of course). The pilot estimates arriving over the airport at 1455 UTC. Unfortunately, he has been unable to obtain a reliable and recent fix, and is not certain that he is on course. So, what should he do if, upon intercepting the 170-degree radial, the airport cannot be found? Should he fly north or south along the radial to find the destination? Since he is running low on fuel, he cannot afford to turn in the wrong direction.

Dead-reckoning (or common sense) navigation offers a logical solution. Approximately 45 minutes prior to ETA, the pilot should make a sufficiently large turn and purposefully intercept the radial north (or south) of the airport.

When the 170-degree radial finally is intercepted, the pilot knows with reasonable confidence which way to turn. By turning off course intentionally, he eliminates the likelihood of turning, searching, and wasting fuel in the wrong direction.

This procedure also is known as the landfall intercept and does not require that the destination be on a VOR radial. The airport could be situated on a river, shoreline, highway, railroad, or anything else that is easily identifiable and is approximately perpendicular to the true course. Nor does the single-line approach have to be reserved for locating a destination. It can be used with equal effectiveness to find a needed enroute checkpoint.

Dead reckoning teaches another valuable lesson: how to avoid a midair collision.

In pre-radar days, a fighter pilot was taught that he could intercept another airplane by keeping the target on a line of constant bearing. In other words, the direction of one aircraft from the other must remain constant (as long as each maintains a constant heading and airspeed).

The same is true of two aircraft on a collision course. Visually, this means that if an aircraft remains fixed at a specific point on your windshield and he is at your altitude, you may expect an encounter of the wrong kind. To avoid such an unpleasantry, change heading so that the "bogie" appears to move across your windshield. When this happens, the two aircraft are not maintaining a constant bearing from one another and an "intercept" is impossible.

DR offers much to the pilot willing to expend a little extra effort. And it will not take him long to learn that DR really stands for Darned Reliable. He will also learn that the big three in navigation are not Collins, King, and Narco; they are Rate, Time, and Distance.

Chapter 22 **Wind and Its Effect on Aircraft**

Not long ago, a Quantas Airlines' Boeing 747-400 flew nonstop from London, England, to Sydney, Australia, setting a world-distance record for commercial aircraft. The 9,720-nautical mile, 20-hour flight was only 1,000 miles shy of flying halfway around the world. The range of this aircraft (and the Airbus 340) is such that we soon can anticipate nonstop flights from any point on earth to any other. There are, of course, an infinite number of great circle routes connecting two cities on opposite sides of the globe, which introduces some novel flight-planning procedures. Political considerations aside, such a flight could take off and head in any direction and still reach its destination. The preferred route, of course, would be the one with the most favorable wind. In other words, if a flight in one direction resulted in bucking a headwind, the captain could turn around and head the other way. Thus, he could arrange for a tailwind no matter where in the world he was going.

General aviation pilots obviously do not have such unlimited flight-planning flexibility. They simply take off and go, accepting the winds Mother Nature has to offer. A round-trip under the influence of any wind, of course, takes longer than the same round-trip made in calm air because more time must be spent fighting the headwind when flying in one direction than taking advantage of the tailwind when flying in the other.

But what about when flying under the influence of a direct crosswind? There is neither a headwind nor a tailwind component. Does this mean that a crosswind has no effect on groundspeed? Obviously not. A crosswind requires that the airplane be turned into the wind to prevent drifting off course. The result of turning into the wind is reduced groundspeed: the stronger the crosswind, the greater the crab angle, the lower the groundspeed. Unfortunately, making a round-trip with a direct crosswind results in reduced groundspeed in both directions.

This leads to an interesting question: what takes longer—(1) A round-trip made under the influence of a direct crosswind (which reduces groundspeed in both directions), or (2) a round-trip made under the influence of an equally strong along-course wind that increases groundspeed one way and decreases it the other? The answer: an along-course wind typically increases round-trip flying time twice as much as an equally strong crosswind.

Speaking of crosswinds and crabbing, assume that a pilot is on final approach to a runway and discovers that he is holding a 10-degree crab angle. Is there any way for him to know the strength of the crosswind component?

Sure. All he needs to know is his approximate true airspeed. Each degree of crab represents one knot of crosswind for each 60 knots of airspeed. For example, a 10-degree crab angle while maintaining 60 knots represents a 10-knot crosswind; 10 degrees of crab while maintaining 120 knots represents a 20-knot crosswind, and so on. For those who use final approach speeds other than 60 or 120 knots, simply divide your airspeed by 60. Multiply the result by the crab angle to obtain the crosswind component. For example, each degree of crab while flying at 90 knots represents 1.5 knots of crosswind. An 8-degree crab angle, for instance, would signify a 12-knot crosswind.

This rule of thumb is particularly helpful in gauging crosswind components at airports where a tower controller is unavailable to provide wind information. It also is useful in cruise flight. You can demonstrate your keen aeronautical prowess to others by always knowing the enroute crosswind component. At 180 knots, for example, you would know that each degree of crab while maintaining track along a VOR radial shows a three-knot crosswind component, and so forth. (Quick now. If a Boeing 747 cruising at 480 knots is crabbing 12 degrees, what is the approximate crosswind component? Did you say 96 knots? You're right.)

On the other hand, gliders make use of the wind rather than buck it. This includes vertical wind, or thermals. A glider being flown in a thermal can remain aloft as long as the pilot can stay awake, but can a sailplane (or a powerless airplane) remain aloft in air that lacks vertical motion? In theory, it can.

Imagine a north/south line sharply separating opposite-direction winds. A strong northerly wind is blowing west of this north/south line and an equally strong southerly wind is on the east side. This north/south line obviously represents a strong wind shear.

A sailplane approaches and then crosses this shear line while on a heading of 350 degrees. As it crosses this north/south line, it leaves the influence of the tailwind and encounters the headwind. The strong wind shear causes an abrupt increase in airspeed. (Flying through a shear from a headwind to a tailwind results in a loss of airspeed.) The pilot uses this sudden surplus of speed to gain altitude while simultaneously reversing course to the right. Just when airspeed returns to normal and while on a new heading of 170 degrees, the aircraft again crosses the shear line, encounters a strong headwind, and is once more treated to a surge of airspeed. By continually recrossing the shear line and gaining altitude in this manner, a pilot could theoretically remain aloft indefinitely. (A species of African bird reportedly has been observed using this procedure, which is called dynamic soaring.)

As discussed in Section Two, there are more practical lessons to be learned by power pilots from those who fly sailplanes. One involves flying in a valley under the influence of a direct crosswind. Sailplane pilots know that this flight should be conducted on the downwind side of the valley because this is where updrafts can be found. Although power pilots do not need updrafts to remain aloft, they can take advantage of rising air to increase forward speed. When flying in updrafts—even weak, imperceptible ones—a pilot places his aircraft in a slightly nose-down attitude to maintain altitude. This results in an increase in airspeed that can be significant, depending on the strength of the updraft. Conversely, flying on the upwind side of a valley places an aircraft in an area of sinking air. This requires flying the aircraft in a slightly nose-up attitude that results in a loss of airspeed.

The vertical assistance provided by a breeze blowing up a hill is much greater than most pilots realize. For example, a 10-knot zephyr wafting up a gentle, 20-degree slope has a vertical component of 340 fpm. Increase the wind velocity to 30 knots, and the vertical component increases to 1,020 fpm. Steeper slopes, of course, provide even stronger up- and downdrafts. Flying on the downwind side of a valley is particularly important if the pilot needs to reverse course, especially when the crosswind is strong and the valley narrow. A 180-degree turn made into the wind has a smaller radius and, therefore, requires less maneuvering room than a turn made away from the wind.

Most pilots have learned that winds-aloft forecasts should be taken with a grain of salt, especially when they are more than a few hours old. So how would you like to have a winds aloft forecast that predicts wind components along various routes for months and even years into the future? Anyone who plans that far ahead might enjoy having a pair of books titled *Winds on World Air Routes* and *Winds on United States Domestic Routes,* both of which are published by The Boeing Commercial Airplane Company. Each of these fascinating volumes presents tables of statistically based headwind and tailwind components for almost every route in the world and for each season.

For example, a pilot flying from Los Angeles to Tijuana, Mexico, at 10,000 feet in the winter can normally anticipate an 11-knot tailwind. Flying from Cairo, Egypt, to Geneva, Switzerland, at 40,000 feet in the fall? Expect a 25-knot headwind. One warning before rushing out to buy either of these expensive books: they do not provide much in the way of low-altitude wind information. For routes more than 500-NM long, winds at 20,000, 30,000, 40,000, and 53,000 feet are shown; for routes less than 500-NM long, winds at 10,000, 20,000, 30,000, and 40,000 feet are shown.

Most pilots realize that airplanes—unlike sailboats, which can be made to tack into the wind—cannot make forward progress against a headwind that is equal to or in excess of true airspeed. Not only does tacking not work with an airplane, it is much worse than that. In the case of a northerly wind of such speed, for example, a pilot could not even track east or west.

Think about it.

Chapter 23 **Pressure-Pattern Navigation Simplified**

Every once in a while a pilot becomes utterly bored with the prosaic chore of navigating a long cross-country trip. So there he sits, mesmerized by the hypnotic wig-wagging of a left/right needle or the blinking digits of a GPS display. Ho hum!

When this happens, it might be time for a change of pace. Perhaps experimenting with a different method of navigation will liven things up a bit.

For the most part, pressure-pattern navigation (aerologation) has been set aside for exclusive use by professionals in long-range aircraft. But the same principle can be applied to cross-country navigation in light aircraft. It is not only a challenging method of navigation, it is also refreshing to learn that expensive avionics are not required.

Most pilots have heard of a technique allowing deviation from a direct route to take advantage of favorable tailwinds or to evade strong headwinds. This is standard procedure on most airline flights more than two-hours long. For example, when a high-pressure system (Figure 60) sits over the central United States, eastbound jets fly north of the high, while westbound jets deviate south of it. In each case, the route—though many miles longer than a direct, straight-line course—requires appreciably less time. Such an off-course track is called the minimum-time route (MTR). It is a classic example of the goal of pressure-pattern navigation—to make the most of existing pressure and wind conditions.

Euclid, the father of modern geometry, might have been correct when he said that the shortest distance between two points is a straight line, but he certainly did not have the airplane in mind. The shortest flying time often is the result of following along a curved and devious MTR.

Many pilots attempt to employ this technique, but few are successful. How far off course should a pilot fly to take advantage of the prevailing winds? A pilot obviously should not fly 100 nautical miles off course during a 200 nautical-mile trip even though strong tailwinds would provide a nice push. The minimum-time route cannot be determined with hunches or guesswork. Most of the time, a pilot is better off flying the direct course rather than guessing. The wind side of an E6-B computer could be used to vectorially determine the MTR, but that would be too much like work. Fortunately, there is a far simpler method available.

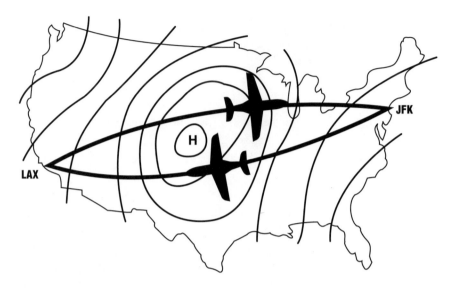

Figure 60. High-pressure system over central United States

Some years ago, a Chicago scientist, Dr. John C. Bellamy, devised a simple formula that caused a navigational revolution. He stated that no matter what wind conditions exist along a given route, the trip can be flown with a single heading. His formula led to what is now the basis for pressure-pattern navigation. By using the Bellamy formula, a pilot can depart on any flight using one and only one wind correction, and this correction ultimately will lead the pilot to his destination, despite the wind shifts (speed or direction) encountered on the way. And the curvaceous track established by an aircraft flying a single heading to the destination closely approximates the minimum-time route.

The magic key to successful pressure-pattern navigation was expressed by Bellamy as follows:

$$\text{Drift (in nautical miles)} = \frac{(P2 - P1)\ K}{TAS}$$

In the formula, P2 is the actual barometric pressure in inches of mercury at cruise altitude above the destination airport, and P1 is the actual barometric pressure at that same altitude above the departure airport. These pressure values generally can be obtained during a pre-flight weather briefing. Should they be unavailable, destination and departure altimeter settings can be substituted with negligible accuracy loss for cruising altitudes of less than 10,000 feet MSL. If the flight is to be conducted above 10,000 feet, the pilot will require access to a constant-pressure chart covering his route of flight.

If station pressure is available only in millibars or Hectopascals, divide the pressure by 34 to obtain the equivalent pressure in inches.

The true airspeed (TAS) must be expressed in knots. K is a factor dependent upon the average latitude of the trip to be flown and is determined from the following table:

Latitude Range	K Factor
22°– 25°	540
25°– 28°	480
28°– 31°	440
31°– 34°	400
34°– 38°	360
38°– 43°	330
43°– 50°	300
50°– 55°	270

Now for a hypothetical problem. A pilot is about to embark on a flight from San Francisco (SFO) to Los Angeles (LAX). The average latitude between these two airports is quickly determined from the aeronautical chart; it is approximately 36 degrees N. The K factor to be used in the formula, therefore, is 360. A cruise altitude of 7,500 feet is selected and the pilot determines during his weather briefing that the barometric pressure at 7,500 feet above SFO is 22.75 inches and above LAX is 22.95 inches. The true airspeed of the aircraft to be used is 100 knots. The known values are then plugged into the Bellamy formula to obtain the anticipated enroute drift.

$$\text{Drift} = \frac{(2{,}295 - 2{,}275)\,(360)}{100} = 72 \text{ nautical miles}$$

Notice that the decimal points in the pressure values are omitted, and that drift is shown in nautical miles. This means that if no correction is made for enroute winds, the aircraft would drift 72 nautical miles off course by the time it arrives abeam LAX, the destination airport. A question now is raised as to whether the 72-nautical-mile drift is left or right. Think carefully. Think of the wind circulation around high- and low-pressure areas. Since destination barometric pressure is higher than that of the departure pressure, the flight effectively will be made from a low-pressure area to a high. Would the pilot expect left or right drift? Proceed to the head of the class if you would anticipate a left drift.

If you are not interested in using logic to determine the direction of drift, just remember these simple rules. When P2 is larger than P1 (P2 – P1 is positive), left drift can be expected. When P2 is smaller than P1 (P2 – P1 is negative), right drift can be anticipated. In the example, P2 is greater than P1. The aircraft therefore can be expected to drift 72 nautical miles to the left of Los Angeles if no wind correction is applied.

The left drift of 72 nautical miles, as determined by Bellamy's formula, is easily convertible to a drift angle with any time-speed-distance computer. Set up the amount of drift (72 nautical miles) on the outer scale opposite the distance to be traveled on the inner scale. For purposes of this example, the distance from SFO to LAX is approximately 300 nautical miles. Opposite 60 (57.6 for those who want greater accuracy) on the inner scale, read the drift angle of 14 degrees on the outer scale. Since drift is left, the 14-degree wind-correction angle must be added to the true course. The true course from SFO to LAX is about 145 degrees, plus a 14-degree wind correction, provides a true heading of 159 degrees to fly the intended route. This is the one and only heading that corrects for all wind conditions between SFO and LAX when the given pressure values exist. The track resulting from flying this heading represents a close approximation of the minimum-time route between those two points.

In the example, it was determined that the drift for the intended flight would be 72 nautical miles to the left. This does not mean that only a left drift would be encountered enroute. The Bellamy formula only states that the net drift at the end of the flight will be 72 nautical miles to the left if no correction for wind is made. During the course of the flight, the aircraft might drift both right and left of course, depending upon actual winds encountered. The net result of all winds acting upon the aircraft, however, produces a 72-nautical-mile left drift.

It might at first be difficult to believe that this one drift correction will provide for arrival precisely over destination. Although it appears that no compensation has been provided for high-velocity winds that might exist enroute, this is not true. The pressure differential between any two points determines the net effect of all winds between them.

Figure 61 shows one of the many possible situations that could exist between SFO and LAX when differential pressure is 0.20 inches Hg (22.95 – 22.75). SFO is located under a low-pressure system, and a pilot would experience a slight right crosswind as he began his trip. The wind is so weak that the 14-degree crab would be considered an overcorrection, and the aircraft would fly slightly right of course. Upon reaching point A, the winds have picked up in strength and begin to blow the aircraft back on course (point B). As the flight progresses toward the high-pressure area, greater drift is encountered, and the aircraft drifts considerably left of course. At point C, the aircraft is abeam the high, and the wind shifts from a right to a left crosswind. Now the aircraft drifts toward the original straight-line course. If everything goes according to Hoyle (or Bellamy!), the reinterception of the direct route should occur above LAX.

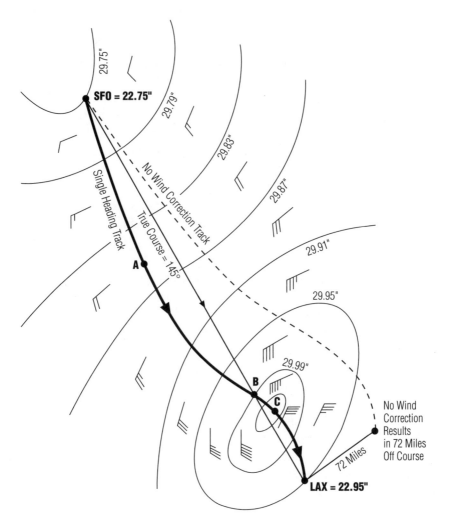

Figure 61. Effect of wind on single-heading flight

Actually, there are an infinite number of pressure patterns that could exist between SFO and LAX, but as long as the pressure differential between them remains the same, the average crosswind or net drift also remains the same.

The dotted line in Figure 61 represents the track that would result from not applying any wind correction while enroute. Note that the aircraft would arrive 72 nautical miles left of LAX, the net effect of all drift encountered enroute.

Single-heading flight reduces time enroute for a very simple reason. During a normal flight along a fixed course, a pilot might have to crab right or left as he progresses to maintain a constant straight-line track. Each time he crabs into the wind, groundspeed is lessened, increasing the time required for the flight. Using a single heading allows the aircraft to drift right and/or left of course without the loss of groundspeed caused by variable crab angles. The actual track flown may be a few miles longer, but it definitely takes less time to fly. It also is easier to execute a flight using a single heading than to compute and fly the several different headings often required to maintain a straight-line course with variable winds aloft.

A quick glance at Dr. Bellamy's formula makes it apparent that if the pressure values at the destination and departure airports are the same, then $P2 - P1$ will be zero and the net drift for the entire flight also will be zero. Under these conditions, a pilot could use absolutely no wind correction and expect to arrive over his destination in minimal time, despite the winds aloft. He might encounter enroute crosswinds, but the net drift effect of all wind encountered would be nil, and he would have flown the minimum-time route. This might seem incredulous, but Figure 62 should dispel any confusion. Notice that a flight conducted between any two points of equal pressure encounters as much left drift as it does right drift. Consequently, wind correction is unnecessary.

The advantage of pressure-pattern navigation is obvious. It provides a method of flying from A to B in minimal time without having to fool around with wind triangles and their resultant and time-consuming crab angles.

But there are some problems. The accuracy of single-heading flight diminishes as the pressure values at the terminal points of the flight change. If they both go up or down, the flight will be unaffected as long as the difference between them remains constant. But if one value should rise while the other drops (unlikely on trips of less than a few hundred miles), then the net drift encountered will change accordingly.

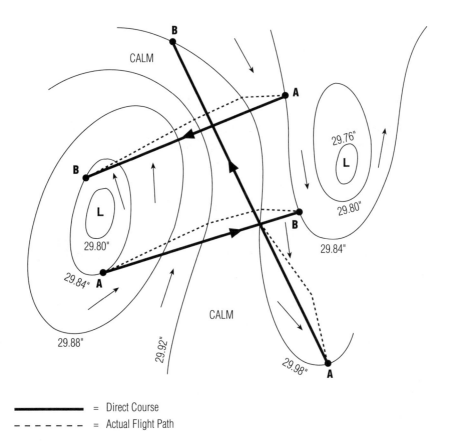

= Direct Course
– – – – – – = Actual Flight Path

Figure 62. Flying between points of equal pressure

Another disadvantage arises when the pilot attempts to plot the MTR. Unfortunately, this requires plotting a series of wind triangles and is a laborious procedure. Instead, I prefer to take off and simply keep track of aircraft position (using visual and radio fixes) while en route. At the end of the flight, I connect all of these fixes with a smooth, curved line to obtain a "picture" of the MTR actually flown.

Determining exactly how long the flight will take also creates a problem. The ambitious pilot can plot wind triangles to predict groundspeeds along the route. A simpler, less accurate technique involves estimating the time en route by conventional methods. Then remind yourself that using the MTR will take somewhat less time. Half the fun is discovering afterwards just how much time was saved.

Consider also that pressure-pattern navigation does not lend itself to flying the airways. The FAA simply refuses to lay out the Victor route structure according to the daily whims and dictates of the wind.

One further word of caution. Pressure-pattern navigation can be used only when the altitude used is more than 2,000 feet AGL. Below this altitude, wind speed and direction are modified by the frictional effects of the terrain. Above 2,000 feet AGL, winds are governed almost exclusively by the direction and spacing of the isobars. That is, winds flow parallel to the isobars, and speed is inversely proportional to the distance between them.

Pressure-pattern navigation works like a charm on long-distance flights. Its benefits have been known for many years. This technique might not replace VOR or GPS navigation, but it is a lot of fun to play with. And who knows? If you become good enough at it, you might want to look into pressure lines of position, or PLOPs, as they are so ungracefully called.

Section 5

The World of Instrument Flight

Although the training for an instrument rating is rigorous, it only scratches the surface. In a sense, becoming proficient on instruments is similar to becoming an experienced VFR pilot. In other words, just as a new private pilot certificate is a license to learn, so, too, is an instrument rating. The following eight chapters are designed to provide some of the additional insight needed to develop IFR proficiency during a variety of situations.

Chapter 24 **The Low-Visibility Takeoff**

As citizens of the United States, we have an extraordinary amount of personal freedom. This applies also to our aviation pursuits, in spite of regulations that occasionally seem excessive and restrictive. But in the exercise of this freedom, it is imperative to recognize that just because something is legal, it might not be safe.

A case in point is the instrument takeoff (not to be confused with an instrument departure—an IFR routing dictated by air traffic control). Instrument-rated pilots operating under Federal Aviation Regulation Part 91 are allowed to take off even when the ceiling and visibility are nil. On the other hand, air-taxi pilots may not take off unless the runway visual range (RVR) is at least 1,800 feet. Frequently, the required visibility is a mile or more. Air-carrier pilots are required to abide by published takeoff minimums, which can be as low as 300 feet RVR, but normally are 1,600 feet RVR. (In some cases, surface visibility must be at least 3 miles.) These takeoff limitations are imposed to provide the paying passenger a minimum standard of safety.

But just because it is legal for private pilots to depart in conditions that would keep commercial flights grounded does not mean that private pilots should do it.

Although many sources refer to the instrument takeoff, none define it. So for the purpose of this discussion, consider that an ITO is any IFR departure where all visual reference to the ground is lost before the airplane is established in a stabilized climb. The pilot must control the aircraft solely by reference to instruments while on the runway or immediately after liftoff.

There are a number of hazards associated with an instrument takeoff. Perhaps the most obvious is the possible loss of runway alignment and aircraft control.

Another significant, infrequently considered danger is runway obstruction. Several years ago, a TWA Boeing 707 was taking off from Tel Aviv's Lod (now Ben Gurion) International Airport in poor visibility at night. As the aircraft gathered speed, the pilots suddenly noticed the ghostly outline of a military KC-97 being towed across the runway. With so little distance between the two aircraft, the captain recognized that an aborted takeoff undoubtedly would result in burying the nose of his aircraft in the fuselage of the other. Without time for further analysis, the captain hauled back on the yoke in an attempt to leapfrog the intruder. Fortunately, the 707 had reached the minimum unstick speed (V_{MU}) and did come off the ground. But not nearly high enough. The belly of the 707 hit the top of the KC-97, and both aircraft were destroyed. The crew survived, and since the 707 was a cargo aircraft, there were no passengers on board.

Hundreds died, however, when two passenger-laden Boeing 747s collided as the result of an attempted instrument takeoff at Tenerife in the Canary Islands.

Many similar collisions have occurred simply because pilots could not see far enough to ensure that the runway was clear. A clearance for takeoff means only that the traffic controller believes the runway is clear. But he could be wrong. An instrument takeoff from an uncontrolled airport can be a big roll of the dice.

When an airline captain departs an airport with visibility so poor that a subsequent return to the airport would not be possible, he is required to file a takeoff alternate. In other words, he must have in mind a nearby airport where a safe approach and landing can be made in case a mechanical difficulty, for example, prevents him from continuing to the destination.

But what about the general aviation pilot? Does he mentally declare a takeoff alternate before an instrument takeoff? Probably not. But what if a door pops open during liftoff, or the landing gear or flaps cannot be retracted, or a passenger becomes seriously ill? How far would he have to go before locating a safe haven? For this reason alone, some pilots never depart unless the visibility is at least sufficient to allow an expeditious return.

Pilots should be aware of a unique hazard when executing an instrument takeoff in a multi-engine aircraft. While researching this subject, I obtained the cooperation of three experienced multi-engine pilots. Each was asked to simulate an instrument takeoff by donning a hood just before brake release. At precisely 70 knots, I retarded a throttle to simulate engine failure and to determine if these stunned pilots could abort the instrument takeoff safely within the confines of the runway. Not one could. In each case, I had to intervene to avoid wiping out a string of runway lights. The lesson here is that a multi-engine pilot probably should not take off unless weather conditions are at least sufficient to allow the aircraft to be guided visually to some minimum altitude above which an engine failure during actual instrument conditions could be handled effectively. (How many pilots, for example, could cope safely with an engine failure at 50 feet AGL without any ground references whatsoever?)

Single-engine pilots, of course, have no such directional problems. An engine failure during an instrument takeoff roll only requires that a pilot keep the aircraft's nose pointed straight ahead and that he apply firm, symmetrical pressure to the brake pedals, which admittedly might not be as easy as it sounds. An engine failure shortly after takeoff, however, would be much more traumatic. With a blanket of fog smothering the terrain, the pilot would have no choice of landing areas. After quickly establishing the aircraft in an optimum crash configuration (if such a thing is really possible), he would be left only with a rabbit's foot, crossed fingers, and an imploring prayer.

Despite these substantial threats to longevity, the greatest hazard of an instrument takeoff is the potential loss of control either during the takeoff roll or within seconds of liftoff.

Although the instrument takeoff is not a required maneuver during the flight test for an instrument rating, many instructors teach their students to take off while under the hood. This may have some training value, but it probably does more harm than good. Unless an instructor drives home the point that such an exercise is strictly a drill and should not be applied in practice, the student concludes that taking off in extremely reduced visibility is acceptable. Since it does not take much effort to master the maneuver, he also develops the notion that an instrument takeoff is safe.

There is a world of difference between simulated and actual instrument takeoffs. To begin with, the hooded maneuver is somewhat of a contradiction. Some visibility is required to align the aircraft with the runway. The student then assumes the visibility is nil and drops the hood prior to brake release. He is not particularly concerned about the outcome of the maneuver because he knows that the instructor will correct any serious tracking excursions.

An actual instrument takeoff, however, begins visually. After all, if a pilot cannot see at least some of the runway, the aircraft cannot be aligned with the centerline. (Sometimes, when visibility is so poor that visual runway alignment is impossible, military aircraft are towed into position and pointed in the right direction by a tug and ground crew.) As the takeoff roll progresses and speed increases, the effective visibility might decrease. This is especially true in heavy rain or snow. Also, fog along the runway may become progressively denser as the aircraft accelerates during the takeoff roll, not an unusual occurrence when departing toward a body of water that is the fog's breeding ground.

At some point, therefore, the pilot must turn to his instruments for guidance before all visual cues disappear. This is more difficult in practice than in theory because pilots tend to maintain visual reference as long as possible. Then—either during the takeoff roll or liftoff—all ground reference suddenly disappears. This rapid, unexpected transition from visual to instrument conditions can lead to spatial disorientation and loss of control. Also, gyroscopic precession can produce an excessive nose-up indication on the attitude indicator during acceleration and compound the confusion.

A similar encounter with vertigo can arise after taking off toward a "black hole" (such as a body of water) on a dark night in VFR conditions when the horizon is not visible.

Although this discussion is intended to discourage instrument takeoffs, the procedure is legal, and pilots will continue to take off in weather conditions that have forced sea gulls to walk. So for those who insist on crapshooting, the following advice might help to improve the odds.

First of all, be certain that all preflight preparations are extraordinarily thorough because you could be on instruments within seconds of brake release. This includes determining that all trim tabs are properly positioned so that the aircraft does not tend to roll, pitch, or yaw on its own. Also, be certain that the pitot heat is turned on before brake release and that all flight instruments are functioning normally. (Yes, pilots have attempted instrument takeoffs with caged gyros and exposed fail flags.) If available and appropriate, engage the flight director to provide the necessary commands.

After the aircraft is lined up with the runway, allow it to roll forward a few feet to ensure that the nosewheel (or tailwheel) is aligned. Set the brakes and take a deep breath. Then rotate the heading bug to the actual aircraft heading so that it points directly down the runway centerline. If such a bug is not available, reset the heading indicator (directional gyro) so that the indicated aircraft heading coincides with a 10-degree increment even if this is slightly incorrect. It is easier to maintain 270 degrees than 273 degrees during a takeoff roll. (Although the heading bug and the heading indicator can be set during runup, they should be fine-tuned after runway alignment to be certain that the proper heading has been selected and that the heading indicator has not precessed in the interim.)

Before takeoff, ask yourself whether the flight is really that important. Before answering, consider that a malfunction that might not be serious during a normal takeoff can take on critical proportions during an instrument takeoff. Finally, double-check all instruments.

After brake release, advance the throttle(s) so that maximum power is set prior to losing ground reference. This prevents having to compensate for increasing power while possibly having to steer solely by reference to the instruments. As the takeoff roll proceeds, be particularly alert for the complicating effects of a crosswind. Also, make it a point to glance frequently at the panel. This helps to ease the transition to guidance by instruments should this suddenly become necessary. Do this, however, with minimal head movement—especially during rotation—to avoid inducing vertigo. Be particularly alert for contrasting light and dark patches of fog. These can be distracting—especially at higher speeds—and may warrant giving up visual reference to the ground in favor of continuing on instruments.

Once a pilot elects or is forced to go on instruments, he should commit himself to the task and resist the temptation to re-establish visual contact with the runway, even though he may sense peripherally that outside conditions have improved temporarily. Taking off visually or on instruments is difficult enough; attempting to alternate between the two may be impossible because of the time, distance, and potential loss of control sacrificed during each transition.

A pilot executing an instrument takeoff should turn his attention to the gauges before liftoff, because if all visual cues have not yet disappeared, they soon will. The rotation technique should be consistent with that normally used for the aircraft being flown, except that a pilot must be certain that sufficient airspeed is available to raise the nose to a predetermined target attitude and hold it there. This is an absolute necessity. Lowering the nose to correct for airspeed decay while on instruments and when so close to the ground cannot be tolerated without risking an inadvertent touchdown. This target attitude, however, should have been determined from previous flights in the aircraft. Guesswork will not suffice.

During rotation, hold the wings absolutely level and be on the alert for the need to add rudder (especially in single-engine airplanes) to prevent skidding. Also, do not be concerned about a slight, momentary dip of altitude and vertical-speed indications caused in some aircraft by a slight increase in static air pressure during rotation. This generally lasts only a second or so and is harmless unless a pilot filled with anxiety overreacts by attempting to pull back excessively on the control wheel. Many pilots are unaware of this phenomenon because they seldom look at their instruments during liftoff.

Once the aircraft has begun to climb, resist doing anything other than maintaining control until some minimum target altitude has been reached. (Many instructors recommend 300 feet AGL.) This includes radio communications, which can be distracting, as well as raising the aircraft's landing gear or the flaps, which can result in pitch changes that may be hazardous while the aircraft is immersed in cloud at such a low altitude. Do not change power settings, do not turn, do not even glance at a chart until reaching this minimum height.

Clearly, the instrument takeoff is dangerous, and anyone who values his or her life would be well advised to decline the option.

Chapter 25 **Flying the ILS Approach**

Believe it or not, there is a similarity between sex and the ILS approach. Not only can each be performed with mechanical movements learned by rote, but experience teaches that—in both cases—the most successful are those who have learned to execute these procedures with finesse and a certain delicate touch.

Most ILS novitiates attempt to keep the cross pointers centered by applying techniques learned while chasing VOR needles on cross-country flights. Although the localizer and glideslope are similar in principle to VOR radials, they are considerably more sensitive and demand a refined mental attitude. The large corrections used during VOR navigation cannot be tolerated during an ILS approach.

To appreciate the sensitivity of a localizer needle, consider, for example, that a VOR radial has an effective width of 20 degrees. In other words, a pilot must displace the aircraft 10 degrees either side of a selected radial to cause the course-deviation indicator (CDI) to deflect fully.

The average localizer, on the other hand, has a width of only 4 degrees. A displacement of only 2 degrees from the centerline results in maximum CDI deflection. In other words, the localizer is five times as sensitive as a VOR radial at any given distance from the transmitter.

In reality, localizer course widths vary from 3 degrees to 6 degrees. Each is tailored so as to be 700 feet wide at the runway threshold. And since a localizer transmitter is usually just beyond the rollout end of its associated runway, it is obvious that short runways have relatively wide localizers and long runways relatively narrow ones.

An appreciation of localizer sensitivity combined with the following suggestions can considerably improve a pilot's ability to execute an ILS approach to minimums.

Figure 63 demonstrates why localizer corrections must be so minimal. When tracking a 4-degree-wide localizer, for example, at a distance of only one nautical mile from the runway threshold, the chart shows that when the needle is deflected one-quarter scale, the aircraft is only 141 feet from being precisely on course.

To a pilot accustomed to VOR flying, a quarter-scale deflection seems like quite a bit. Between VOR stations, a return to course might require a 10-

Localizer Needle Deflection	At the Runway Threshold	Distance from Runway Threshold					
		1/4 nm	1/2 nm	3/4 nm	1 nm	2 nm	3 nm
1/4-scale deflection	88 ft.	101 ft.	114 ft.	127 ft.	141 ft.	194 ft.	247 ft.
1/2-scale deflection	175 ft.	202 ft.	228 ft.	255 ft.	281 ft.	387 ft.	493 ft.
3/4-scale deflection	263 ft.	302 ft.	342 ft.	382 ft.	422 ft.	581 ft.	740 ft.
Full deflection	350 ft.	403 ft.	456 ft.	509 ft.	562 ft.	775 ft.	987 ft.
Localizer width	700 ft.	806 ft.	912 ft.	1,018 ft.	1,125 ft.	1,549 ft.	1,974 ft.

Figure 63. To find the distance of the aircraft from the center of the localizer, enter table with amount of needle deflection and distance of aircraft from runway threshold. (Note: This table is based on a 4°-wide localizer.)

degree correction (or more) to be held for several minutes. This previous experience with the CDI has an adverse effect on the pilot because it creates the tendency to make similarly large corrections when tracking an ILS.

The same correction (10 degrees) applied to a localizer when only 141 feet off course results in such a rapid return to the centerline that overshooting the localizer is almost impossible to avoid.

With respect to a localizer (and not a VOR radial), a quarterscale deflection is not that big a deal. When 141 feet off course, the aircraft is only 41 feet from being lined up with the edge of a 200-foot-wide runway.

Putting this in proper perspective, consider how small a correction would be required when a plane is 141 feet from the extended runway centerline during a VFR, straight-in approach. Very little. The heading change would be barely noticeable. Quite obviously, the same minor correction should be made during an actual ILS approach.

This, then, is what is meant by the need to adopt the proper mental attitude. Heading changes during an ILS approach should only be a small fraction of what is normally required to center an equally displaced VOR needle.

Most pilots who have difficulty keeping the localizer needle within reasonable limits are usually guilty of chasing the needle. They have not learned that the secret of a successful ILS approach is the result of logical, minimal, predetermined heading changes.

For example, assume that a pilot is intercepting the localizer. He rolls out on the ILS heading just as the needle centers in the bull's-eye. The published magnetic course of the ILS becomes what is called the temporary reference heading, which—in this case—shall be 095 degrees.

Under no-wind conditions and with an error-free heading indicator, this heading theoretically would lead the aircraft precisely along the localizer. Such is rarely the case, however.

Expecting some drift, the pilot pays careful attention to needle behavior, while flying the reference heading with flawless determination. He knows that an inadvertent heading change causes the localizer needle to move and leads to the false impression that wind drift is the responsible culprit. An accurate "picture" of the wind cannot be drawn unless the reference heading is precisely maintained.

The heading is 095 degrees, and the needle slowly moves left. There are two possible reasons for this: a left crosswind or an improperly set heading indicator (or a combination of both). But this pilot is sharp. Once on the localizer, he knows that to subsequently reset the HI can only interfere with his plans to execute the perfect ILS approach. Once the HI has been synchronized with the compass, prior to localizer intercept, he will assume that all needle movement is caused either by wind drift or heading change.

As the needle moves left, the pilot rolls into a very shallow turn toward the needle. His immediate intention is not to center the needle, but simply to stop it dead in its tracks.

After 5 degrees of turn, in this case, the needle stops and the pilot rolls the wings level. He precisely maintains the new heading (090 degrees) and again begins his vigil of the localizer needle. If the needle remains in its displaced position, the pilot knows that this new heading (090 degrees) is causing the aircraft to essentially "parallel" the localizer. He knows also that whatever heading "parallels" the localizer also can be used to track the localizer when the needle is centered later. This new heading (090 degrees) becomes the revised reference heading and quite accurately compensates (within a degree or two) for any prevailing wind and/or any discrepancy between the compass and the heading indicator.

If the needle continues to move, however, it is at a much reduced rate, and the pilot can make whatever smaller correction is necessary to stop needle movement. The end result becomes the new reference heading.

Since it is his desire to center the needle, the pilot turns farther left to a heading of 085 degrees. Obligingly, the needle moves toward the bull's-eye. As the needle centers, does this pilot have to guess at what heading shall be required to track inbound? Of course not. He turns to the reference heading (090 degrees) and smugly observes the captured localizer. He is now ready to intercept the glideslope and continue with this, the thinking man's approach.

This two-step maneuver of (1) turning to stop needle movement and then (2) turning farther to intercept the localizer can be accomplished by a savvy pilot in one smooth move. He turns toward the digressing needle and simply notes the reference heading at that point during the turn when the needle comes to a halt. But the turn continues briefly and without interruption to reverse needle movement. When the needle returns to the bull's eye, a turn is made to the reference heading noted during the initial turn.

As the descent begins, no one can be so naive as to believe that wind drift will not change. Count on it. The point is that unless a strong wind shift (or shear) exists between the ground and 1,500 feet AGL, drift change will be gradual. As the localizer needle begins to react accordingly, a pilot must similarly turn to stop the needle and establish a new reference heading, one that can be used until conditions again require a change. The idea is to fly logical headings, based on observations of needle behavior, and not to take arbitrary, random swipes at the localizer.

As the aircraft descends on the glideslope, it also gets closer to the localizer transmitter, which further increases needle sensitivity. Although the same techniques are used when the localizer moves off center, heading changes must be proportionately smaller. A 2-degree heading change near minimums, for example, has about the same effect on needle movement as a 6-degree "bite" when near the outer marker.

As the aircraft approaches decision height (DH), it becomes increasingly more important to fly a specified heading and to not chase the needle. The most urgent requirement is that the needles not be in motion, because this indicates cross-tracking and is usually more responsible for missed approaches than arriving at minimums with slightly offset yet motionless needles.

If the localizer is slightly left or right (and motionless), it is better to accept being a few feet off course than to risk initiating a cross-track correction that could result in a larger needle displacement in the opposite direction. In other words, do not be so precise that a slight needle deflection cannot be tolerated (unless you can make exacting 1-degree or 2-degree turns or are below the glideslope). The obsession to exactly center the needles can blow an approach. (This applies, of course, to Category I approaches only; the lower minimums associated with Category II and III approaches do require substantially more precision and equipment.)

The glideslope is another breed of cat, similar to the localizer but even more sensitive. It has an effective width of only 1.4 degrees. In other words, a vertical deviation of only 0.7 degree fully deflects the horizontal needle.

Figure 64 graphically displays glideslope sensitivity. When an airplane is 2 nautical miles from the runway touchdown zone, for example, a needle deflected half-scale indicates that the aircraft is only 74 feet above or below the glideslope. When only 1/2 mile from the touchdown zone, the same needle deflection translates to only a 19-foot deviation from perfection.

Glideslope Needle Deflection	Distance from Runway Touchdown Zone					
	1/4 nm	1/2 nm	3/4 nm	1 nm	1-1/2 nm	2 nm
1/4-scale deflection	5 ft.	9 ft.	14 ft.	19 ft.	28 ft.	37 ft.
1/2-scale deflection	9 ft.	19 ft.	28 ft.	37 ft.	56 ft.	74 ft.
3/4-scale deflection	14 ft.	28 ft.	42 ft.	56 ft.	84 ft.	111 ft.
Full deflection	19 ft.	37 ft.	56 ft.	74 ft.	111 ft.	149 ft.
Glideslope thickness	37 ft.	74 ft.	111 ft.	149 ft.	223 ft.	297 ft.

Figure 64. To find the distance of the aircraft above or below the glideslope, enter table with amount of needle deflection and distance of aircraft from runway touchdown zone (not runway threshold).

To put it another way, the glideslope is 14 times as sensitive as a VOR needle and three times as sensitive as the localizer at equal distances from the station transmitters. Think about it this way. When tracking a glideslope 1 mile from the touchdown zone, the needle has the same sensitivity as when tracking a VOR radial when only 0.07 nautical mile from the VOR transmitter (if that were possible).

Such sensitivity requires thinking about the controls (or perhaps breathing on them) more than it does moving them. Tracking the glideslope also requires the proper mental attitude.

Instead of requiring a reference heading (as does the localizer), the glideslope demands a reference sink rate. The vertical-speed indicator (VSI) is often ignored, but it is the magic key required to unlock the airport when ceiling and visibility conspire against you.

Prior to glideslope intercept, determine from the approach plate the recommended sink rate required to slide down the glideslope at the ground-speed anticipated during the approach. Figure 65 shows, for example, that a 4-degree glideslope (the steepest in the U.S. is actually 3.9 degrees) requires a 709 fpm sink rate when groundspeed is 100 knots.

Usually, however, a pilot can predict the required sink rate without referring to a chart. Since most glideslopes are on the order of 2.25 degrees to 3 degrees, this handy rule of thumb can be used: "Cut the approach ground-speed (knots) in half and add a zero." When using a 3-degree glideslope with a groundspeed of 80 knots, for example, sink rate should be approximately 400 fpm. Figure 65 indicates a required sink rate of 425 fpm, but there are not many pilots who can control a VSI quite that precisely.

As the glideslope is intercepted, immediately establish and attempt to maintain the recommended sink rate. If this is done correctly and if ground-speed remains constant, the glideslope needle will require no further attention. But this happens only in textbooks; the glideslope undoubtedly will move off center.

Quite obviously, variations in sink rate are required to arrest a displaced glideslope needle, but it is the method and amount of correction that require emphasis.

Groundspeed	Glideslope Angle				
	2°	2-1/2°	3°	3-1/2°	4°
60 knots	212	265	319	372	425
70 knots	248	310	372	434	496
80 knots	283	354	425	496	567
90 knots	318	398	478	558	638
100 knots	354	442	531	620	709
110 knots	389	487	584	682	779
120 knots	425	531	637	744	850

Figure 65. To find the recommended sink rate (fpm), enter table with anticipated groundspeed and glideslope angle (from approach plate).

What I am about to say is certain to raise eyebrows and attract scowls from the purists, but the best and easiest way to recapture a displaced glideslope needle is to simply apply the appropriate elevator pressure without regard to airspeed and power. Allow airspeed to vary (within reason) and to hell with power adjustments. Why complicate the issue by trying to rub your tummy and the top of your head simultaneously? Simply nudge the yoke and adjust sink rate slightly. Do, however, keep a ready hand on the throttle in case airspeed starts to get out of hand. Unless a wind shear is present, however, airspeed usually takes care of itself rather nicely.

The required sink-rate adjustment rarely exceeds 200 fpm. So, if a 500-fpm sink rate is being used and the glideslope needle begins to rise, change the sink rate to 300 fpm and watch needle behavior. Usually, it will return toward the bull's-eye, at which time the original 500-fpm sink rate (or slightly less) should be resumed.

If the needle stops or only slows a little, then reduce sink rate an additional 100 fpm. Very little change in sink rate is usually all that is necessary to recapture the glideslope. Just tickle the yoke; don't horse around with it.

Unless the glideslope needle is fully deflected upward, do not reduce the sink rate to zero. Such an abrupt change requires subsequent abruptness (and sloppy technique) to prevent the needle from dropping rapidly toward the bottom of the instrument.

Unless wind conditions change dramatically and unless an aircraft is dangerously below the glideslope, varying sink rate by more than 200 fpm is rarely necessary.

To appreciate the finesse required to do this properly, concentrate on varying sink rate by increments of 100 or 200 fpm during a visual, straight-in approach. Learn how little control movement is required. Observe also— during a visual approach—how little the elevator is used to remain in the slot. It is no different when the aircraft is engulfed in cloud and the glideslope is being used for descent.

So you see, flying the cross-pointers is sort of like sex. Each requires the proper mental attitude, a soft touch, and the ability to put it all together (meaning the localizer, the glideslope, and the ILS bull's-eye, of course).

Chapter 26 **The Low Visibility Transition from Approach to Landing**

The obvious purpose of instrument training is to acquire the proficiency to operate an aircraft safely in IFR conditions. Some of this training, however, falls short of the mark, because it is almost impossible to simulate or duplicate many of the hazards an instrument pilot is likely to encounter in real weather.

A prime example is the technique most often used to prepare pilots for actual ILS approaches. After sliding down the electronic banister and arriving at decision height (DH), students are told either to execute a missed approach or to remove their hoods and land. In no way does this prepare them for the low-visibility environment they eventually may encounter between DH and touchdown during an actual ILS approach. It proves only that they can follow instructions and land an airplane in VFR conditions.

The accident files bulge with statistics proving that the most hazardous phase of an IFR approach is the visual segment. This is because—contrary to what a pilot has been trained to expect—visual conditions often do not suddenly appear at DH. Instead, indistinct visual clues may emerge slowly from obscurity and be difficult to interpret. Since the approach lights are more or less in sight, the pilot breathes a sigh of relief and descends below DH. Once pilots shift their attention to the outside world, they may discover that the visual cues do not provide the guidance needed to control aircraft attitude and flight path. Certain illusory effects may compound the problem and dangerously mislead even the most experienced pilots.

To appreciate the potential hazards associated with the visual segment of an ILS approach, it is necessary to understand how visual cues are used during VFR approaches.

When descending toward a runway, a pilot needs lateral (offset), roll, and vertical (pitch) guidance. Lateral cues are provided by observing ground objects moving across the windshield. The idea, of course, is to line up with the runway and then keep it positioned in front of the aircraft (plus or minus any drift correction). The horizon provides roll guidance and allows a pilot to constantly monitor bank angle.

The most difficult aspect of the approach is vertical control, which is establishing and maintaining a desirable slot to the touchdown target. Without realizing it, pilots receive vertical (and some lateral) guidance from the

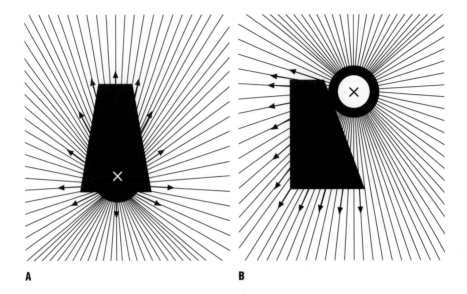

Figure 66. Visual cues for vertical guidance on approach appear to spread outward from projected touchdown point

way in which objects on the ground seem to spread outward from the projected touchdown point during descent. Figure 66A shows an aircraft descending toward the touchdown zone of a runway; the touchdown target appears stationary in the windshield while surrounding visual cues spread outward. In Figure 66B, the projected touchdown point is to the right of the runway's departure end.

Once pilots are aware of this visual spreading, they can use the phenomenon to control more accurately the approach slot during all visual approaches.

At night and when relatively close to the runway, pilots are aided by parafoveal streamers. (Parafoveal is a medical term referring to the area of the eye controlling peripheral vision.) These streamers are the apparent spreading away of runway lights from the projected touchdown point, as seen through the pilot's peripheral vision, and provide a reliable source of vertical guidance during the final segment of a visual approach (even though pilots may not be aware of it). Figure 67A shows streamer behavior as the aircraft approaches the runway touchdown zone while Figure 67B represents a laterally displaced approach.

Although the spreading of visual cues and parafoveal streamers are important to the success of a visual approach, they often are unavailable when breaking out of an overcast at DH in limited visibility. This is because so few visual cues are available to generate the necessary spreading. Approach lights usually provide adequate lateral and roll guidance, but they offer little vertical assistance. In other words, pilots may be unable to detect a developing glideslope excursion when only the approach lights are in sight.

Consequently, descent guidance normally is unavailable until at least a portion of the runway can be seen. Pilots breaking out at 200 feet with a reported runway visual range (RVR) of 1,800 feet can see only to a point 3,000 feet short of the touchdown zone and 2,000 feet short of the runway threshold. And if the slant-range visibility along the glideslope is less than the reported RVR, they cannot even see that far. (A slant-range visibility of 3,800 feet is required to see the touchdown zone when arriving at a 200-foot decision height on a 3-degree glideslope.)

Pilots also may be subjected to optical illusions that almost compel them to push the nose down, which can lead to a catastrophic undershoot.

When pilots descend from an overcast into low-visibility conditions, they perceive a relatively low horizon. Since everything they can see—which is not much—appears in the lower portion of the windscreen, they sense that the airplane is in a nose-high attitude. Pilots "correct" this by lowering the nose, a common reaction known as tucking. Unfortunately, the increasing sink rate is difficult to detect visually because of the insufficient vertical guidance mentioned previously. When pilots finally recognize that they are about to land in the lights, it may be too late.

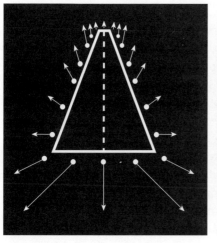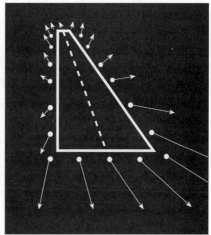

A

B

Figure 67. "Parafoveal streamers" aid night visual approaches

A sudden reduction in visibility—such as when flying through variable-density fog—also can be misinterpreted as a rising nose (lowering horizon) and result in an untimely tuck.

An overly steep descent can result from a left crosswind. In most airplanes (depending on the shape of the windshield), sighting the approach lights toward the right gives the illusion of being high. Conversely, crabbing right and sighting the lights to the left often give the impression of being low.

A host of other illusions exacerbate the problem of maintaining a safe descent profile during those last 200 feet. Unusually narrow or long runways, for example, create the impression of being high, while wide or short runways have the opposite effect. Similarly, upslope runways create the illusion of being high, while downslope runways cause a pilot to believe he is low.

Less predictable are the illusory effects of precipitation. Blowing snow, for example, eliminates the contrast between the runway and its surroundings, which substantially reduces depth perception. (The largest attitude changes typically occur when approaching a runway through blowing snow.) A rain-spotted windshield can make an airplane seem high or low (depending on droplet size, concentration, and the resulting refraction of light). Equally unpredictable are the pitot/static system errors that are known to develop when flying through heavy precipitation. These can lead to erroneous indications of airspeed, vertical speed, and altitude.

Sequence flashers often are the first approach lights to be seen when descending through fog. Pilots occasionally are disoriented by these pulsating, glare-producing strobe lights, especially when they flash diagonally across the windshield (such as when one is crabbing or cross-tracking the localizer).

Speaking of lights, pilots occasionally contribute to their own confusion by light mismanagement. Strobe lights should be turned off when flying on instruments to avoid the vertigo that stroboscopic reflections can produce. Landing lights should not be turned on until a safe landing is assured and to avoid the blinding glare they can create in low-visibility conditions (especially fog and snow). Excessively bright cockpit and instrument lights increase the time required for the eyes to adjust to the outside world.

Another hazard in the low-visibility environment is wind shear. This does not necessarily refer to the dramatic variety that can quickly change airspeed. During an ILS approach to minimums, pilots should be prepared for the more insidious type of shear, the type caused by wind gradient.

Since wind speed typically and predictably decreases as altitude decreases within 2,000 feet of the earth's surface (the frictional layer), pilots routinely encounter a headwind loss during approaches into the wind. This normally is of little consequence, but when such a loss-of-headwind shear combines with the other potential hazards already discussed, it can be the straw that breaks the airplane's back.

The message should be clear: an ILS approach to minimums can be dangerous. The hostile environment of low visibility is no place for instrument pilots who are either inexperienced or not current.

The airlines have had their share of accidents resulting from disorientation during the visual segment of ILS approaches. As a result, numerous regulations have been created to minimize an airliner's exposure to hazard. For example, airline pilots are not allowed to execute an ILS approach to Category I minimums unless an autopilot or dual-display flight director is used. Also, a captain checking out in a new airplane must raise his personal minimums no matter how experienced he may be—until he has logged 100 hours in that aircraft.

General aviation pilots might take advantage of this conservative operating philosophy by raising their own personal minimums until substantial weather experience is attained. For starters, many instructors recommend minimums of no less than 400 feet (DH) and a 4,000-foot RVR. As proficiency in poor visibility develops, these minimums gradually can be reduced. Pilots who do not regularly fly IFR, however, might consider never descending below DH unless the runway is in sight (even if the approach lights are visible).

Preparation for the low-visibility environment found between DH and touchdown begins prior to the approach. This includes studying the missed-approach procedure. A pilot should be as familiar with that as he is with the approach itself. Spend a few more moments studying the list of lighting aids associated with the runway to which the approach is to be made. Knowing what to expect when breaking out of an overcast or obscuration helps to smooth the transition from instruments to visual flight.

When tracking the localizer inbound, determine if the crab angle (if any) is in accord with the tower-reported wind. If so, anticipate that when the approach lights appear; they will be off to one side of the aircraft and skewed diagonally across the windshield. Such anticipation can avoid disorientation.

If the crab angle is not in accord with the reported wind, some form of wind shear or gradient can be expected on the way down. (Crab angle also can be used to estimate the crosswind component using the "rule of sixty," which states that each degree of crab per 60 knots of airspeed represents a 1-knot crosswind.)

Although an applicant for an instrument rating can pass the flight test simply by not allowing the ILS needles to reach maximum deflection, such performance is unacceptable when visibility is really low. Every effort must be made to keep the needles within one fourth of maximum deflection (near the bull's-eye) so that cross-tracking of the localizer or glideslope is unnecessary at DH.

When approaching DH, inexperienced pilots may sense the appearance of a peripheral visual cue that is either real or imaginary. Since some pilots often are so anxious to establish visual contact, they prematurely shift their attention to the outside at a time when they should be increasing their concentration on the instruments.

Such an initial sighting should not be relied upon for visual reference. Much more than a few lights are needed to provide even marginally suitable guidance. The inexperienced pilot, however, is tempted to rivet his attention on what can be seen. He abandons the instruments and begins to inadvertently wander from the localizer and to tuck beneath the glideslope. The severity of these excursions and the altitude at which they occur can determine where and how a flight will terminate.

When a visual sighting is made, it should be used—if possible—only to confirm what the instruments say. The pilot might be better off not looking out at all. According to the U.S. Flight Dynamics Laboratory, almost five seconds are required to abandon instrument flight and absorb visual data. If the visual cues are inadequate, dangerous vertical deviations can occur. An additional two seconds are required for the pilot to revert to instruments and absorb what they indicate.

If visual cues become available prior to DH, resist the temptation to look at them (unless it is apparent that the visibility is dramatically better than reported). Pay attention to keeping the needles centered and stabilizing heading, airspeed, sink rate, and power.

Upon reaching DH, you must make an immediate and significant decision. Look out and quickly determine if the legal requirements for continuation of the approach are met and if the aircraft is in a position from which a safe landing can be made. If not, execute the missed approach without hesitation. If the approach can be continued safely, return to the instruments and verify that no inadvertent or incorrect control inputs have been made. Then look outside once again. It is hoped the "picture" will have improved to the point where sufficient cues are available to assess visually the aircraft's position, attitude, and flight path. If these factors cannot be determined readily, or if excessive corrections are required, execute the missed approach.

Unfortunately, instrument pilots usually are trained to initiate a missed approach only at DH and not when below it. Numerous accidents could have been prevented if pilots were as spring-loaded to pull up (when below DH) as they were determined to land.

Throughout the visual segment of the approach, pilots should remind themselves that visual guidance might be only marginal at best and that they might experience an urge to descend more steeply (tuck). One way to combat this is to monitor aircraft attitude and sink rate. Do not allow the aircraft to descend more rapidly than was required to maintain the glideslope prior to reaching DH. In other words, when breaking out of the overcast, "hold what you have." Correct the heading as necessary, but resist yielding to what may appear to be a compulsive need to lower the nose. The worst that can result from an insufficient sink rate is a slightly long landing. The result of tucking can be fatal.

Many runways served by an ILS also are equipped with a visual approach slope indicator (VASI). Since VASI provides excellent vertical guidance, it is the only visual cue that can be totally relied upon to prevent undershooting (or a hard landing).

Many pilots rely heavily on an autopilot. Most corporate and air-carrier flight managers encourage it. This relieves pilot work load during an ILS approach, but it also encourages some pilots to become so preoccupied with establishing visual contact that they fail to adequately monitor autopilot performance. Since a coupled autopilot can wander, become decoupled, make unwarranted control inputs, and respond poorly to wind shear, total reliance is unfounded. An autopilot is a marvelous aid, but it never should be allowed to fly a pilot into conditions beyond his own ability to handle them.

The transition from instrument to visual conditions in very poor visibility is one of the most challenging demands made on an instrument pilot. To simplify the task, many airlines have adopted a procedure called the monitored approach (to be used when the ceiling is less than 400 feet and the RVR less than 4,000 feet).

During a monitored approach, the first officer is responsible for monitoring the instruments and autopilot. When nearing DH, the captain looks out the window and concentrates only on establishing visual contact. In the meantime, the first officer keeps his head in the cockpit. Upon reaching

DH, the captain—who is still looking out the window—says either, "I've got it," or "Continue the approach" (assuming that the conditions needed to descend below DH are met). If the captain says nothing before or upon reaching DH, the first officer automatically executes the missed approach (without looking up).

Unfortunately, the advantages of a monitored approach are unavailable to the pilot trying to do it alone. His only weapons for survival are proficiency, experience, and recognizing before it is too late that he might have bitten off more than he can chew.

Chapter 27 **Executing Nonprecision Approaches**

There is a strange misnomer in IFR flying called the nonprecision approach. The term seems to suggest that there is something sloppy about an IFR approach that does not utilize an electronic glideslope.

In practice, the opposite is true. The nonprecision approach often is more demanding and requires more precision and technique than the ILS or so-called precision approach.

Accident statistics seem to bear this out. Considerably more fatalities result from nonprecision approaches than from ILS approaches. This is not because the VOR approach, for example, is inherently more dangerous than the ILS. Every IFR approach—irrespective of the type navaid used—is safe as long as the pilot complies with the published procedure.

The nonprecision approach is the more difficult because it requires a pilot to devise his own glideslope and use judgment to establish a visual slot, techniques requiring more skill and IFR discipline than chasing perpendicular needles. Time and again, I have observed professional pilots shooting near-perfect ILS approaches, only to find that these same pilots invariably have more difficulty with nonprecision approaches.

The reasons for this are numerous and lead to the purpose of this discussion—to offer suggestions that can simplify the demands of a nonprecision approach.

Pre-solo pilots are taught that good landings result from good approaches. So it is that the quality of an IFR approach is related to the time spent planning for the procedure, an activity best performed while en route to the destination airport.

After reviewing and becoming familiar with the approach plate, check for notations warning of unusual conditions. These notes often go unnoticed.

The Detroit (Metro Wayne) VOR Runway 9 approach plate, for example, contains this interesting caution: "Brightly lighted street in town 1.5 NM short of runway may easily be confused for Runway 9." An often overlooked notation on the Hayward (California) VOR-A plate says, "Final approach course aligned 1,150 feet left of approach end Rwy 28L." Reviewing such notes can eliminate undesirable and dangerous surprises at the bottom end of an IFR approach.

The mental gymnastics of computing the time required to fly from the final-approach fix (FAF) to the missed approach point (MAP) also should be accomplished while en route. Unfortunately, this chore usually is left until the last minute, a practice that can result in dangerous error.

Assume, for example, that a pilot is preparing for a VOR Runway 8 approach to Albuquerque (Figure 68). He scans the bottom of the plate and notes that 6 minutes and 45 seconds are required to fly from the VOR to the missed approach point (based on an approach speed of 80 knots). Sounds simple enough, but such simplicity incorporates error.

This approach calls for passing over the VOR at 7,500 feet and descending to an MDA of 5,660 feet, which means that the average altitude during the approach is roughly 6,500 feet. A quick spin of the computer reveals that 80 knots of indicated airspeed is equivalent to a true airspeed of more than 90 knots.

Now consider that even though the wind at the surface may be calm, the wind over the VOR could be a westerly tailwind of 10 or 20 knots, which further increases groundspeed to more than 100 knots.

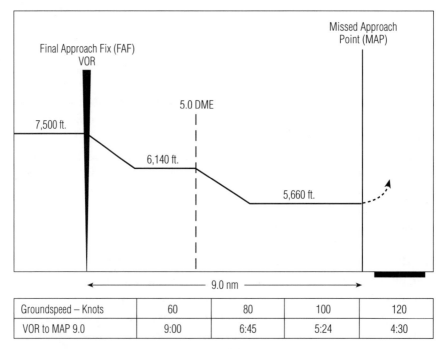

Groundspeed – Knots	60	80	100	120
VOR to MAP 9.0	9:00	6:45	5:24	4:30

Figure 68. VOR approach to Runway 8, Albuquerque

It is the groundspeed, not the indicated approach speed, that must be used to enter the "time to MAP" table at the bottom of the plate. At 100 knots groundspeed, the time required to fly the 9-nautical-mile final approach course is 5:24, not 6:45, as calculated earlier. Without realizing it, the pilot in this example would fly beyond the missed approach point for almost a minute and a half—a potentially lethal error.

Conversely, failure to consider the effects of a headwind could result in flying an abbreviated final-approach course. During conditions of minimum visibility, this might require having to execute a pullup before getting close enough to the airport to establish visual contact.

Assume that a pilot considers all factors and determines his average groundspeed on final will be 73 knots. After consulting the table, he determines it is necessary to interpolate between 60 knots (9:00) and 80 knots (6:45). The actual time required, therefore, is 7:32, a number easier to determine in your living room than while flying solo in the clouds.

Fortunately, there is a clever way to eliminate the need for laborious interpolation. In this case, for example, simply increase approach speed by 7 knots to arrive at a planned groundspeed of 80 knots and read the time required directly from the table. Adjusting approach speed is simpler than juggling numbers and prevents mathematical errors from ruining an otherwise good approach.

If the approach procedure requires timing the final approach segment, do not use a clock or watch with a sweep-second hand because this adds unnecessary hardship. Assume, for example, that such a clock indicates 12:57:33 when passing over the final-approach fix at the beginning of a 6:46 final-approach course. Quickly now, at what time will the aircraft reach the missed-approach point? The answer is 1:04:19. But a pilot should not have to make such mental calculations during such a critical phase of an IFR approach. Instead, use a reverse timer, set it to 00:06:46 (in this case), and begin timing down when passing over the final-approach fix. The aircraft will pass over the MAP when the timer indicates 00:00:00.

If a reverse timer is unavailable, a conventional stopwatch or timer is next best. But do not simply begin timing from "zero" when passing over the FAF because this requires having to remember the specific time required to fly to the MAP. There is a better method.

While en route, subtract the determined time (6:46) from 10 minutes, which results in 3:14 (in this case). Then—while still en route—start the stopwatch. Then hit the stop button at precisely 3:14. When over the final approach fix, start timing again. When the missed-approach point is reached 6 minutes and 46 seconds later, the stopwatch will indicate 10 minutes.

If such a technique is employed prior to every timed approach, the stopwatch will always indicate 10 minutes when the missed-approach point is reached. This relieves the pilot of having to remember a specific time interval, one that varies from one approach to another. The effect is that of reducing all timed approaches to a common denominator.

Another number that is often hard to keep in mind is the minimum-descent altitude (MDA). It usually is an odd figure such as 1,620 feet or 770 feet. And since it often is necessary to fly low and slow at this altitude for up to several minutes, it is a number that is vital to a pilot's health and well-being. But there is no need to commit this number to memory either.

Before your next IFR flight, visit a stationery store and buy a box of small, red, self-adhesive arrows. Prior to an IFR approach, peel off the protective backing from one of these markers. Then place the arrow on the altimeter so that it points directly at the MDA. With this simple act, you have eliminated something else to remember. (Be sure to buy the type of adhesive markers that peel easily from the glass face of the altimeter)

This technique is used by virtually every air-carrier pilot. But instead of using stickers, he uses a mechanical "bug" built into the altimeter. Frankly, I cannot understand why every IFR aircraft does not have an altimeter (and airspeed indicator) with these extremely helpful devices.

By employing these suggestions, a pilot is relieved of having to memorize a string of unrelated numbers and is less encumbered during the approach.

There is another item to be covered during the planning stage. Glance at the circling MDA even when planning to execute a straight-in approach. Occasionally, the circling MDA is the same as the straight-in MDA. When this is the case, a pilot who establishes visual contact with the runway from too high an altitude to land straight-in has the option to circle and land (should he so desire).

Conversely, if the circling MDA is higher than the straight-in MDA, a pilot has no such option when flying at the lower minimum-descent altitude.

Here is another tip. Assume that the straight-in MDA is 500 feet and the circling MDA is 600 feet. A pilot makes a straight-in approach and descends to 500 feet. He spots the airport, but is too high to land straight-in. He is also 100 feet below circling minimums. Is a missed approach necessary? Perhaps not. If the pilot can climb to the higher, circling MDA prior to reaching the missed-approach point and can still see the airport at this higher altitude, he is then in a legal and safe position from which to commence a circling approach.

Fortunately, most of the preceding considerations are unnecessary during an ILS approach; the glideslope needle solves many of the problems associated with nonprecision approaches, but not always.

Should a pilot encounter a glideslope failure (either the transmitter or receiver), he is suddenly compelled to either abandon the ILS or continue by executing a nonprecision, localizer approach. The latter, of course, requires preparation. It is extremely difficult to convert from a precision to a nonprecision approach without first having become familiar with the minimum-descent altitude and the time required to fly from the outer marker to the missed-approach point.

The prepared pilot will, prior to executing an ILS, become acquainted with the "glideslope-out" requirements and begin timing his approach when passing the outer marker—just in case.

It should be obvious by now that the success or failure of a nonprecision approach often hinges on the quality of preparation.

When approaching the final-approach fix, airspeed, altitude, and heading should be stabilized. The pilot should spend a moment reviewing what must be done once the FAF is crossed, because this is the busiest portion of an IFR approach. To simplify a pilot's workload at this point, a system of five Ts has been developed. Each T represents a required action.

(1) TIME. Begin timing the final approach segment when directly above the final-approach fix. This step comes first because timing must commence at the FAF and no later.

(2) TURN. Turn the aircraft to the new course (if a dogleg turn is required at the FAF). This must be done as soon possible to remain within the obstruction-free approach corridor.

(3) TUCK. This is a cute term used to describe the beginning of descent. It is not mandatory that the descent begin precisely upon passing the FAF, but it is in a pilot's best interest to descend rapidly to the MDA (or to an intervening altitude) for reasons explained later.

(4) TWIST. Twist or rotate the course selector to the desired radial and make whatever final corrections are necessary to bracket and track the final-approach course.

(5) TALK. This has the least priority because communicating with a tower controller has little to do with a successful IFR approach. Although approach control usually will ask a pilot to contact the tower when passing the FAF, do not be intimidated into conversation before the first four of the five Ts have been completed. The FAA should revise its procedures so that—during IFR conditions—approach control can issue landing clearance to a pilot before he reaches the final-approach fix. The final moments of an IFR approach are not the best time for talking.

Once the tower is contacted, however, always ask for the latest altimeter setting because this can be different from the setting obtained earlier from air traffic control or an outdated ATIS broadcast. Remember, each error of 0.01 inches represents 10 feet on the altimeter.

A pilot who can remember his five Ts (time, turn, tuck, twist, and talk) has an organized method of getting lots done in minimal time. The system also helps to prevent forgetting an important step.

The method of descending to MDA is a source of controversy. Many pilots descend so as to reach the MDA just prior to the missed-approach point. This results in a relaxed, gradual descent but is illogical during minimal weather conditions.

Figure 69 is the profile view of a typical VOR approach. The pilot must pass over the VOR at 2,000 feet and then descend to a 600-foot MDA. The distance between the VOR and the missed approach point is 6 nautical miles, which, at a groundspeed of 90 knots, for example, requires four minutes.

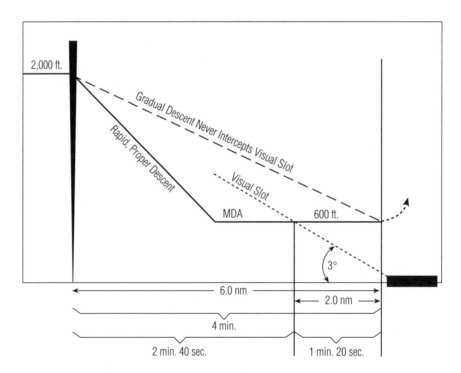

Figure 69. Profile view of a typical VOR approach

Quite obviously, if the pilot breaks out of the 600-foot overcast immediately prior to reaching the missed-approach point, he will be too high to continue and will be forced to pull up.

Proper planning dictates that a pilot level off at the MDA prior to intercepting a 3-degree approach slot (the dotted line in the figure), from which point a normal, visual descent to the runway can be executed.

The problem, therefore, is to determine how soon one must arrive at the MDA in order to intercept such a slot. The solution is not difficult.

A 3-degree slot simply means descending 300 feet during every nautical mile of flight. To be in a normal, visual slot when approaching the example airport, therefore, it is necessary to level off at the 600-foot MDA when at least 2 nautical miles prior to the MAP.

At a groundspeed of 90 knots, 2 nautical miles requires a flying time of 80 seconds. This means that it is necessary to arrive at the MDA, in this case, at least 80 seconds (1:20) prior to reaching the missed-approach point. Since it will take 4:00 minutes to fly from the FAF to the MAP, a pilot should plan to be at the MDA at least 2:40 (4:00 – 1 :20) after passing the final-approach fix.

The suggestions offered here cannot be found in FAA manuals. Instead, they represent a gathering of techniques developed by professionals whose survival depends on the precise execution of nonprecision approaches.

Chapter 28 **The Hazards of Circling Approaches**

The circling approach is not an instrument approach. It is a contact approach, a maneuver used after the airport is sighted during a conventional instrument approach (VOR, ILS, GPS, and so on) in cases where the final-approach course angles too far off the runway heading for the pilot to make a straight-in landing.

The circling approach is not an easy or particularly safe approach. An inherently hazardous procedure, it involves low-altitude maneuvering during slow flight under a low overcast with limited visibility. The procedure is not easy even under optimum conditions, but when attempted on a turbulent, showery night, the circling approach demands highly disciplined, sharply honed skills.

This maneuver is unique because it cannot be simulated. Although the mechanics of a circling approach may be practiced in VFR conditions, this drill bears little similarity to reality. In fact, practicing in good weather can even add to the danger of an actual circling approach. This is because an inexperienced pilot could be misled into believing the maneuver is easier than it really is.

Most major U.S. air carriers recognize the hazards of circling approaches and have revised their policy manuals to prohibit line pilots from executing the maneuver in less than VFR conditions. There is a message here that applies to general aviation pilots who are allowed to perform circling approaches when the weather is considerably less than this.

Most commonly, circling is required because the final-approach course (to or from a radio facility) makes more than a 30-degree angle with the runway in use. This is typical of VOR approaches and explains why corresponding approach plates contain only circling minimums.

When the final-approach course makes an angle of 30 degrees or less with the active runway, "straight-in" minimums usually are published.

If the final phase of an IFR approach requires an abnormally steep descent (because of obstacles on final), FAA publishes only circling minimums even though the procedure would otherwise qualify as a straight-in approach. This does not mean that a pilot must circle to land. If the runway is sighted sufficiently early in the approach and the pilot considers it safe to do so, he has the option to either land straight-in or circle to land.

Most approaches that require circling are obvious. A pilot can determine from a glance at the approach plate that a circling maneuver is required. What often traps the unsuspecting pilot is an ILS approach to Runway 18, for instance, at a time when Runway 27 is the active runway.

When preparing for the ILS, the pilot is preoccupied with setting up the radios, reducing airspeed, and establishing the aircraft in an approach configuration. He expects to be cleared for an approach to Runway 18 but may not be prepared for the words that follow: "...circle to land Runway 27."

The pilot is suddenly thrust into a new game with a different set of rules. He must shift from a relatively low decision height (DH) to a higher minimum-descent altitude (MDA). Also, he must determine the allowed flight time from the final-approach fix to the missed approach point and decide which circling method to use.

It is logical to ask why a pilot might be required to circle and land on a runway other than that served by the ILS (or other approach facility). There are several reasons. Sufficiently strong, adverse winds might warrant the use of another runway, or the ILS runway might be closed due to construction or blocked by a disabled aircraft. A preflight analysis of weather forecasts and notices to airmen often indicates when a pilot might anticipate a circling approach and its associated higher minimums and hazards.

Listening to an ATIS broadcast sufficiently far from the airport is a more accurate source of information and allows the pilot time to study the approach plate before becoming involved in the demanding complexities of an IFR arrival.

Not all circling approaches are difficult and inherently dangerous. The unusually high circling minimums at Palm Springs, California (1,352 feet AGL and 3 miles), for example, make the procedure relatively simple: descend to VFR conditions, enter the traffic pattern, and land.

The most important aspect of any approach that requires circling is to be prepared for what must be done after establishing visual contact with the airport. Prior to initiating the instrument-approach procedure, study the airport diagram and create a mental picture of the runway layout and how to distinguish the active runway from among the possible matrix of others.

Next, determine in advance the best circling procedure to use once the runway has been sighted. Those recommended by the FAA are shown in Figure 70.

Procedure 70A is used when landing opposite to the direction of the approach. But by following this recommendation, the runway ends up on the right side of the aircraft where it might be difficult to see, especially

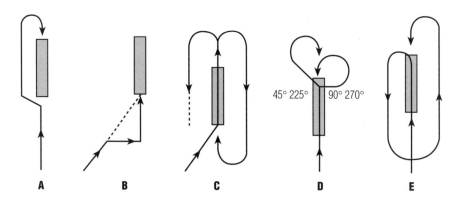

Figure 70. Circling procedures recommended by the FAA

when visibility is poor. Unless the presence of obstacles dictates otherwise, plan a counterclockwise (left) circle.

Although the minimum visibility for circling approaches might exist on the ground (where it is measured), visibility at circling altitudes (the MDA) may be less. Once the runway is in sight, keep it in sight with the tenacity of a cougar stalking its prey. Losing visual contact with the airport mandates an expeditious missed approach (unless losing sight of the airport results only from a normal bank of the aircraft during the circling approach).

While a left-hand circle is recommended, do not ignore notations on the chart that might dictate otherwise. A comment such as, "NA East of RWY 18-36" in the Circle-To-Land Minimums section of the approach plate is often overlooked and warns that circling must be confined west of this particular runway because of obstacles on the east side.

Maneuver 70B is used on an approach course that intercepts the runway centerline at less than a 90-degree angle and when the airport is sighted sufficiently far away so as to allow a simple turn onto base leg.

There are times, however, when a pilot does not sight the runway until almost above it. Since he is too high to use 70B, it is necessary to circle as shown in 70C. If allowed, he should avoid the right-hand pattern and execute a left-hand circuit.

The FAA once recommended maneuver 70D, which unfortunately still can be found in some training manuals. Presumably, this method of course reversal to the runway was used when a pilot broke out of the overcast over the approach end of the runway and was heading in the opposite direction. Whether using the 90- or 45-degree breakaway, as shown, the pilot temporarily severs his visual connection with the airport and must trust (to luck?) that he will find it once again after completing the turnaround maneuver.

This technique is an invitation for vertigo and disorientation, especially at night. A better way to accomplish the same thing is shown in 70E. When over the approach end of the runway, make a left turn to the upwind leg and completely circle the runway until established on final.

Circling maneuvers following ILS and GPS approaches are easier than those following VOR and ADF approaches. The localizer, for example, leads a pilot precisely along the final-approach course to the airport. VOR radials and ADF bearings frequently do not.

Most pilots appreciate that outbound ADF tracking rarely coincides with the course printed on the chart, but they probably are not aware of the inaccuracies that can be experienced when tracking a radial.

Every IFR pilot knows (or should know) that a VOR receiver is allowed up to a 4-degree error when tuned to a VOT test signal. What he may not know is that the VOT transmitter is allowed a 1-degree error. Additionally, a conventional VOR transmitter is allowed up to a 2.5-degree error. Unless exceptionally sharp, a pilot is not likely to keep the needle precisely centered throughout an approach. A quarter-scale needle deflection is an acceptable deviation and represents another 2.5-degree error. And if this were not enough, an FAA study reveals that nondigital omni-bearing selectors are frequently as much as 2 degrees in error.

If all these potential errors were to accumulate in the same direction and conspire against an unsuspecting pilot, his aircraft could be 12 degrees off course at any given point during a VOR approach. Curiously, FAA protects a pilot from enroute obstacles only when within 4.5 degrees of the published course.

There is more to this than chastising the FAA and reviewing potential VOR-bearing errors. An error of several degrees can result in being considerably off course. Since many circling approaches are associated with VOR approaches, it is distressingly obvious that a pilot could execute a VOR approach with superhuman precision, establish ground contact and because of restricted visibility, sail past the airport without being close enough to see it.

Pilots tracking along a final-approach course also should not limit their search to the left of the aircraft, for example, simply because the approach plate says that is where the airport should be. Once a pilot establishes ground contact, he should search for the airport in all directions. Even experienced pilots have passed an airport and executed a missed approach simply because of psychological blinders riveting their attention in only one direction.

After passing the fix from which a descent to MDA is authorized, it is important to descend rapidly. The idea is to level off at the MDA and establish a stabilized attitude and airspeed at least 1 mile prior to reaching the airport. This affords ample time to conduct a thorough search for the airport. If a gradual sink rate is used, the MDA and the missed-approach point might be reached simultaneously. This allows no time to scan for the runway.

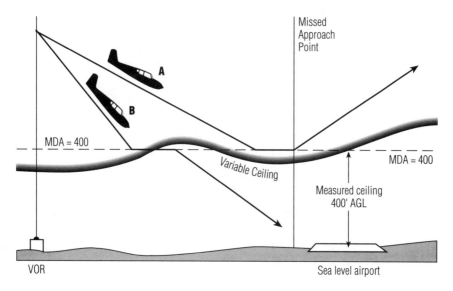

Figure 71. Flying an approach with a variable stratus overcast

Another reason to descend rapidly applies primarily to straight-in, nonprecision approaches but can, at times, apply to circling approaches. Figure 71 shows a typical stratus overcast. At the airport, the ceiling is measured as 400 feet overcast. But this is not necessarily the height of the cloud base at any given point along the approach corridor. For example, Aircraft A descends gradually to the MDA and, because of a lower ceiling at this point, the pilot never establishes ground contact and is forced to execute a missed approach.

The pilot in Aircraft B, however, is more savvy. He descends rapidly to the MDA, levels off and eventually spots the runway.

If the descent to MDA is made with full flaps, consider retracting them to the 50 percent position (in most light aircraft) when leveling at MDA. Circling with full flaps at a constant altitude requires considerable power. This leaves little power in reserve to compensate for inadvertently lost altitude or to initiate an expeditious missed approach.

One danger associated with circling is the temptation to descend beneath the MDA simply because the airport has been sighted. Unless the aircraft is in a position from which a normal descent to landing can be made, a premature descent can be fatal.

When the FAA establishes circling minimums, it does so on the basis of providing only a 300-foot obstacle clearance within a 1.3-mile radius of the runway (for Category A aircraft) on the circling side of the airport (if designated). Dropping down an extra 50 or 100 feet to avoid a lowering cloud base, for example, erodes this already marginal obstacle clearance. Therefore, if maintaining MDA results in cloud re-entry, accept the inconvenience and execute a missed approach.

Once the airport is in sight, maneuver so as to keep the active runway on your left (unless otherwise prohibited). Plan to always be within one mile of the active runway. This guarantees adequate obstacle clearance and probably will prevent losing sight of the airport when visibility is poor.

Should a large turn be required, it might be a good idea to temporarily play ostrich. Keep your head in the cockpit and execute the turn on instruments and with precision. It is not difficult to lose control in a turn because of a visual fixation with the ground when the weather is 400-and-1. An occasional glance at the airport during the turn is all right, but most attention should remain in the cockpit.

During the circling maneuver, airspeed should be stabilized at normal approach speed (1.3 V_{S0}). This provides adequate stall protection, obviates the need to lose both airspeed and altitude when turning final, prevents the need for massive trim changes, and, finally, keeps the turn rate relatively high. This final item is particularly important. Increased airspeed decreases the turn rate (at a given bank angle). This increases turn radius, which can result in an excessively wide pattern and loss of visual contact with the airport.

Another area demanding extreme care is the missed approach. It is of paramount importance that a pilot be thoroughly familiar with the procedure prior to beginning an approach. If it is necessary to consult an approach plate after inadvertently entering clouds at less than 400 feet AGL, you are in serious trouble.

Since the need for a missed approach can occur at any point while circling, confusion often rises as to the method of initiating the miss. Simply stated, turn toward the runway (even though it cannot be seen) and intercept the missed-approach procedure when over the airport. This can require some imagination and again stresses the need to be familiar with the missed-approach procedure.

A final word of caution. The published missed-approach procedure guarantees terrain clearance only when initiated at the designated missed-approach point (MAP). Pulling up prematurely might sacrifice this protection. So, if you are engulfed in cloud and tracking toward the airport at MDA when the tower advises that the field has just gone to zero-zero, do not abandon the approach. A climb may be initiated, but avoid making any turns until reaching the MAP.

The sidestep maneuver is often confused with the circling approach. These procedures are related but—like brothers—should be treated individually. A sidestep maneuver follows an IFR approach to one of two parallel runways less than 1,200 feet apart. A pilot is allowed to "sidestep" and land on the other parallel runway, provided it is in sight when at or above the published "Minimum Sidestep MDA" and the appropriate clearance has been received.

Generally, sidestep minimums are higher than those for straight-in approaches and less than those for circling approaches.

Any pilot who considers making his first circling approach when the weather is reported as 400-and-1 should either hire an experienced professional to ride shotgun or cancel his planned flirtation with fate. The circling approach can be a hazard to your health and should be respected accordingly.

Chapter 29 **Busting Approach Minimums**

The limbo is a popular pastime in the West Indies. The challenge, as you may know, is for dancers to remain on their feet as they lean back and writhe and slither under a wooden pole suspended between two uprights. Use of the hands is not allowed. The pole is lowered progressively until only one remaining player can squirm from one side to the other without dislodging the pole. Unfortunately, some pilots feel similarly challenged when executing IFR approaches, a game with potentially lethal consequences.

Minimums for IFR approaches are not established arbitrarily. They are painstakingly calculated to provide the lowest possible decision height (DH) or minimum-descent altitude (MDA) under a given set of circumstances. The resultant IFR procedure, if followed carefully, assures minimum acceptable safety margins. By descending below DH or MDA without having any of the required visual cues in sight (Figure 72), a pilot erodes these safety margins and so places himself in jeopardy.

Consider a VOR approach, for example. If the terrain surrounding an airport is as flat as a billiard table and no obstructions are near the airport and a very reliable VOR transmitter is situated on the airport, the FAA might allow an MDA to be as low as 250 feet with a required visibility of only half a mile. Certainly no one would want to shoot a nonprecision approach to lower minimums.

Acceptable Visual Cues for the Runway of Intended Landing

1. Approach light system	7. Runway touchdown zone
2. Runway threshold	8. Touchdown zone markings
3. Threshold markings	9. Touchdown zone lights
4. Threshold lights	10. Runway
5. Runway-end identifier lights (REILs)	11. Runway markings
6. Visual approach slope indicator (VASI)	12. Runway lights

A pilot may not operate an airplane below DH or MDA unless at least one of the above cues is distinctly visible and identifiable to the pilot.

Figure 72

But when approach characteristics are less than ideal, minimums are elevated. This might be necessitated by obstacles near the airport, the absence of approach lights, a distant VOR that does not provide sufficient guidance, or any of a number of other variables.

Minimums for a given approach are determined initially, using a very complex set of criteria outlined in the FAA publication, *Terminal Instrument Procedures* (TERPS). After these theoretical minimums are calculated, the FAA flight tests the approach to guarantee that these results apply to the real world. If it is determined that the radial defining the final-approach course does not lead the pilot accurately, minimums might be increased further. Even though the resultant minimums may seem unreasonably high, logic was responsible for each 20-foot increase in the MDA and 0.25-mile increase in required visibility. To violate these minimums is as irresponsible as ignoring the red line of an airspeed indicator or any other operational limit.

Although it might seem that the relative simplicity and precision of an ILS approach would allow minimums in every case to be 200 feet and 0.5-mile visibility, there are factors that necessitate raising these minimums, too. For example, the ILS approach to Runway 7 at Burbank, California, has published minimums of 250 feet and 1 mile. A pilot who foolishly descends below DH would have a problem. The localizer transmitter at Burbank is situated at the approach end of the runway, not at the departure end, as is the case almost everywhere else. As an aircraft approaches and passes over the transmitter, the localizer becomes extremely narrow and sensitive. Unless the pilot is in visual conditions at such a time, the result is likely to be dangerous low-altitude crosstracking. The point is that there is a very good reason for establishing a specific DH or MDA. To bust these minimums is to invite a confrontation with a variety of hazards.

Fortunately, not many pilots ignore safety limits during IFR approaches. Those who do generally are reacting to the influence of job pressure, "get-home-itis," or an inflated ego. Others are subjected to peer pressure. This is especially prevalent when an arriving pilot learns that a preceding aircraft has just completed the approach. He may develop an attitude of "well, if he can make it, so can I." If the weather has deteriorated since the first aircraft completed its approach, this false pride could compel the pilot to complete the approach by busting minimums "just a little bit."

The only time busting minimums can be justified is during an emergency, such as when a low fuel supply precludes the possibility of going elsewhere.

Although some of aviation's grim statistics are caused by those who feel more skillful (or luckier) than the rest of us, it appears that most instrument approach accidents are caused by those who violate minimums unintentionally. This probably seems incredulous. After all, if a pilot follows faithfully the dictates of an approach plate, he should not be exposed to risk. Although true in theory, it does not always work out that way. This is because an IFR approach is a relatively complex procedure requiring total attentiveness and concentration. One of my early instrument instructors went so far as to say, "If you are not doing something at all times during an approach procedure, then you are doing it wrong." But keeping busy is not enough. Equally important is being aware of the variables and keeping up with the changes.

For example, most pilots obtain the altimeter setting from the automatic terminal information service (ATIS), at airports where it is available. When the pilot reaches the airport, barometric pressure may have changed significantly, resulting in an inaccurate altimeter indication. This can be especially hazardous when the pressure is falling or rising rapidly. Or perhaps the altimeter setting was transcribed incorrectly. (I once heard the ATIS at Lambert Field in St. Louis broadcast a setting of 29.98 when it should have been 29.68.) Since each .01 inch of error equates to an altitude discrepancy of 10 feet, this kind of error cannot be tolerated. If destination weather is marginal, request and confirm—even if you have the current ATIS information—the latest altimeter setting when approaching the final-approach fix.

Since the DH or MDA is such a critical altitude, be certain to engrave it on your mind prior to executing the approach. Better yet, buy an altimeter "bug" that attaches to the face of the altimeter and can be adjusted to indicate DH or MDA throughout an approach. This increases altitude awareness considerably. A pilot then only has to be certain that he does not misread the altimeter while descending. Do not scoff at such a warning. Air carrier pilots, especially tired ones, have misread altimeters by 1,000 and even 10,000 feet, resulting in everything from embarrassment to an unexpected swim to a rendezvous with the Grim Reaper.

Be cautious also about recognizing, during runup, altimeter errors that might have developed since the last biennial test of the static system. And if this certification has expired, all instrument flying is illegal no matter how accurate the altimeter might appear to be. A combination of an inaccurate altimeter, an incorrect altimeter setting, and a little sloppy flying easily can erode the obstacle protection afforded pilots during an IFR approach.

VOR receiver and display accuracy also should be verified before an IFR approach in marginal conditions; maximum obstacle protection is available only when within 4.5 degrees of a final-approach course.

Many pilots use radio (absolute) altimeters as another way of increasing altitude awareness during IFR approaches. Some of these devices even provide altitude warnings with synthesized voices. Unfortunately, many of these well-intentioned pilots misuse their radio altimeters in such a way as to bust minimums without realizing they are doing so.

Despite implied claims, radio altimeters cannot and should not be used to determine the MDA during any nonprecision approach.

Assume, for example, that a pilot is shooting a VOR or GPS approach to an airport (Figure 73) where the MDA is 300 feet HAT (height above touchdown). He has no way of knowing that the terrain in the approach corridor is considerably below runway elevation. In the meantime, the pilot descends until the radio altimeter indicates 300 feet. Notice that the airplane is actually well below the MDA and is much closer to possible ground obstacles than it should be. Even when the terrain appears relatively flat, an undetected slope could lead a pilot to descend 50 or 100 feet below the MDA.

In the case of rising terrain, a pilot relying on a radio altimeter might level off too high, conclude he needs to make a missed approach, and deprive himself of a successful approach.

Similarly, radio altimeters must not be used to determine DH during a Category I ILS approach because of the uncertainty of terrain slope in the approach corridor.

Radio altimeters can be used to determine DH on some Category II and all Category III ILS approaches. In these special cases, the terrain in the approach corridor has been surveyed carefully. Pilots read from the approach

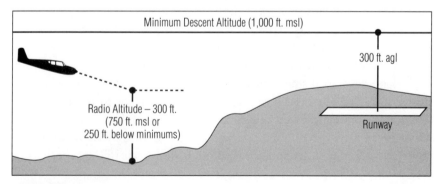

Figure 73. Incorrectly relying on a radio altimeter during a non-precision approach

plate exactly what radio-altimeter indication (to the nearest foot) corresponds to the DH as shown on the barometric altimeter.

Most unintentional violations of MDAs probably occur when otherwise conscientious pilots fail to arrest aircraft sink rate sufficiently upon reaching a minimum-crossing altitude on final or the MDA itself. This is not surprising. When the airplane is in landing configuration (gear down and flaps fully extended), more pitch change and power are required to level off than many pilots anticipate. This is particularly true when steep descents are required. The result is a busted minimum. If this occurs during a flight test, the applicant can remove his hood and try again some other day. But if it happens during an actual approach, the pilot may not be afforded the luxury of a second chance.

There are two ways to avoid this problem. The first is to resist using full flaps during an approach until landing is assured. Second, practice recovering from high-drag, low-power, steep descents at various target altitudes (without allowing the airplane to get one foot too low).

There are times, too, when even a careful pilot is seduced by fate into leaving the haven of an MDA. This occurs most frequently when a pilot in cloud catches glimpses of the ground out of the corner of his eye. He senses that he could escape the overcast simply by dropping "just a few more feet." But what if the cloud base ahead is much lower (as it so frequently is)? Then how much lower can the pilot go? The game of limbo has begun.

The rule is explicit; descent from MDA is not allowed unless one or more of the official visual cues can be seen and visibility ahead is at least as much as that specified for the approach. There can be no compromising without eroding minimum safety margins.

It is possible for a pilot to bust minimums by descending from the MDA with the runway clearly in view, but only if the subsequent descent to touchdown requires either an unusually steep or a flat descent. The regulations state that a pilot may not leave the MDA until in a position from which a visual approach can be executed at a normal sink rate. The FAA justifiably claims that unusually steep or shallow descents near the ground are hazardous during marginal weather.

For this reason, the FAA developed a visual descent point (VDP) for selected nonprecision approaches. Upon arrival at the VDP, a pilot can leave the MDA and know that a normal 3-degree descent profile will lead him safely to the runway threshold (as long as other requirements for leaving the MDA are satisfied). In other words, a descent initiated significantly beyond the VDP requires a steep descent and vice versa.

From a practical standpoint, the VDP is a form of missed-approach point. The regulations specify that steep descent profiles are not allowed (and can be hazardous). So if a pilot passes the VDP and still is engulfed in cloud, he should give serious thought to executing a missed approach even though the actual missed approach point (MAP) has not yet been reached.

Once a pilot spots the airport and descends from the MDA or DH, it is entirely possible for him to reenter clouds or pass unexpectedly into an area where visibility is less than specified as a minimum for the approach. At such a time, pilots tend to press on, assuming the airport will reappear just as quickly. Is such a pilot busting minimums? Absolutely. A missed approach is mandatory. Unfortunately, once the airport has been located visually, pilots are reluctant to give up the chase.

When a pilot busts minimums during a nonprecision approach, he risks colliding with an obstacle. Doing the same during an ILS approach, however, does not subject the pilot to the same risk (as long as the aircraft is kept on the glideslope). But this does reduce dangerously the time and distance available to transition from IFR to visual conditions. When descending at 600 feet per minute, for example, a pilot slipping out of the overcast at 200 feet AGL has only 20 seconds to make this transition, correct any cross tracking or lateral-offset errors and assess landing conditions. Losing any of this valuable time and altitude by remaining in cloud below the DH is extremely risky.

The final seconds of an ILS approach can be so critical that most airlines suggest that their pilots use autopilots to make a coupled approach whenever the reported weather is less than 400 feet and 0.25 mile.

Executing an instrument approach when reported weather conditions are below minimums is a popular hangar-flying topic. This is legal, but only during noncommercial operations. Pilots who take advantage of this opportunity must recognize the probability of a missed approach and be all the more prepared. But what if the pilot arrives at the MDA or DH and determines that in-flight visibility is at least as great as that required for the approach, even though the reported visibility is less? He can continue the approach and land but might be called upon to justify his actions. On the other hand, the FAA might have difficulty proving that the pilot did not have the required minimum visibility. This is because visibility as determined from the control tower often is different than that experienced by a pilot during an approach.

It is the pilot's responsibility to determine if minimums really exist. This is a classic example of the honor system. But if a pilot cheats, he is the one most likely to suffer.

Published minimums are just that—minimums. Inexperienced pilots and those who do not maintain razor-sharp proficiency might consider establishing personal, higher minimums until they feel more comfortable with marginal conditions. If the minimums for an ILS approach to San Francisco are 200 feet and 0.5 mile, why not voluntarily raise them to 300 and 0.75? Pilots not only are taught to abide by FAA limitations, they also are encouraged to recognize their own.

After a first officer on an airline is promoted to captain, the FAA requires him to abide by higher-than-published minimums during his first 100 hours in the left seat, even though he might have had thousands of hours in the right seat of the same airplane and might have executed at least as many instrument approaches while there. General aviation pilots can improve their safety record considerably by adopting a similarly conservative philosophy. After all, there is much more at stake than dislodging a limbo pole.

Chapter 30 **Holding Patterns Simplified**

Murphy created two inescapable laws especially for aviation. The first states that headwinds shall increase in proportion to the pilot's anxiety to get home. The second says that when fuel reserves are low, an IFR pilot can expect to be sent to a holding pattern.

We have no choice about accepting Murphy's first law; it is merely an expression of Mother Nature's whimsical ways. The second axiom is less tolerable and more aggravating because the holding pattern is a man-made shackle. After all, an air traffic controller has to put an airplane somewhere when he doesn't know what else to do with it.

Holding clearances usually are issued when excessive traffic converges on a terminal area or when the destination weather is below landing minimums. Also, a pilot might be instructed to hold when the IFR runway is closed temporarily because of snow plowing or is blocked by a disabled aircraft. At such time, a pilot can either proceed to an alternate airport or etch racetracks in the sky while waiting patiently for conditions to improve. The holding pattern is ATC's stop sign and is flashed whenever an aircraft cannot proceed.

A corollary to Murphy's Holding Law states that a holding clearance shall be issued only when the pilot is completely submerged in cockpit activity and is least prepared. Somehow, controllers always manage to comply with this rule. Whether he's driving a 747 into San Francisco or a Cessna into Santa Monica, the holding clearance always seems to catch a pilot off guard.

The inbound course of a holding pattern usually lies along the route of flight. In such a case, entering the pattern is no more complex than making a 180-degree turn at the holding fix. But occasionally a satanical controller sends a pilot to a pattern requiring either a teardrop or parallel entry. And that's when the suds hit the fan. The average instrument pilot hasn't had to worry about such procedures for so long that he's probably forgotten how.

After the pilot finally locates the holding fix, he usually consults a hieroglyphic holding pattern diagram. But such a guide looks confusingly similar to an Aresti aerobatic diagram and, if followed, can result in a teardrop entry to a lomcovàk. Desperately, the victim pilot searches the cockpit for a template or holding pattern computer to resolve his difficulties. But by the time he locates one and figures out how to use it, the holding fix has been left behind.

Fortunately, there are simpler, less confusing ways to enter holding patterns. There is no reason to be intimidated by the FAA's recommended methods, because no regulatory muscle has been created to enforce their use.

When the FAA devised its entry procedures, it did so with the objective of confining the aircraft as closely as possible to the lateral limits of the holding pattern. Every holding pattern is surrounded by a large womb of airspace to protect the holding aircraft. The exact size of this area varies according to altitude, distance of the farthest VOR defining the fix, and the type of aircraft (propeller-driven or jet-powered).

Figure 74 shows the airspace protecting the pilot of a propeller-driven airplane while holding at 5,000 feet at a fix 20 nautical miles from the farthest VOR defining that fix. The pilot is offered a 14 by 8 nautical-mile area within which to maneuver his machine into a racetrack pattern that measures only 1.0 by 2.5 nautical miles (assuming a 90-knot holding airspeed, one minute legs, and a no-wind condition).

Clearly, he can use any reasonable method of entry without having to worry about violating the limits of protected airspace.

Figure 75 illustrates one extremely simple method that can be used to enter any holding pattern regardless of the direction from which it is approached. It is the only method to use (even during an FAA flight test) when ATC issues a holding clearance just as the aircraft passes over the holding fix. All the astonished pilot has to do (after crossing the fix) is to turn to the

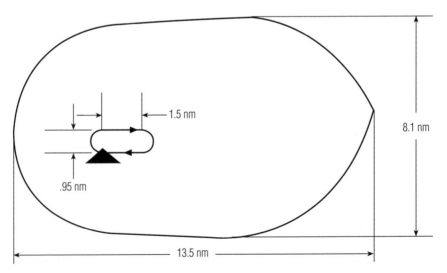

Figure 74. Protected airspace surrounding a propeller-driven aircraft in a holding pattern

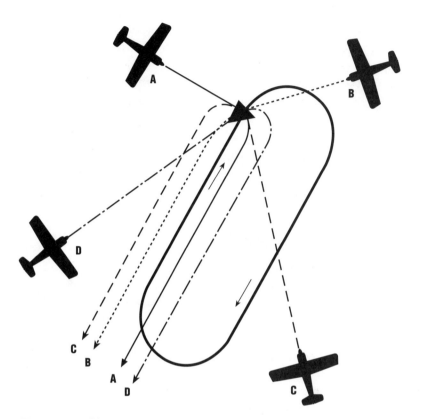

Figure 75. Holding pattern entry procedure

outbound heading of the holding pattern and remain on that heading for one minute. This initial procedure requires no mental gymnastics and is foolproof.

During the minute of outbound flight, set the VOR course selector to the inbound course of the holding pattern and decide which way to turn to intercept that radial. At the end of the minute, turn toward the radial, intercept it, and track inbound to the fix. That's all there is to it. The airplane has been established in the holding pattern with a minimum of fuss and bother.

This technique of "turning to the outbound heading" can be used without fear of recrimination whenever a pilot is doubtful about which of FAA's three recommended entry methods to use. It is an easy, safe, and legal technique. (Although FAA examiners prefer that instrument rating applicants demonstrate standard entries during a flight test, they won't fail anyone who uses reasonable procedures and remains well within protected airspace.)

If a pilot desires to use the FAA's entry procedures, he can do so with much less effort by slightly modifying those techniques. The suggestion that follows doesn't require correlating those 70-degree and 110-degree relative bearings and sectors to aircraft heading and holding pattern alignment. Instead, use 90-degree quadrants because they are so much easier to visualize.

For example, assume that a pilot has been cleared to hold at Delay Intersection (Figure 76). According to the FAA's recommendations, there are three ways to enter the pattern depending upon the direction from which the fix is approached: the teardrop, the parallel, or the direct entry.

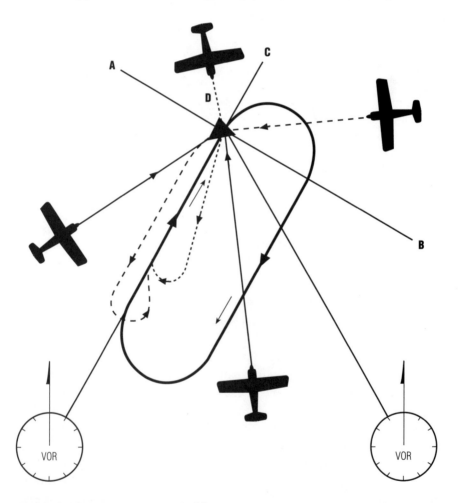

Figure 76. Three ways to enter a holding pattern

To simplify the holding problem the pilot should draw the racetrack pattern on his chart. For some unknown reason, pilots protect their IFR charts from pencil marks as if they were priceless Picassos. IFR charts are revised and replaced so frequently that revising the Jeppesen manuals is almost a sideline profession: there's no reason not to write on them.

So, when a holding clearance is received, immediately draw the pattern on the chart—with a red crayon if that helps to make the pattern stand out. Once the pattern is illustrated, half the battle is won.

Next, slash a line through the fix perpendicular to the holding radial (represented by line AB in Figure 76). Then extend the inbound course of the pattern beyond the holding fix (line DC). With a modicum of practice, these lines won't have to be drawn, but for now they help to visualize what follows.

If the aircraft approaches the fix from the holding side of the perpendicular line (AB), simply make a direct entry. In other words, turn to the outbound heading of the holding pattern upon reaching the fix. The direction of the turn should coincide with that of the holding pattern. That is, turn to the right for standard patterns or to the left for nonstandard patterns. That's all there is to it. You're in the pattern and have only to remain in orbit until ATC mercifully allows continuation of the flight (to another holding fix, no doubt).

If the fix is approached from within the quadrant bounded by lines AD and DC, the aircraft nose will be inside the holding pattern upon crossing the fix. So take a hint; stay inside the pattern and execute a teardrop entry.

The only other possibility is to approach the fix from within the quadrant bounded by the lines BD and DC. Upon crossing the fix, the nose of the aircraft will be pointed outside the holding pattern. So, take another hint; stay outside the pattern and execute a parallel entry.

This modified version of FAA's recommended entry procedures works equally well with right- and left-hand patterns. Happily, it requires considerably less mental wizardry.

The truth is that a pilot is free to choose whatever method of pattern entry is easiest for him. There are no requirements other than to be careful about not getting too far from the holding pattern and violating the limits of protected airspace. To preclude this possibility, maneuver into the holding pattern at reduced airspeed. Since there is ample maneuvering room for aircraft holding at 175 knots IAS (maximum-allowable holding speed for propeller-driven airplanes), flying at 100 knots (or less) results in using proportionately less airspace and allows much more room for error.

Savvy instrument pilots not only know how to simplify holding procedures, they also know how to occasionally escape from having to hold at all.

If a pilot is relatively far from the holding fix when he receives the holding clearance, he should immediately advise ATC that he's reducing airspeed. He then slows to the aircraft's best endurance speed. This airspeed is very nearly the same as that used for a power-off glide and results in the use of minimal engine power.

This serves three purposes. First, it gives the pilot more time to prepare for the holding entry. Second, it reduces the per-minute fuel consumption and conserves fuel at a time when it might be desperately needed. Finally, reducing airspeed consumes part of the holding delay en route and reduces the amount of holding necessary at the clearance limit. It is certainly far more comfortable to cruise in a straight line at reduced airspeed than to chase your tail around a holding pattern.

With some luck, a pilot might be able to consume the entire delay en route and not have to hold at all. This technique, by the way, is common practice among airline pilots, and controllers have become used to it.

Once established in a holding pattern, it usually is necessary to begin timing the inbound and outbound legs. The duration of the outbound leg is adjusted so the inbound leg is one-minute long (when holding at or below 14,000 feet MSL). When above 14,000 feet, the inbound leg should be a minute-and-a-half long.

Timing the legs, however, is a pain in the empennage. There is a better way, but only when holding on a VOR radial and when the airplane is equipped with operable distance measuring equipment (DME).

At such times, a pilot has only to request holding with 5-mile DME legs, for example. Controllers almost always comply with this request. Subsequent turns in the pattern are then made with respect to DME indications, not the clock. The procedure is considerably simplified.

If DME is unavailable, a pilot might request five- or even ten-minute legs. If approved, this eliminates the drudgery of having to hold in relatively small patterns which have only minute-long legs.

With respect to time, be very skeptical about Expect Further Clearance (EFC) times issued by controllers. Never plan on having sufficient fuel reserves solely on the basis of this estimate. When the EFC expires, you might be issued further holding instructions with a new and extended EFC.

In other words, don't continue holding and burning into the fuel reserve needed to divert to an alternate on the basis of an optimistic EFC. When the time comes to divert, do so without hesitation. It is tempting to continue holding with the thought that an approach clearance probably is imminent. But the result could be a case of fuel exhaustion.

Consider a pilot holding in a pattern situated at right angles to the prevailing wind. The wind causes turn radius to increase when the turn is initiated over the holding fix. Conversely, a turn at the opposite end of the pattern is into the wind, which reduces turn radius.

Pilots often attempt to correct for this drift by using a steep bank when turning downwind and a shallow bank when turning into the wind. This is improper and makes the job of holding unnecessarily difficult. All turns in the pattern should be at the standard rate (3 degrees per second for light airplanes) or with a 30-degree bank angle, whichever requires the shallowest bank angle (unless a flight director is used).

The easiest way to correct for wind drift is to first determine the crab angle necessary to track the inbound course of the holding pattern. Then, triple this wind correction angle and apply it to the no-wind heading normally used to fly the outbound leg.

For example, if the pilot uses a 5-degree left crab to track the inbound course, he should correct 15 degrees to the right while flying outbound.

A final note of caution concerns the holding "stack," a situation where numerous aircraft are holding at the same fix, but at different altitudes (hopefully).

When the bottom man in the stack is cleared to leave the pattern, clearances are usually issued—one at a time—for successive aircraft to descend 1,000 feet to the next lower altitude. A problem can arise when one pilot is slow to initiate the descent while an impatient pilot only 1,000 feet above makes like a dive bomber. The result can be a near miss or worse.

To prevent such a conflict, never report vacating a holding altitude until actually doing so. Also, make descents in the stack at 500 fpm—no more, no less. These simple steps can go a long way toward preventing an encounter of the wrong kind.

Unfortunately, there is no advice available to help a pilot totally circumvent Murphy's Holding Law. Hopefully, however, some of this advice can be used to ease the burden of compliance.

Chapter 31 **Strange and Amusing Instrument Approaches from Around the World**

Most instrument pilots have been told that one IFR approach is essentially the same as every other. "Master the local procedures," they are advised, "and you will have no difficulty elsewhere. It simply is a matter of following the lines on the chart and abiding by the constraints."

As do most generalizations, this has notable exceptions. As you fly farther afield, you will discover some fascinating, amusing, difficult, and even hazardous IFR procedures that make those at home seem prosaic by comparison.

Some approach plates and area charts are so cluttered with teardrop turns, sweeping arcs, segmented routes, and racetrack patterns that they appear to be creations of a cartographer gone mad. Some are so complex, they almost dare a pilot to accept the challenge. Such charts, which resemble Count Aresti's blueprint for an aerobatic routine, should be studied on the ground because reviewing them in the air could induce vertigo or airsickness.

Perhaps the world's most absurd IFR approach is at Ipoh, Malaysia. Upon reaching the missed approach point (MAP) at 372 feet above ground level (AGL), the pilot must proceed visually over and between obstacles to the airport, which is 36 miles away. There is no minimum visibility specified for this straight-in, nondirectional, radiobeacon (NDB) approach, which is just as well. Under the best of conditions, a pilot cannot see that far from such a low altitude.

Despite the obvious advantages of VOR, GPS, and ILS, the NDB remains a common approach aid outside the U.S. Not long ago, there was even one approach based on the archaic, four-course range. When shooting the range approach to Chihuahua, Mexico, the pilot had to follow the A (· —) side of the north leg from the cone of silence to the 7-mile-distant airport. This probably sounds like gibberish to new pilots, but it may coat the eyes of older ones with a nostalgic mist.

In contrast, Chicago's O'Hare International Airport holds the record for the most full-ILS approaches: eleven.

One must be careful when planning to execute a VOR approach to Kennedy International Airport, because many general aviation aircraft are not capable of maintaining the 13,900-foot minimum descent altitude. By the way, *this* Kennedy Airport serves La Paz, Bolivia, where the elevation is

13,310 feet above sea level and a portable oxygen bottle is needed just to preflight the airplane. (The main runway is as long as the airport is high.)

Some approaches keep a pilot flying in circles. The NDB approach to San Vincente del Caguan, Colombia, for example, requires a pilot to descend for several thousand feet to the MDA and MAP while in a holding pattern. A missed approach requires him to remain in the pattern and shuttle back up to the starting point (and continue holding).

A missed approach in Russia involves flying a rectangular pattern around the airport and includes instructions to execute another approach; no further clearance is necessary. In case of communications failure, therefore, a pilot may be destined to execute a series of approaches and misses until fuel runs out. He has to keep trying until he gets it right.

Until the demise of the Soviet Union, the enroute, IFR chart of that country showed only one east-west airway spanning this vast country, it extended from Moscow to Yedinka, a navaid on the east coast. Airway Red 22, which seemed an appropriate name, was 3,558 nautical miles long and had a VOR at each end. En route, the pilot had to follow a chain of 21 radio-beacons; many of these were hundreds of miles apart. Some superhuman navigation was required because cross-track excursions of more than 5 kilometers (2.7 nautical miles) from the airway centerline were *verboten*.

When in Russia—and also the People's Republic of China—pilots must maintain metric altitudes (such as 4,500 meters), so have a metric conversion chart handy.

Although some missed approaches require complex maneuvering, none are as ominous as those at Cape Newenham and Utopia Creek, Alaska. Because of the surrounding terrain, the approach plate for each of these airports contains this foreboding note: "Successful go-around improbable."

An IFR approach to Castlegar, British Columbia, is not fun either. To find the airport, a pilot must follow a segmented trail of NDBs while descending into a long, deep, narrow valley.

On a more amusing note, there are at least two approaches in the world where the final-approach course consists of a DME arc from a nearby VORTAC. These are at Wallops Island, Virginia, and Pinang Island, Malaysia.

A few places do not use the MDA as it is used elsewhere. A pilot shooting an NDB approach to Nosy-Be, Madagascar, for example, must execute a missed approach as soon as he reaches the MDA. The MDA there is treated as a form of decision height. Too bad. Upon reaching the MDA, the pilot probably will be too far from the airport to see it.

The most common reason for an approach procedure to be complex is high terrain near the airport. Nowhere is this more true than at Innsbruck, Austria. The airport and the city lie at the bottom of a bowl rimmed by lofty, alpine granite. The IFR approach to Innsbruck's only airport can be so treacherous that the Austrian government advises all pilots intending to use the procedure to practice it first during VFR conditions. Some who have heeded this advice have opted never to repeat the procedure when flying in instrument conditions.

After intercepting the Innsbruck localizer inbound, the pilot uses DME indications (there is no glideslope) to program descent along a steep, 4.7-degree (500 feet per nautical mile) profile. While descending, however, the aircraft will pass over the airport and continue toward an NDB, the missed-approach point. At the beacon, the pilot must either execute the miss (which requires a maximum-gradient climb) or continue visually to the airport, which is 7 miles behind the tail.

The flip side of the double-size approach plate details the visual portion of the procedure. Upon reaching the MAP, a pilot desiring to proceed visually must execute a 180-degree turn using a radius of less than 1 mile. Upon completing this turn, the aircraft passes over the second decision point, where the pilot is given one last chance to look toward the airport and quickly decide if he really wants to continue. (If not, the turn is maintained, and he returns to the beacon, the original MAP). Consider that the airport will be 7 miles away and that the minimum visibility required for the approach is only 3,000 meters (less than 2 nautical miles). Complicating matters is a note on the approach plate stating that a strong wind from the southeast may produce severe turbulence and downdrafts. (At Cape Lisburne, Alaska, surface winds in excess of only 10 knots produce severe turbulence on final approach; at Vestmannaeyjar, Iceland, pilots can expect "peculiar" wind behavior at all times because of a nearby volcano.)

A pilot approaching Innsbruck knows that he will pass over the airport and have to reverse course. But what about the hapless pilot approaching Wonderboom Airport at Pretoria, South Africa? He is advised that "upon breaking cloud, the aerodrome could be behind the aircraft." With only 1-mile visibility, where does he look? If the airport is not in sight, should he turn around?

Terrain also plays a major role in the design (probably by a sadist) of Hong Kong's infamous Cheung Chau (or "Charlie Charlie") approach. The procedure requires a figure-eight descent pattern over the "CC" NDB until reaching visual conditions at 780 feet above the wind-swept waters of the

South China Sea. The pilot then tracks inbound to a second NDB, where he begins another descent while aiming for a 400-foot hill adorned with a pair of large, illuminated, orange-and-white checkerboards. When these warning signs swell to fill the windshield and the copilot begins to squirm, a sharp right turn is made to avoid the hill and to align the aircraft with the runway, which is less than a mile away. When pilots depart in the opposite direction, they are cautioned not to turn right after takeoff unless planning to penetrate the People's Republic of China and be "fired upon without warning."

Although terrain poses some unusual problems, there are other hazards with which to contend. When approaching Gambell, Alaska, for example, pilots must monitor the NDB's aural identifier to ensure they are not homing in on signals being transmitted from within Russia, which is only 41 miles away. (At their closest points, Russia and the United States are only 3 miles apart.)

When flying near Rio de Janeiro, "false station passage may be indicated by local radio aids due to the aerial tramway on Pao de Acucar Mountain."

When nearing Veracruz, Mexico, pilots should be aware of possible oscillation of their instruments due to a powerful electrical substation located only a mile from the airport. But when flying to Kwajalein in the South Pacific, they must avoid an area north of the airport where strong electromagnetic radiation could harm equipment and those on board.

When approaching Maracaibo, Venezuela, pilots must not overfly nearby oil fields, because a crash landing there could ignite more than local excitement. Pilots also are admonished not to overfly at too low an altitude certain cities, zoos, royal palaces, game reserves, and historical sites. But nowhere are the warnings as harsh as those in Seoul, Korea.

There is a small prohibited area just east of Seoul's Kimpo International Airport that must be given wide berth. Anyone trespassing there and ignoring the warning tracers fired at him can expect to be shot down.

Since the airport is only 23 miles south of the 38th parallel, pilots are warned of possible harassment from North Korea. A note on the Seoul Area Chart says to beware of unreliable navigational signals and communications. "Pilots receiving warning calls such as 'turn to [such and such] a heading or you will be fired upon' should exercise extreme caution in reacting to these calls."

Care also is advised when nearing Kwangju, Korea. The airport is surrounded by a high-angle firing range.

For whatever reason, the folks at Tarbes Airport in France are neither compassionate nor hospitable. Aircraft with one engine inoperative are prohibited from landing there. Does this mean that the pilot of a Piper Warrior having an engine failure while approaching Tarbes is expected to pull up and go elsewhere?

At a latitude of 82.5 degrees north, in Canada's Northwest Territories, Alert is the world's most northerly airport. (The most southerly is at the South Pole.) But Alert and other nearby facilities are so close to the magnetic pole that ordinary compasses are useless. Consequently, all bearings, directions, and courses shown on the approach plates are referenced to true north. Pilots should not even contemplate approaching these airports in IFR conditions without having the means to reference their gyroscopic heading indicators to true north prior to beginning a descent.

At one time, there reportedly was a military landing site on the ice pack north of Canada. But since ice drifts, pilots approaching this base had to tune in an NDB first and listen for a Morse code message advising them of the airport location and runway alignment for that day.

A pilot desiring an IFR approach in most places must first obtain an air traffic control clearance, but this is not applicable everywhere. At Sfax, Tunisia, and Skukuza, South Africa, for example, ATC services are not available. Pilots should broadcast their intentions in the blind on a discrete frequency prior to beginning an approach and arrive at a mutually agreeable method of separating themselves from one another.

Caution is advised when receiving weather information from Entebbe Tower in Uganda. Always ask if the reported ceiling is the height of saturated air or the height of the clouds of swarming insects that drift over the airport from adjacent Lake Victoria. If it is the latter, prepare for a dogged pitot tube on final approach.

Pilots are accustomed to warnings about animals on the runway. These usually refer to deer, antelope, and cows. But when landing at some foreign airports, pilots may have to compete for space with kangaroos, hyenas, "strolling dogs," monkeys, and holy cows. In New Zealand, sheep are so abundant on some airports that pilots are warned, "Caution: runway greasy—braking action poor." A strip in Africa is slick because of worms.

Birds can be a problem, but at Salalah, Oman, pilots must be alert for "large, predatory birds" (eagles, condors, or F-5s?). At Comox, British Columbia, bird activity on the airport is particularly intense when ceilings are low. The birds apparently recognize foul weather and ground themselves accordingly, which is more than can be said about some pilots.

Finally, be careful when flying into Bahrain International Airport on the Persian Gulf. Lesser sand plovers and sandpipers that migrate from Russia (probably without clearance) roost on the airport and often fly back and forth across the runway in such great numbers that they are visible on radar.

When the runway finally is in sight, an instrument pilot's problems usually are over, but not always. Imagine landing at Eskilstuna, Sweden, only to discover that a road—complete with traffic—crosses the runway. Also be careful at Minchumina, Alaska; in the winter, snow is removed only once a week to facilitate mail delivery. The airport at Kuala Lumpur, Malaysia, has a unique feature: a runway used only by those who need to make a gear-up landing.

At Point Barrow, Alaska, the runway consists of 5,000 feet of stainless-steel planking. To prevent the surface from becoming slick during rain and snow, the center third of the length is coated with antiskid paint. Imagine braking heavily with one wheel on wet steel and the other on antiskid paint; the pilot might get a panoramic view of the airport that he did not expect.

Most pilots should avoid the VOR-A approach to Kenmore Air Harbor, Washington, unless they want to go for a swim. This approach, like a few others in Maine and Louisiana, leads only to a seaplane base. But even seaplane pilots should avoid the NDB approach to Nortrym. After breaking out of the overcast, they will find themselves over the turbulent waters of the North Sea (near Norway) with only an oil rig on which to land.

When approaching Barton Airport at Manchester, England, pilots are advised not to overfly the nearby cemetery (who there would be disturbed?). On the other hand, the cemetery at Yurimaguas, Peru, is on the airport and, according to local gossip, is for the convenience of pilots who fail to survive their own carelessness.

Section 6

Emergency Tactics

Like other forms of insurance, emergency training is something that we hope never has to be used. Nevertheless, the proficient pilot must be prepared for whatever unlikely situation develops when the Fickle Finger of Fate points his way. These five chapters deal with subjects seldom given sufficient attention during conventional training. Hopefully, this knowledge will prove to be another insurance policy that is never needed.

Chapter 32 **Flight Control Failure**

It happened during the student pilot's fifth lesson. The instructor was demonstrating an accelerated stall when the control wheel suddenly fell limp in his hand. As the nose plunged earthward, the instructor desperately pulled the wheel full aft. But there was no response. It was impossible to raise the elevator.

Or was it? During those agonizing moments of panic, the instructor caught a mental flash of a technique often discussed but rarely practiced. He reached for the pitch-trim wheel on the floor and rotated it rearward. The crippled aircraft reacted sluggishly, total nose-up control had not been lost.

For the next half hour, the crippled Cessna 152 was nursed toward a nearby airport. But during the landing approach a burst of power was applied to prevent an undershoot. The resulting pitch-up could not be countered sufficiently with trim. The beleaguered aircraft stalled 50 feet in the air and impacted the tarmac nose first. Both occupants were critically injured.

A portion of every pilot's training is devoted to the most common emergencies, especially engine failure. Unfortunately, there are other potential crises that are given little or no attention. One of these is the partial or total failure of a primary flight control.

Such an emergency occurs infrequently, but not so rarely that it can be ignored. National Transportation Safety Board records annually reflect numerous accidents attributable to flight-control difficulties.

The most serious such problem, of course, is the loss of elevator control. Yes, the trim tab can be used to control pitch within limits, but few pilots appreciate how difficult it can be to land without a fully functioning elevator. Anyone who makes light of such a problem probably has never done it. This was demonstrated dramatically during a series of test flights with experienced pilots in the left seat. One of them was Cal Pitts.

Pitts is a veteran pilot and seasoned flight instructor. After we had discussed a recent accident involving a failed elevator cable, Pitts expressed confidence in his ability to take off and land an airplane without touching the control wheel. A five-dollar wager flew out of my hip pocket and landed neatly on the coffee table between us. It was met with an equal amount, and we headed for a rented Cessna 152.

With his right hand, Pitts opened the throttle; his left hand—itching to grasp the control wheel—remained in his lap. At 50 knots, he cranked in a bit of nose-up trim. The 152 lifted off nicely. But at 20 feet AGL, the Cessna pitched up unexpectedly. Rapid nose-down trim was applied and a stall averted, but now the Cessna was heading downhill. Nose-up trim was frantically added. After more porpoising and trimming, the aircraft was stabilized in a normal climb. Pitts smiled smugly, not realizing that the most difficult challenge had yet to be met.

He skidded the 152 around the pattern with light rudder pressures and positioned us on the downwind leg. With one hand on the trim wheel, Pitts retarded the throttle with the other. The nose pitched down. Pitts decided it would be easier to raise the nose by reapplying power rather than bothering with excessive use of the trim wheel. Good thinking.

We were both surprised at the large amount of pitch change resulting from so little as a 100-rpm power change. In practice, aircraft attitude can be controlled, within limits, solely by judicious use of the throttle. Add power to raise the nose; reduce power to lower it.

While on base, Pitts made a big mistake; he extended the flaps. As soon as the spring-loaded switch was depressed, the nose pitched skyward—insistently. Considerable trim was required to return the nose to the horizon. But it didn't stop there. It kept going down. Nose-up trim was applied. Again, the nose returned to the horizon and failed to stop at the desired attitude. Several oscillations later, Pitts finally brought the Cessna under control. A lesson was learned: flap deflection can create pitch changes much larger than can be controlled by trim alone. If flaps are used during stick-free flight, they must be used gingerly, extending or retracting them only 1 or 2 degrees at a time.

After stabilizing the aircraft on final approach at a modest sink rate, Pitts felt his confidence return. As the wheels neared the concrete, he gradually applied nose-tip trim. But at 10 feet AGL and without warning, the plane began nosing toward the concrete. Pitts countered with rapid nose-up trim, but it was too little, too late. He reluctantly admitted that had I not grabbed the wheel, the aircraft would have landed nosewheel first. Damage, we concluded, would have been likely.

After cleaning up the aircraft (both inside and out), we taxied back to Runway 21 for another try. Six attempts later, Pitts made his first hands-off landing to a full stop. And his progress was better than other pilots tested.

Preparing for this type of emergency is difficult. Handling characteristics vary considerably from one airplane to another. Simply because a pilot can make a stick-free landing in one aircraft does not necessarily mean that he can do it in another. But some practice in any airplane helps to understand the complexities and variables. Stick-free landings, however, must never be attempted without a capable pilot with sharp reflexes in the right seat. Unfortunately, a stick-free landing cannot be simulated at altitude, for reasons explained later. Also, be extremely careful during a hands-off missed approach. A gross and uncontrollable pitch-up usually occurs when full power is applied rapidly.

Five variables affect pitch: flaps, power, center of gravity, trim, and ground effect. Each must be understood if a pilot is to successfully land an aircraft without a fully functioning elevator.

Consider a wing with flaps retracted. The center of gravity is forward of the center of lift. Visualize what would happen without a horizontal stabilizer. The lift would pull up on the center of the wing while the weight of the aircraft, acting through the center of gravity, would pull down on the leading edge. The result would be a nose-down pitching moment. To prevent this, the horizontal stabilizer is designed to produce a downward force (negative lift) that maintains equilibrium.

Now imagine what happens when flaps are extended. The airflow from the trailing edge of the wing (downwash) is deflected more sharply downward. The increased downwash strikes the upper surface of the horizontal stabilizer. This increases the tail-down force, which causes the nose to rise and explains why flap extension causes a pitch-up and retraction a pitch-down, a characteristic of most light aircraft. Some aircraft, however, behave oppositely (that is, flap extension causes nose-down pitching) because of an aft shift in the center of lift. This is most typical of aircraft configured with cruciform or T-tails.

The probability of a successful stick-free landing, however, is increased when flaps are not used at all. With the flaps retracted, it is easier to maintain a nose-high landing attitude. Approaching the runway with flaps extended usually results in a nose-down attitude, requires larger pitch changes during the flare, and increases the likelihood of landing nosewheel first.

The ability of the horizontal stabilizer to produce a downward aerodynamic force depends on wing downwash, the free airstream, and propeller slipstream. It stands to reason, therefore, that when propwash weakens during a power reduction, the horizontal stabilizer loses some effectiveness. This is why power reduction causes the nose to pitch down; the horizontal surfaces cannot provide as much negative lift as when the propeller slipstream is stronger. Conversely, applying power results in a greater downward force on the tail, which causes the nose to rise.

With practice, a competent pilot should be able to counter the effects of flap extension or retraction by the timely reduction or addition of power, in such a way as to maintain a relatively constant attitude. This is a challenging exercise to try at a safe altitude.

The downwash from a wing that helps to produce a download on the horizontal stabilizer (on low- and high-wing aircraft) is altered when the airplane enters or leaves ground effect (about 20 feet above the ground for most lightplanes). When entering ground effect, downwash is reduced, which causes a nose-down pitching moment. It was this unexpected attitude change that caught Pitts off guard during his first attempt at a hands-off landing.

Conversely, when climbing out of ground effect, wing downwash increases to produce a nose-up pitching moment.

These pitching forces created by changes in downwash occur during every takeoff and landing, but the pilot is rarely aware of them. Necessary corrections are made subconsciously with subtle pressures on the control wheel. But when making a hands-off landing, this effect must be anticipated. It can be countered only by a perfectly timed application of nose-up trim and/or a few timely jabs of power.

Another variable is center of gravity. Landing without up-elevator capability can be simplified by shifting the adjustable cabin load aft. By moving heavy items to the rear, for example, it is easier to make a hands-off approach in a nose-high attitude, a particularly important consideration when flying taildraggers.

Finally, there is the elevator trim tab. Little can be added to what a pilot already knows about this supplemental control except that the effect of a trim tab varies considerably from one aircraft to the next. It might prove interesting to determine just how well the trim tab can control pitch attitude in the plane you fly regularly. A practice exercise involves stabilizing the airplane in a full-power climb. Then retard the throttle and see how rapidly the aircraft can be stabilized in a normal glide attitude (using trim only). Then reverse the procedure and reestablish the climb. Most pilots tend to overreact to this problem. Several roller-coaster-type oscillations usually are induced before an aircraft is brought under positive control.

A single broken or disconnected elevator cable usually doesn't result in a complete loss of pitch control. In most airplanes, a failed cable represents only a partial loss. For example, it is usually possible to apply "up" elevator even though "down" elevator capability has been lost, or vice versa.

Assume that the up-elevator cable has failed. The wheel moves aft easily, but produces no response. Forward wheel movement beyond the neutral position produces a nose-down attitude. In such a case, the pilot should apply considerable nose-up trim, enough to produce a moderately nose-high attitude. From then on, any desired attitude can be obtained by either relaxing forward pressure on the control wheel (for nose up) or increasing forward pressure (for nose down). This technique essentially restores total pitch control to the control wheel. Conversely, if only nose-up elevator is available, pitch control can be maintained by applying considerable nose-down trim (refer to Figure 77).

Loss of Up-Elevator Control	Loss of Down-Elevator Control
1. Apply *excessive* nose-up trim	1. Apply *excessive* nose-down trim
2. Push control wheel forward to maintain desired attitude	2. Pull control wheel aft to maintain desired attitude
3. Push harder to lower nose	3. Release back pressure to lower nose
4. Release forward pressure to raise nose or flare for landing	4. Increase back pressure to raise nose or flare for landing

Figure 77. Controlling pitch with a failed elevator cable

Belonging to the same class of emergency is the more serious jammed elevator. Although various combinations of power and flap extension offer limited pitch control, the prospects of a successful landing are poor.

One incident serves as an example of this problem. A student was on his second solo cross-country flight. All sorts of paraphernalia were strewn on the cockpit floor: a plotter, a computer, a clipboard, a bag of sandwiches — you name it, he had it on board. During a period of moderate turbulence, the E6-B computer was lifted off the floor and came to rest in a crevice behind the instrument panel in such a way as to prevent the application of down elevator. The frightened pilot used all of his strength in a frantic attempt to move the control wheel forward and lower the nose. Fortunately, the plastic computer gave under the strain and crumbled to the floor in pieces.

There is a popular theory that circulates among hangar flyers. It states that "reverse trim" can be used to control pitch in the event of a jammed elevator. If the elevator is jammed, so the hypothesis goes, the application of nose-down trim, for example, would cause the tab to rise. In effect, it would act as a mini-elevator and cause the nose to rise somewhat.

This theory was tested and debunked in a Cessna 172. The effect of trim application alone (the control column was held firmly in place) caused no detectable attitude change. This effect, or lack of it, is attributable to slop in the elevator control system. Nose-down trim, for example, causes a very slight movement of the elevator in the opposite direction as the slack is taken up in the cable. This minute elevator deflection cancels any effect the "reverse trim" technique might have.

This procedure might work, however, in aircraft with larger tabs, adjustable horizontal stabilizers, or rigid push-rod control systems.

The closest I ever came to a jammed control was on a flight to Las Vegas, Nevada, in a Luscombe 8E. My friend, Joe Stanley, sat in the right seat. He spent most of the trip maintaining a navigation log to break the monotony of a slow flight across the bleak Mojave Desert.

East of Clark Mountain, we encountered strong thermal activity. The left wing dipped, and I countered by moving the control stick to the right. Klunk! It stopped dead center. I tried again, but further attempts to move the stick to the right failed. Klunk! Klunk! Still no luck. The Luscombe was now in a steep left turn. Stanley looked to me for an answer, but I had none. Fifteen seconds and 180 degrees later, I was attracted to a reflection on Stanley's lap. I reached over to his right knee and slapped away the aluminum clipboard positioned between his stick (the dual control) and the right sidewall. For one brief moment, we had felt that hollow sickness that creeps into the stomach when aircraft controllability seems lost. It's a feeling neither of us is likely to forget.

Although a loss of aileron or rudder control is not normally as serious as an elevator problem, it can be. Case in point: a charter pilot was departing Oakland after the Beech 18 ("Twin Beech") had been in the shop for major maintenance. After liftoff, the control wheel was moved to the right to counter a small gust that had lowered the left wing. The airplane rolled farther left. The pilot turned the wheel farther right, but the big twin demonstrated a contrary will of its own. The left wingtip scraped the runway surface as the pilot suddenly realized what was wrong.

Reacting brilliantly and courageously, he turned the wheel toward the lowered left wing. The ship righted itself, and the pilot nursed the aircraft around the pattern, substituting right aileron pressure when left was needed, and vice versa. Investigation revealed that a mechanic had rigged the ailerons in reverse. The whole problem could have been avoided by a more careful pre-flight inspection.

Loss of total or partial aileron control because of mechanical failure can be combated by making shallow, skidding turns using rudder only. Another interesting technique can be used in airplanes with two cockpit doors. By opening both doors and allowing them to trail freely, directional control can be maintained by pushing on one door or the other. Pushing open the left door of a Cessna 172, for example, results in a surprisingly coordinated right turn, and vice versa.

A combination of doors and ailerons can be used in case of rudder failure, but avoid crosswind landings.

Irrespective of the type of control difficulty, land only at an airport with long runways and crash/rescue facilities. Most importantly, reduce the possibility of such an emergency by increasing the diligence of preflight inspections.

Chapter 33 **Coping with Pitot-Static Difficulties**

An accident investigator from the National Transportation Safety Board claims that many more fatalities are caused by pitot-static icing than is possible to determine.

With resigned frustration, he adds, "We often accuse a pilot of disorientation and loss of control when we know instinctively that the accident was really caused by erroneous flight data resulting from blocked pitot-static lines. But the ice usually melts before an investigator arrives at the crash site. The proof is gone forever."

A spectacular example of such an accident occurred in 1974 when a Northwest Airlines' Boeing 727 was being ferried from New York's JFK International to Buffalo, New York. Although the aircraft was cleared to FL310 (31,000 feet), the ill-fated jetliner never reached its assigned attitude. At 24,800 feet, the trijet entered a spin and crashed only 83 seconds later (the average rate of descent was more than 17,000 fpm).

Were it not for the voice and flight-data recorders salvaged from the strewn wreckage, it might have been inconceivable to conclude that such a disaster was caused by a simple yet lethal overdose of pitot icing. But that's exactly what happened. And if a professional airline crew flying an elaborately equipped aircraft can fall victim to such a fate, then so can the lone, general-aviation pilot flying a less sophisticated machine.

The Boeing pilots were deceived by erroneous airspeed indications. Because of ice-clogged pitot probes, both airspeed indicators behaved like altimeters and responded only to changes in altitude (for reasons explained later). During the climb, indicated airspeed increased steadily and persistently. This caused the pilots to raise the nose farther in an attempt to arrest what appeared to be a dangerously high airspeed. This resulted in an increased climb rate, which compounded the problem. As altitude increased, so did indicated airspeed. The pilots continued to raise the nose until they had unwittingly forced the aircraft to stall.

There are three lessons to be learned from this accident.

(1) Adhere diligently to checklists. (The 727 crew failed to turn on the pitot heat even though this item was on their taxi checklist.)

(2) When various instruments disagree, initially believe the one that indicates the most adverse condition. (Both attitude indicators in the 727

apparently operated properly and reflected the dangerous 30-degree pitch angle prior to stall.)

(3) Distrust instruments that indicate performance beyond the capability of the aircraft. (Near the top of the 727's abbreviated climb, the pitot-static instruments indicated a continuous 5,000-fpm climb at an indicated airspeed of 340 knots, a generally impossible feat unless the airplane is caught in a thunderstorm.)

We should not, however, be too quick to criticize the 727 crew for not recognizing their problem. Contradictory instrument indications can be totally bewildering.

During subsequent experiments in a simulator, several professional pilots were subjected to similar flight conditions and instrument indications. More than half of them fixated on the erroneous airspeed indicator while ignoring the properly functioning attitude indicators.

Surprised? Don't be. When a pilot takes his first flying lesson, he begins to develop the deep-seated habit of observing and reacting to airspeed indications. Airspeed becomes his primary key to survival. Later, he is introduced to the attitude indicator, a relatively complex device that is more subject to mechanical failure than the simpler, more reliable airspeed indicator. It is little wonder that—in a pinch—many pilots revert to airspeed.

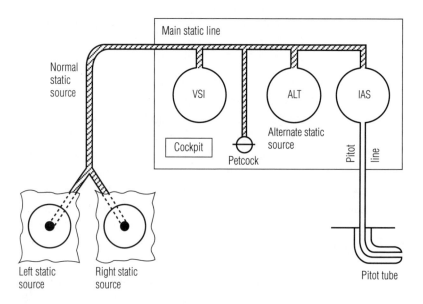

Figure 78. Typical pitot-static system

Figure 78 is a diagram of a typical pitot-static system. Its purpose is to provide static (ambient) air pressure to the altimeter, vertical-speed indicator (VSI), and airspeed indicator as well as to provide pitot (ram air) pressure to the airspeed indicator.

Many pilots are of the impression that two static ports (one on each side of the fuselage) are provided for system redundancy. Not so. Otherwise, considerate airframe manufacturers also would provide a backup pitot tube because this item is most prone to icing, for example. Dual static sources are necessary and equalize (balance) pressure variations that occur on both sides of the fuselage when the aircraft slips and skids (such as during turbulence).

To determine the effect of having available only one static source, I enlisted the aid of aviation attorney Robert Cleaves. In addition to owning a Cessna 185 that would be ideal for simulating various types of pitot/static difficulties, Cleaves had been an experimental test pilot.

Prior to our first flight, we placed masking tape over the right-hand static source. During the subsequent climb, all instruments functioned normally, using air pressure from the left-hand static source.

After leveling at 4,000 feet, Cleaves alternately stabbed at the left and right pedals. This caused all three pitot/static instruments to behave erratically. Why they did so is not mysterious.

During a yaw to the right, the only operational static source (on the left) was turned partially into the relative wind. This allowed the airstream to blow into that static port. This increased the pressure in the static line and was interpreted by the altimeter—in this instance—as a loss of 400 feet. Also, the VSI indicated a substantial sink rate and the indicated airspeed dropped 13 knots. (The behavior of the IAS gauge is explained later.)

Conversely, during a yaw to the left, the open static source was on the "downwind" side of the fuselage and sensed a decrease in pressure. As a result, the altimeter rose, the VSI indicated a climb, and the indicated airspeed increased.

In turbulence, the three instruments were extremely sensitive and fluctuated wildly between high and low indications.

Should all three of these gauges act similarly during a normal flight, the odds strongly favor that one static port is clogged. By yawing the aircraft and observing the readings, a pilot can determine which of the two static sources is plugged.

Prior to a second flight, both static sources were covered with tape to simulate heavily iced static ports. During the takeoff roll, everything seemed normal. But during the climb from sea level to 5,000 feet, the VSI remained at zero, and the altimeter insisted that we were still on the ground. The IAS gradually decreased from 78 knots at sea level to about 52 knots at 5,000 feet, even though attitude and power settings remained constant.

Since the static sources were sealed at sea level, sea-level pressure was trapped in the static lines and prevented the VSI and altimeter from sensing an altitude change.

Totally blocked static sources are extremely hazardous. Without an altimeter, how can a pilot execute an IFR approach or maintain an assigned altitude or remain clear of obstacles?

At such a time, a pilot has two choices. The most obvious is to use the alternate static source. This is simply an extension of the main static line that is routed into the cockpit and installed within easy reach of the pilot. This tube is sealed with a petcock so that cockpit air cannot normally enter the static system. However, when the normal static source is blocked, the petcock can be opened. This introduces cockpit air to the static instruments. Since the air pressure in an unpressurized cabin is nearly the same as the ambient pressure outside the aircraft, this restores reasonable accuracy to the pitot-static instruments. (In pressurized aircraft, the alternate static pressure obviously must be routed to the instruments from outside the pressure vessel.)

These instruments, however, will not be quite as accurate as when the normal static source is used. This is because ambient pressure in the cockpit varies slightly with airspeed, attitude, and the positioning of ventilation controls.

When the vents are open, for example, air rushing into the cockpit tends to pressurize the cabin. This increased pressure is sensed by the altimeter as a lower altitude. Closed vents, on the other hand, often result in cabin air having slightly less pressure than the air outside. This produces a higher-than-actual indication of altitude.

When using the alternate static source during an IFR approach, open the vents fully, no matter how cold it is outside. In this way, the altimeter probably will read lower than true, a safe-side error.

Unfortunately, some lightplanes used for IFR flight are not equipped with alternate static sources. This is ludicrous. Aircraft owners spend thousands of dollars on electronic redundancy. It is illogical that they not install an inexpensive alternate static source and provide a backup supply of static air for the single most important IFR instrument—the altimeter.

Lacking an alternate static source, a pilot with an ailing static system has an emergency alternative—break the glass on the face of the VSI. Doing so allows cabin air to enter the instrument and then the normal static-system plumbing to the altimeter and airspeed indicator. (When breaking the glass, try to do so without damaging the VSI needle.) Although the altimeter and airspeed indicator will operate reasonably well, the VSI will be out of phase with respect to actual aircraft performance. For example, a 500-fpm climb rate will be indicated by a 500-fpm descent, and vice versa.

Cleaves's airplane has an alternate source. So, with the normal static ports still sealed at 5,000 feet, the petcock was opened. All three instruments sprang to life. After the needles stabilized, we closed the alternate source, which "froze" the static system at 5,000 feet. As the flight continued, there was no way to detect gradual altitude changes. A subsequent steep, intentional descent was detected only by a significant increase in airspeed and noise level. As we leveled off a few hundred feet above the Pacific, the altimeter and VSI were still at 5,000 feet.

Many pilots contend that if icing conditions are so severe as to clog up the normally ice-free static sources, then unusually heavy structural icing would have created an earlier emergency. This is not always true, because static sources are subject to other, more insidious forms of icing.

Consider, for example, a pilot who flies after a recent rain or after his aircraft has been washed. Water droplets and/or condensation in the static lines may freeze after a climb to a sufficiently cold altitude in VFR or IFR conditions. Bugs, dirt, wax, and blowing sand are other culprits that attack the reliability of the static system.

A partially clogged static system also is hazardous because the symptoms are difficult to detect and vary according to the degree of blockage.

To simulate this condition, we retaped the static ports and poked tiny holes in the tape to allow only a restricted flow of static air pressure to the instruments.

During the climb, we noted that the altimeter and airspeed indicators were lagging and indicated less than true values; also, the VSI indicated less than the actual rate of climb. This was because the static pressure outside the aircraft changed faster than could be sensed through the pin pricks in the masking tape used to cover the larger static ports.

After leveling off, the instruments slowly caught up and indicated correctly.

The danger of partially blocked static lines was accentuated during descent. The IAS was higher than actual, the lagging altimeter indicated higher than actual, and the VSI indicated less than the true rate of descent. We were deceived into believing that conditions were safer than they really were.

One way to combat this problem is to temporarily open the alternate static source at least once during every IFR descent. If the needles move significantly when this is done, a static pressure problem exists, and the alternate source should be used for the remainder of flight.

Figure 79 is a simplified diagram of the airspeed system and is useful in analyzing IAS errors resulting from partially or fully blocked pitot/static air sources.

When ram air enters the pitot tube, it flows into a sealed diaphragm within the airspeed indicator housing that expands with increasing pitot pressure. It is the expansion and contraction of this diaphragm that causes the airspeed needle to move. The ram air entering the pitot tube actually consists of two types of pressure: the static or ambient atmospheric pressure of the air outside the airplane and the dynamic pressure of the air caused by forward motion.

To prove this, consider an airplane at rest. Static air pressure enters the pitot tube and the diaphragm. Since the diaphragm is filled by static air pressure, why doesn't it expand? Because the static pressure—from the static ports—enters the case of the instrument and surrounds the diaphragm. Since the pressure inside the diaphragm is equal to the surrounding pressure, the diaphragm is "relaxed" and indicates zero airspeed. For the airspeed indicator to operate properly, static air pressure must be allowed to enter the case of the instrument to counteract the static—not the dynamic—pressure that enters the diaphragm through the pitot tube in flight.

Assume that an airplane is in a steady climb during which the entire pitot tube freezes over with ice. The air in the diaphragm is trapped. But as the climb continues, static air pressure surrounding the diaphragm decreases. This reduction in surrounding pressure allows the diaphragm to expand and causes indicated airspeed to increase, even though actual airspeed remains constant.

Conversely, during a descent without pitot pressure, the static pressure in the instrument case increases and compresses the diaphragm, resulting in a reduction of indicated airspeed.

In this manner, the airspeed indicator behaves like an altimeter—the problem encountered by the Boeing 727 crew mentioned earlier.

Many pitot tubes are provided with a drain hole (see Figure 79) to allow water to leave the system. Assume that the main pitot entrance is clogged but the drain hole remains clear. What then? Only static pressure enters the diaphragm through the drain hole, pressure exactly equal to the static pressure surrounding the diaphragm. As a result, the diaphragm relaxes (contracts) and indicated airspeed drops to zero.

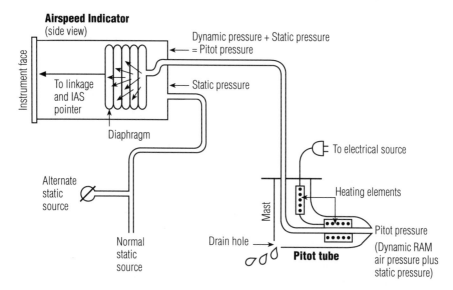

Figure 79. Effect of pitot and static pressure on the airspeed indicator

To prevent icing, pitot heat should be used at all times when flying in visible moisture. Turn it on also before takeoff if there's a chance that taxiing through a puddle might have splashed the probe.

Frequently check the operation of the pitot heat on the ground by feeling the pitot probe—but don't grab it: a properly operating heater heats the tube sufficiently to burn the skin. Also check the pitot tube before every flight for foreign matter that might clog the works.

Unless the static source of an airplane is located on the pitot probe, an iced-over pitot does not affect altimeter and vertical-speed indications. A static system that is not free and clear, however, does affect indicated airspeed even when the pitot is clear.

Assume the static ports are blocked during a climb. As a result, static pressure surrounding the diaphragm does not decrease as it should. The diaphragm, therefore, cannot expand as much as it should. Consequently, indicated airspeed is less than it should be.

Conversely, during a descent the static air pressure surrounding the diaphragm does not increase as it should. As a result, the diaphragm expands more than it should, and indicated airspeed is greater than it should be.

When a pitot or static source becomes impaired, the instruments can present a bewildering display of flight data. The best preparation for such an emergency is to understand the system and know how to interpret its messages.

Chapter 34 **Engine Failure After Takeoff in a Single-Engine Airplane**

It is characteristic of man to ignore certain facts of life, even though his fate may be determined by them. He is reluctant, for example, to think about cancer, AIDS, and obesity, to name just a few threats to his welfare.

Among such unpleasant and frequently avoided topics is the pilot's nightmare—an engine failure after takeoff in a single-engine airplane. But unless such problems are discussed and understood, we might not learn to cope with them.

Engine failures occur more frequently than many pilots realize. The National Transportation Safety Board states that during a recent five-year period, 4,310 accidents resulted from engine failures in the U.S. That's an average of 862 per year, or more than two every day. Of these 4,310 reported powerplant failures, a significant percentage occurred during or shortly after takeoff. In fact, many more engine failures occurred during this period. But these were not included in the report because they did not result in either aircraft damage or bodily injury.

Much has been written about enroute engine failure, and many techniques have been developed for dealing with such emergencies. Pilots are taught, for example, to plan flights so as to avoid hostile terrain and always to be within gliding distance of a landing site suitable for an emergency landing.

But what advice has been developed for the hapless pilot who finds himself behind a stilled engine shortly after takeoff? Damned little! Virtually everything taught about this potentially catastrophic event can be summarized in a single sentence: "If the engine fails after takeoff, land straight ahead; do not turn back to the airport."

This "rule," however, is not so golden that it must be accepted without question or criticism. This is a controversial subject that requires substantial analysis. This is because there are times when a pilot should return to the airport and not land straight ahead.

The accident records are replete with case histories that describe in graphic detail the often fatal results of those who choose to make a 180-degree turn back to the airport from too low an altitude. In most cases, stalls or spins are entered inadvertently by frightened pilots with an aversion to flight near the ground. Many others have returned successfully, but these events go unnoticed because they do not become accident statistics.

Altitude is the primary difference between success and failure. When a pilot has sufficient altitude, a turnaround to the airport might not only be safe, but it also might be his only recourse (especially when the terrain ahead offers little hope of a survivable forced landing).

If the pilot does not have sufficient altitude, a turnaround should not be attempted. It is wiser to accept a controlled crash than to risk spinning uncontrollably into oblivion.

But how high is high enough? What is the minimum altitude above which a return to the airport can be executed safely?

This depends not only on aircraft glide characteristics, but also on the turnaround technique. For example, should bank angle be shallow, medium, or steep? To answer these and other questions regarding the controversial turnaround, I enlisted the aid of several veteran flight instructors to obtain flight data for a variety of general aviation singles.

To simulate an engine failure after takeoff, we flew each aircraft in take-off configuration and at its best-angle-of climb speed. At an arbitrarily chosen altitude (usually, 2,000 feet AGL), the throttle was abruptly retarded.

The pilot flying the aircraft did nothing for four seconds. According to FAA studies, it takes this long for a pilot to recognize an engine failure and initiate action. After the four second delay, the aircraft was established in a 30-degree banked, gliding turn. At the completion of a 180-degree turn, the sink rate was arrested to simulate a landing flare. Subsequent tests were conducted using 45-degree, 60-degree, and 75-degree banked turns. The net altitude loss during each turnaround was recorded and compiled.

According to these findings, the minimum altitude loss (in most cases) results from a steeply banked turn. The altitude loss in a Cessna 172, for example, is 380 feet when a shallow bank is used, but only 210 feet when the bank angle is steepened to 75 degrees.

It might seem incongruous that a shallow bank results in more altitude loss than a steep bank. After all, the sink rate during a gliding turn does increase with bank angle. The explanation involves the element of time. When a Cessna 172 is banked 30 degrees while gliding at 70 knots, the rate of turn is only 9 degrees per second. As a result, the time required to execute a 180-degree turn is 20 seconds—sufficient time for substantial altitude loss even though the descent rate is nominal.

Conversely, the turn rate increases to an astonishing 58 degrees per second during a 75-degree bank. In this case, a 180-degree turn requires only three seconds, insufficient time to lose substantial altitude even with a relatively high descent rate.

The results seem to favor using a steep bank angle. But another factor must be considered—stall speed. Increased stall speeds result from progressively steepened bank angles. During a 30-degree banked turn, stall speed increases only fractionally, from 50 to 53 knots in a Cessna 172L, for instance. In a 75-degree banked turn, stall speed increases by a dramatic 97 percent (in all airplanes). It is obvious that steep bank angles must be avoided during any low-altitude maneuvering.

Another argument against the steep turn is the difficulty a pilot would encounter while attempting to arrest a high sink rate near the ground. With the aircraft already dangerously close to stall, added elevator pressure is required to overcome the airplane's substantial vertical momentum. This aggravates the problem by increasing the probability of a high-speed (accelerated) stall near the ground.

Test results and calculations indicate that the optimum bank angle is a compromise between the altitude-losing effects of the shallow bank and the rising stall speeds associated with steep bank angles. The optimum bank angle, therefore, is 45 degrees because this divides wing lift evenly between turning and supporting aircraft weight. It provides a moderate turn rate and altitude loss, combined with only a 19 percent increase in stall speed.

(Although it seems logical that the optimum glide speed should be used during the turnaround maneuver, research by David F. Rogers, a professor of aerospace engineering at the U.S. Naval Academy, indicates that the minimum altitude loss during the turn results from maintaining an airspeed only 5 percent above stall. (I winced, too.) Such an airspeed apparently results in the minimum altitude loss per degree of turn, reduces turn radius, and reduces lateral distance from the runway. After completing the turn, airspeed should be increased to the normal glide speed. Although this research appears to be accurate, I am reluctant to recommend the use of such a low airspeed to anyone not specifically trained in the maneuver. Otherwise, most pilots probably would be better off to simply maintain the normal glide speed throughout the maneuver.)

During this investigation, other turn methods were explored: half-spins, wingovers, and skidding turns. In most cases, these exotic maneuvers proved unacceptable and resulted in greater altitude losses than were experienced during coordinated turns. So to those who envision a wingover back to the runway following an engine failure, good luck. The maneuver itself might not cause an excessive altitude loss, but consider that a turnaround maneuver is not complete until a normal flare arrests the sink rate and places the aircraft in a normal landing attitude. Aerobatic maneuvering usually fails to allow for this final, vital necessity.

One important exception was noted when we flew a Cessna 150—the skidding turn. It is a technique recommended only for highly experienced pilots who are intimate with this popular aircraft.

Once the nose has been lowered following an engine failure and normal glide speed has been attained, place the Cessna 150 in a 30-degree banked turn. Slowly add bottom rudder. Simultaneously apply whatever amount of top (opposite) aileron is needed to maintain a constant 30-degree bank angle. Continue cross-controlling until full bottom rudder has been applied. The result is a skidding turn with a rapid turn rate and nominal sink rate. The aircraft is fully controllable and shows no tendency to stall or spin. The altitude loss after recovery and simulated landing flare is only 200 feet. No one should experiment with this maneuver unless accompanied by a flight instructor.

The applicability of this technique is peculiar to the Cessna 150. Similar techniques would not necessarily be satisfactory in other aircraft. We experimented with skidding turns in a Piper Super Cub and a Cherokee 140 and experienced altitude losses of 500 and 480 feet, respectively. In these aircraft, and probably in most others, the 45-degree banked turn is safer and more efficient.

It must be emphasized that no two aircraft types behave or perform similarly, even though they may have similar design features. The optimum turnaround technique for any specific aircraft type must be determined experimentally and be suitable for the experience level of the individual pilot.

Figure 80 shows the position of a Cessna 172L at the completion of three 180-degree gliding turns using bank angles of 30, 45, and 60 degrees, respectively. As bank angle steepens, lateral displacement from the extended runway centerline decreases. After completing a 45-degree banked, 180-degree turn, the aircraft is displaced 854 feet from the runway. Because of this lateral offset, it is obvious that a pilot with barely enough altitude to execute a 180-degree turn is still in jeopardy because additional altitude is needed to continue the turn beyond 180 degrees (as shown).

It was initially suspected that an extra 25 percent of altitude, beyond that lost during the turnaround itself, would be required to return to the airport. For example, we determined that a Cessna 172L loses 300 feet during a 45-degree banked turnaround. We believed that an extra 25 percent (75 feet) added to the 300-foot altitude loss during turnaround would be suffi-

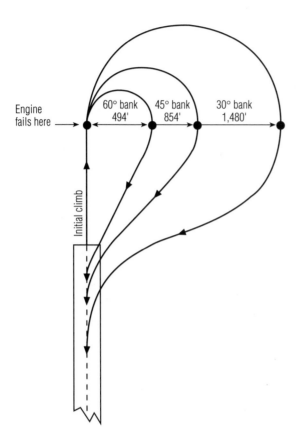

Figure 80. Effect of bank angle on turn radius during gliding turns

cient to jockey the aircraft into a position from which a safe landing could be made. But this was wrong. Further flight testing revealed that an extra 50 percent of altitude is needed. Instead of 300 feet, a Cessna 172L in a 45-degree bank needs at least 450 feet before a turnaround can be performed safely under ideal conditions.

Once a pilot determines how much altitude a particular type of aircraft loses during a 180-degree turn, he should increase this figure by at least 50 percent (and perhaps 100 percent!) to determine the minimum safe turnaround altitude. By adding this result to the airport elevation, a pilot at least has a target altitude that must be attained before a return to the runway is contemplated. If a Cessna 172 pilot were departing an airport at 1,900 feet MSL, for example, he would add a turnaround altitude of at least 450 feet to arrive at a target altitude of 2,350 feet MSL. Below this altitude, a turnaround would not be recommended. Above 2,350 feet, a turnaround probably would be safe.

A turnaround normally should not be made to a very short runway because the pilot is afforded so little margin for error. And since a turnaround usually results in a downwind landing, the problem of "deadsticking" into a short field is compounded. Furthermore, a pilot should not consider turning around unless he reaches the altitude required to execute a turnaround maneuver (excluding the 50-percent safety margin) at or prior to reaching the end of the runway.

When taking off into strong headwinds, a turnaround is risky because of the possibility of overshoot and the considerable runway length required to dissipate fast groundspeeds. Under these conditions, it is advisable able to lower the nose and accept the terrain ahead. If initial impact groundspeed is cut in half by a strong headwind, the destructive energy of the aircraft is reduced by 75 percent, increasing the probability of survival. Doubling touchdown groundspeed, however, quadruples destructive potential and proportionately increases the likelihood of injury.

If a turnaround results in excessive altitude on final approach, it can be dissipated conventionally by S-turning, flap deployment, slipping, or a combination of these. On the other hand, if a pilot winds up with a slight altitude deficiency and he is not sure whether the landing gear will clear the fence or destroy it, he might wait until the last possible second to extend flaps to the takeoff position. This last-ditch effort causes a slight ballooning in most aircraft and might be what's needed in a pinch. But since you don't get something for nothing, watch out for an increased sink rate after the fence has been left behind (hopefully intact).

Figure 81 shows why a turnaround should be made into a crosswind (if any). Turning into the wind decreases lateral displacement from the runway and allows the aircraft to be more easily aligned with the centerline after the 180-degree turn is completed. A downwind turn, however, allows the aircraft to drift farther from the runway, decreasing the likelihood of a safe return to the airport.

If the wind is blowing straight down the runway, then turn in whichever direction is most comfortable (left for most pilots). Consider, however, that as altitude is gained in the lower layers of the atmosphere, Mr. Coriolis makes the wind veer clockwise (in the Northern Hemisphere), suggesting that a right turn is more practical.

If a pilot departs from a parallel runway, he probably should turn toward the other parallel and land on it. He must not have a fixation about landing on the departure runway. When a pilot's one-and-only engine fails, no holds are barred. If a taxiway or another runway or a clear area between seems a better choice, then by all means, exercise your options. Put the airplane on any surface that appears survivable.

As the landing is begun, do not allow a prolonged flare to eat up valuable terrain. Put the airplane down—firmly if necessary—and stomp on the binders. If obstacles loom ahead, raise the flaps to kill lift, consider groundlooping, and if necessary, allow either or both wings (but not the nose) to strike an object, assisting in deceleration.

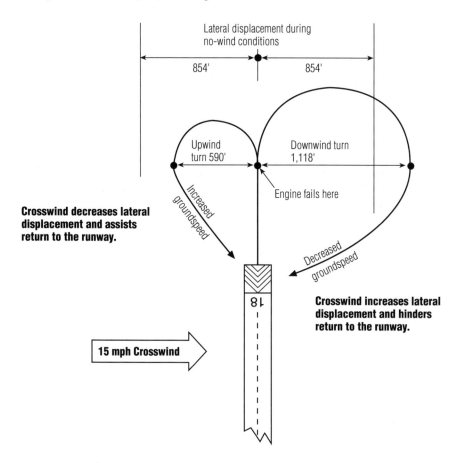

Figure 81. Effect of a 15-mph crosswind on lateral displacement when gliding in a 45°-banked turn at 80 mph.

Do anything to stop the aircraft while keeping the fuselage intact. Some experts even consider a gear-up landing when deadsticking into a very short field. That will slow down the airplane quite rapidly. The idea is to save lives. To hell with the airplane; it can be replaced.

Tradition claims that landing is more hazardous than takeoff. Landing, we have learned, usually requires more finesse and expertise and has been compared to threading a needle. A takeoff, on the other hand, frequently is compared in simplicity to withdrawing thread from a needle. But when it comes to relying on the structural integrity of aircraft and engine, the takeoff offers more risk. This is when the powerplant and its related systems are first put to the crucial test, and when we learn if everything is going to hold together. Maximum performance is required when engine stresses and strains are at a maximum. A pilot is not as concerned about powerplant reliability during an approach because he has been assured of its structural integrity while en route.

Once a pilot acknowledges the risk of an engine failure during takeoff and initial climb, the least he can do is prepare for the possibility. One ace up his sleeve is knowing the minimum safe turnaround altitude of his aircraft.

Having a target altitude provides a psychological advantage during a time when a pilot is burdened with an assortment of departure chores and is least prepared for an engine failure. With a target altitude in mind, he is not forced to make an immediate "turn/no turn" decision. That determination was made where it should have been made—on the ground. If he is below target altitude, the pilot knows—without guessing—the inadvisability of a turnaround. Above this altitude, he can turn with some assurance of safety and, as a result, perform more calmly and efficiently than were he to turn without knowing anything about the probability of his survival. An engine failure after takeoff is extremely frightening and can reduce mental sharpness to pudding with the snap of a connecting rod. Take it from someone who's been there—twice! Armed with a target altitude, a pilot is considerably ahead of the game.

When conditions suggest using the turnaround maneuver, a pilot can ill afford the luxury of guesswork. He must know that he can make it safely or not attempt the turn. Once committed to a course reversal, he must perform with cool, calculated precision, turning at the desired bank angle while maintaining closely the optimum glide speed. Large variations in pilot performance can drastically erode valuable altitude.

A pilot might be advised to keep his head in the cockpit and stay on instruments while establishing the gliding turn. This helps to ensure proper entry. Neck-craning to locate the runway doesn't do any good until some of the turn has been completed. He must firmly resist the temptation to steepen the bank and/or reduce airspeed. An excessively nose-high attitude does not avert ground contact. On the contrary, it may rush things a bit. (A 5-percent variation in glide speed does not cause any appreciable erosion of glide performance.)

When a pilot follows a calculated course of action, his mind is less encumbered with fear, offering him the opportunity to attempt a restart of the failed engine. Perhaps the problem can be eliminated by switching fuel tanks or adding carburetor heat. But to maneuver the aircraft and simultaneously analyze an engine failure requires a clear head. Preparation can help to make this possible.

As you read this, you no doubt will consider arguments against a turn after takeoff. Many of these are valid and have been reviewed, but what about the arguments favoring a return to the airport? There are many, including the most obvious temptation: the availability of a long, smooth landing surface. Also, a disabled aircraft can be handled better on an airport than off, and the airport may have firefighting equipment and an ambulance available. An off-airport crash can delay assistance, making a timely rescue difficult or even impossible.

Additionally, it is instinctive in man to want to return to the comfort and security from which he began. Babies want their mothers; pilots want airports. Surprise a pilot by retarding the throttle during a routine departure and the chances are excellent that he will instinctively initiate a turnaround without regard to altitude.

To emphasize the influence of this subconscious, instinctive desire to return, it is worthwhile to draw from the crash experience of the airlines. When an airliner makes a survivable crash landing at night, most of the passengers usually flock toward the single front door through which they entered originally. Never mind that a flight attendant urges them to leave through a closer, more suitable exit; they're not listening. Shocked passengers are often hellbent for leather to travel the entire length of the fuselage (even through an over-wing fuselage fire) to get to where it all began—the front door.

When a pilot is below the minimum safe turnaround altitude, he must fight this natural, often overwhelming instinct to return to the airport.

One procedure far superior to the turnaround maneuver is simply to avoid the engine failure in the first place. Since fuel starvation or exhaustion is more common than structural or mechanical failure, a pilot should modify his normal thorough preflight to include setting the fuel selector valve on the fullest tank prior to engine start. Once this is done, the valve should not be moved again until the aircraft is in cruise flight.

Many pilots reposition the selector valve during runup. Wrong! When a tank is selected so soon before takeoff, a pilot has no assurance the engine is operating on an unrestricted flow of fuel. There might only be sufficient fuel in the lines for the plane to become airborne before sudden silence stuns the pilot into quiet, unnerving reality.

By selecting the desired fuel tank before engine start, a pilot can test fuel-flow integrity before departure. Sufficient fuel is used during engine start, normal taxi, and runup to guarantee fuel from the tank is indeed flowing freely to the engine.

As the throttle is advanced during the initial takeoff roll, the pilot should consider the possibility of an aborted takeoff. After maximum power is stabilized, he should listen carefully for unusual roughness and judiciously scan engine gauges. Unfortunately, too few single-engine pilots are mentally prepared for an abort; they are "wired to go" and tend to either ignore or contend with abnormalities until it is too late to simply retard the throttle and brake to a safe stop.

One year I administered 24 biennial flight reviews. It became my practice to pop open the right-hand door at approximately 30 knots during the takeoff roll. Of the 24 pilots I checked, only five rejected the takeoff. The other 19 persisted with the takeoff even though more than 4,000 feet of usable runway remained ahead. This demonstrates that many pilots lack mental preparation during takeoff and fail to consider that an abort might be necessary. A problem on the ground is rarely serious, but when taken aloft, a pilot has the devil as copilot.

The initial climb should be made as steeply as is practical and safe. Relatively flat climbs reduce the likelihood of a return to the departure runway should an engine failure occur even when above the turnaround altitude.

Many pilots habitually retard the throttle almost immediately after liftoff. This should be avoided unless required by local noise-abatement procedures. If the engine is operating normally at maximum power, don't disturb a thing. Leave the engine alone and use it to achieve maximum climb performance. Do not reduce power until safely above the minimum turnaround altitude. Don't worry about damaging or overheating the engine. This procedure has no adverse effect on the modern engine.

Once airborne, get into the habit of looking for a place to land. It might be difficult to think about a forced landing during the early moments of flight, but this simple procedure can pay off handsomely. If a spot has been selected, the shock of an engine failure at low altitude is not quite so traumatic. Suitable landing sites are not always ahead or behind; they may be off to the side. The point is that the pilot should look for one while he has the opportunity to do so. It's like insurance; hopefully he'll never use lt.

No one can be so presumptuous as to tell a pilot exactly what to do when his engine fails after takeoff. It is for each pilot to decide what course of action is best for him. The foregoing provides some techniques and data resulting from a rather lengthy and exhaustive investigation of the available options. Hopefully this will be of use to those who acknowledge the risk we assume during every takeoff.

Fortunately, the modern engine can tolerate considerable abuse and mismanagement before failing its master. But—like cancer and heart disease—engine failures do occur. The thought of an engine failure after takeoff might be frightening; ignoring the possibility can be fatal.

Chapter 35 Engine Failure at Night or When IFR in a Single-Engine Airplane

Is there a prospect more chilling than an engine failure that occurs while flying at night or IFR (or both) in a single-engine airplane? A daytime failure is serious enough but generally is survivable. At night or when above a low ceiling, the same emergency can be catastrophic.

Pilots are trained to cope with engine difficulties during daylight VFR conditions. Who hasn't had an instructor pull the throttle to simulate engine failure? It catches us by surprise but is not alarming, because the engine really isn't dead. And isn't every multi-engine pilot trained to manage a twin on one engine?

These exercises are reminders that although the modern piston engine is superbly reliable, it can fail, and we need to be prepared for such a possibility. Paradoxically, however, we are taught nothing about handling a similar emergency at night or when IFR. The subject is virtually ignored.

The military, however, offers this advice to its single-engine pilots: "If the engine fails at night or when above a low ceiling, bail out."

One fatalistic instructor offers this suggestion about an off-airport, dead-stick landing at night: "When you get to within a few hundred feet of the ground, turn on the landing lights. If you don't like what you see, turn 'em off."

Fortunately, engine failures are remarkably rare, but they do occur, however infrequently. When taking off into an ebony sky or a low ceiling, the possibility must be considered.

A pilot who flies single engine at night or over an extensive area of low cloudiness does so because of his faith in the engine. Every hour, every day, and every year of uneventful flight reinforces this belief. Experience tends to isolate a pilot from the concept of engine failure.

But should such a failure occur while he is enshrouded in darkness or cloud, he might have difficulty overcoming the shock of such cruel reality. He has had little or no preparation for the cataclysmic, terrifying silence. Plane and pilot simply descend helplessly toward an uncertain fate.

This is not intended to frighten night pilots or those who fly extensive IFR in single-engine airplanes. Rather, the purpose is to focus attention on the reality that an engine can fail at any time, which dictates the need for preparation at all times.

Preparation begins with planning. Unless a pilot is willing to bet his life (and those of his passengers) that his engine will not fail, flights should be avoided over areas of very low ceiling and visibility. There should be enough maneuvering room beneath the clouds for a pilot to locate a landing site of his choice. Descending blindly and powerless into zero-zero conditions puts lives totally in the hands of fate.

This is because an emergency landing is generally survivable only when the pilot can control the aircraft and select the softest point of impact; crash landings in the blind usually are terminal.

If a flight over extensive fog cannot be avoided by selecting an alternate route, consideration might be given to postponement until conditions improve.

Remember that although enroute stations might be reporting a 1,000-foot overcast, for example, hilly or mountainous terrain between those stations might rise to above the base of the overcast or higher. Flying above a 1,000-foot ceiling might be safe when over the Great Plains, but not necessarily when over the Alleghenies or the Rockies. The character of enroute terrain should be considered.

Night flying also requires planning that enables a pilot—in case of engine failure—to see the projected landing area.

This, however, is not a universally held opinion. Many pilots—professionals included—prefer gliding into a "black hole" instead of landing in an illuminated area. Their theory is that a dark spot is probably undeveloped and, therefore, reasonably flat. Landing "in the lights," they claim, offers a greater risk because of automobiles, structures, and other man-made obstacles.

Others (myself included) disagree because of our reluctance to plunge blindly and unexpectedly into a boulder, ravine, or unlit structure. When he can "see" impending obstacles, a pilot is at least able to point the aircraft in the least damaging direction and direct the wings to absorb the initial shock in an attempt to preserve the fuselage and its fragile contents.

A multilane highway is a popular haven for powerless pilots. Admittedly, however, these lengthy "runways" were more suitable when the speed limit was higher. The best technique suggests landing into the wind (if possible) and with the traffic. Descend to a point between two cars and begin a speed reduction (flare) before settling between them. Hopefully, the driver of the car behind will see the aircraft and decelerate. As groundspeed decreases, the car in front should pull ahead of the airplane leaving sufficient room for a safe landing (power lines and bridges notwithstanding).

If highway traffic is heavy and slow, land elsewhere.

Another good alternative on a dark night is a body of water located by lights reflecting from its surface. Ditching near the edge of a body of inland water offers a high probability of survival, even to nonswimmers. The idea is to escape the crash; worry about subsequent problems later. (When ditching in a river, land with the current, not against it, unless strong winds dictate otherwise.)

If a landing must be executed on totally dark terrain, select a spot as near to civilization as possible. This increases the likelihood of early rescue and medical attention.

Soaring over a carpet of lights under a mantle of black sky can be intensely rewarding—an aesthetic, introspective experience. But night flying requires unique considerations. Paramount among these is route selection. To maximize safety, courses should be altered to follow major highways, fly over or near as many enroute airports as possible, and avoid extensive areas of totally dark terrain. This latter point is particularly important over mountainous terrain. An engine failure here could find a pilot gliding unwittingly toward the Grand Canyon or trying to bore a hole in Mt. Granite. A near-full moon is particularly helpful when flying single-engine aircraft at night.

Once under way—whether at night or when on instruments—a pilot must be acutely sensitive to the behavior of the powerplant and related systems. At the first indication that something might be amiss, proceed to the nearest airport. Minor discrepancies that might be acceptable on a daytime VFR flight can be totally intolerable at other times.

Fortunately, most power losses are only partial engine failures. With the exception of fuel exhaustion, it is unusual for an engine to quit without warning.

Should a partial loss occur, proceed to the nearest suitable landing area (which might or might not be an airport) and land as soon as possible.

The most horrendous situation is, of course, total power failure at night or when IFR. Your most immediate and pressing adversary is panic because of its detrimental effect on pilot performance. Contrary to initial reaction, you will not be helpless. There are many factors to consider and actions to take. These require as unencumbered a mind and body as is possible to organize. Difficult as it might be, calm down. Take a deep breath and get to work.

The first step is to determine if you have really had an engine failure. Sound silly? It's not. A massive power loss might feel like total failure, but the engine could be producing sufficient power with which to either maintain altitude or hobble toward a nearby airport in a gradual descent. Juggle the engine controls in an attempt to find a combination that maximizes available power.

If the engine has failed totally and attempts to restart it are fruitless, then you are faced with a full-scale emergency and have precious few moments to consider many variables.

The first step involves establishing the proper priority: aviate (fly and maintain control of the airplane!), navigate, and then communicate. The latter involves (1) turning on the emergency locator transmitter (don't wait for a crash to activate this electronic plea-for-help; the internal switch may fail to operate), (2) selecting the emergency transponder code (7700) post haste, and (3) attempting to establish voice communications with a radar facility that could vector you to a nearby airport.

Incredibly, an IFR pilot gliding through cloud can (either alone or with radar assistance) execute a dead-stick, IFR approach to a safe landing. Yes, it has been done.

I recall once surprising an advanced instrument student (who was wearing an IFR hood) with a retarded throttle. Because he had an abundance of altitude, he was able to orient himself, select the appropriate approach plate, and guide the aircraft to the threshold of a nearby airport. The trick, we concluded, was to remain substantially above the minimum crossing altitudes shown on the approach plate until reasonably close to the airport. Curiously, and using a technique described later, such a feat is easier when the engine is really dead and not just idling.

A dead-stick, IFR approach may not be successful, but there's not much to lose by trying. When engulfed in cloud, where else is there to go?

A major consideration (at night or in the clouds) is the vacuum instruments (the gyroscopic attitude and direction indicators). Without engine power, the vacuum (or pressure) pump might produce less than the minimum airflow required for proper gyro operation. As an unpowered descent continues, be on guard for erroneous attitude information (or tumbled gyros!) by cross-checking the electric turn coordinator or indicator. Rapid and large attitude changes should be minimized. Maneuvering adds precessional forces to gyroscopic instruments that makes them even more unreliable when the vacuum pump has marginal output.

Gyro failure is a serious problem not only when IFR, but also perhaps when VFR at night. Although the horizon might be visible at altitude, it could disappear from view during descent because of terrain irregularities.

The electrical system also warrants attention. When the engine fails, rpm decreases to less than that required for generator operation. Windmilling rpm, however, usually allows an alternator to carry the load. Therefore, if the aircraft is equipped with a generator and not an alternator, only battery power will be available.

Batteries, however, are severely weakened when coldsoaked at high altitude or when exposed to winter temperatures. Consider that at 32 degrees F, a fully charged, lead-sulphuric acid battery loses 35 percent of its stored energy; at 0 degrees F, 60 percent of its electrical potential is lost. And this assumes a healthy battery. If the battery is cold-soaked and weak to begin with, electrical power could be in short supply.

To prevent total electrical loss during an engine-out descent, it is important to reduce electrical load as much as possible. Turn off everything that isn't essential. When transmissions are made, keep them brief and to the point. Avoid using landing lights until close enough to the ground for them to be useful.

If your aircraft utilizes an engine-driven hydraulic pump to extend the landing gear and flaps, consider that when the propeller is windmilling, there might not be sufficient hydraulic pressure available to extend the landing gear prior to landing. Save enough time for a manual extension.

Pilots have been trained since Year One to glide at the best angle-of-glide speed. This is fine if trying to reach some distant point. But if there are no airports within gliding range or if a pilot cannot find a landing site (because he is still in cloud), then he has an alternative.

By reducing airspeed to about stall speed plus 10 or 15 knots, sink rate decreases dramatically. This slower airspeed is familiar to all glider pilots as the "minimum-sink speed." True, the airplane does not glide as far (horizontally), but this speed does substantially postpone ground contact. This allows more time to communicate, more time to calm down, and more time to select a landing site.

If the terrain is so dark or the clouds so low that a pilot must land "in the blind," such reduced speed and sink rate also reduce impact forces (vertical and longitudinal Gs) and increase survival probability.

When and if the pilot finally sees a place to land, airspeed should be adjusted to a normal approach speed (when no lower than 1,000 feet AGL) to increase aircraft maneuverability.

If structural icing is expected or encountered during descent, sink rate should be increased until below the icing level to minimize exposure to this added risk.

A powerless pilot has yet another life-saving technique available. If there is absolutely no hope of rekindling the engine and if the aircraft is at a relatively high altitude, shut off the mags, adjust the mixture to idle cutoff, and reduce airspeed until the propeller slows to a halt. (This occurs near the stalling speed in most lightplanes.)

Stopping the prop is almost as effective on a single as feathering a propeller on a twin; total airframe drag is reduced substantially.
If it is desirable to reach a distant airport, stopping the prop could make the difference, because this typically increases glide range by a whopping 20 percent (in most cases).

Or, if you are descending at the minimum-sink speed, such drag reduction decreases sink rate substantially. When I flew a Cessna 185 with a stilled prop, the aircraft floated earthward (and very quietly) at a modest 300 fpm. The sink rate in that airplane—which had a cargo pod—during a normal glide with the propeller windmilling was 900 fpm.

Short of stopping the prop, glide performance in some aircraft can be increased slightly by positioning the propeller in maximum pitch (low rpm).

One subject of controversy is the position of retractable landing gear during an off-airport, emergency landing. Unless specific conditions warrant otherwise, touch down on land with gear extended. This allows the gear legs to absorb some of the initial shock. A water landing should be made with wheels up.

Flap position also is a controversial subject. Generally, and shortly before touchdown, they should be extended. Remember, flaps hinder glide performance but reduce touchdown speed.

To minimize fire potential, fuel pumps, selector valves, and the master switch (if practical) should be turned off prior to touchdown.

It is interesting that some countries prohibit night and/or IFR flight in single-engine airplanes. Fortunately, the FAA imposes no such ban on U.S. pilots because night and IFR flying is a safe, rational activity—but only when tempered by conservative planning.

There can be risks, however. It is for each pilot to weigh the purpose of a specific flight against those risks to determine if and when the end justifies the means.

Chapter 36 **Precautionary Landings**

Every pilot has an ace up his sleeve—the precautionary landing. Simply stated, this is a premeditated landing, on or off an airport, when continued flight is possible but inadvisable.

Consider, for example, the low-flying VFR pilot who becomes engulfed in deteriorating weather while relatively far from an airport. He has a choice: continue into potentially worsening conditions (ahead or behind), or make an off-airport landing.

The second choice often is the safest. Yet the records show that a noninstrument-rated pilot caught in such a situation rarely exercises this option. Instead, he plunges onward, passing up one farmer's field after another until visual contact with the ground may be irretrievably lost. Eventually, he may collide with an immovable obstacle or lose control of the aircraft.

The National Transportation Safety Board, which has the task of investigating and tabulating general aviation's fatalities, states: "Any pilot who becomes trapped in weather and does not give serious thought to the feasibility of a precautionary landing (on or off an airport), frequently accepts the most dangerous alternative—continued flight."

Consider also the pilot running low on fuel. He thinks he has enough remaining to reach the nearest airport, but he isn't absolutely certain. Yet he often is willing to bet his life (and those of his passengers) on the unknown quantity of avgas sloshing in the tanks. This individual also has a choice: make a premeditated, off-airport landing with power or continue until a forced landing without power eliminates the option.

Such a pilot is a natural candidate for exercising discretion by opting for a precautionary landing. But will he? The statistics say no and indicate that a pilot is much more likely to risk fuel exhaustion than to make an off-airport landing while the engine is still developing power.

The records also show many pilots go so far as to overfly enroute airports until the last drop of fuel is consumed, an often fatal syndrome known as "destinationitis." (One reason why airline pilots so rarely run out of fuel is that they have no personal involvement with the destination and are not compulsively motivated to continue when common sense dictates otherwise.)

All of this leads to a logical question. "Why do so few pilots take advantage of the precautionary landing?" Countless lives could be saved by the timely employment of such a technique.

Part of the answer is that a precautionary landing is not a technique at all. Rather, it is a state of mind. It is the willingness to consider and possibly accept an interrupted flight plan and the damage that could result from landing on unimproved surfaces. But the rational mind must be prepared to at least weigh this alternative against the potentially lethal consequences of flying into increasingly adverse conditions.

Off-airport, precautionary landings are rare because pilots are not mentally prepared to consider this alternative; the subject seldom is discussed seriously. Pilots do learn about forced landing procedures during their presolo instruction, but not about precautionary, off-airport landings with power. We are programmed to consider landing only at airports...unless the engine fails. It's one extreme or the other.

Many situations that might justify an intentional, off-airport landing often develop into the drama of a forced landing under more difficult circumstances simply because pilots are reluctant to correctly evaluate their difficulties. Some are afflicted with either the "I-can-make-it" or the "it-won't-happen-to-me" syndrome, which is known also as the inability to face reality.

There is no doubt about how extremely difficult it is to land in a pea patch while the engine is still running. But there are occasions when the hazards of continued flight are less desirable. This is when a heads-up pilot will weigh the variables and arrive at the safest conclusion before the passage of time, distance, and fuel eclipse the option. In short, he must be the captain of his fate, not the victim.

The primary objective of this discussion is not to recommend a precautionary landing under any specific set of circumstances. Rather, it is an attempt only to bring attention to a lifesaving procedure that is not implemented as often as it should be. Being aware of the alternative at least helps to simplify the decision, should it become necessary.

An objective discussion of this nature requires playing the devil's advocate. In other words, a precautionary landing might not be the best alternative. Perhaps there is enough fuel on board to hobble to the nearest airport. Perhaps the VFR pilot flying into worsening weather will find improving conditions on the other side of the pass. Perhaps continued flight would be the safest course of action.

Another reason not to land on the nearest highway is that we know from experience that a pilot usually is able to extricate himself from most difficulties. If every pilot who ever became nervous were to make a precautionary landing, there might be more planes than cars on some highways.

Also, a precautionary landing is not without hazard. Aircraft damage is not unlikely, and injury to those on board is certainly possible. A pilot who intentionally lands in a wheat field, totals the aircraft, and later finds that he did have enough fuel remaining to reach an airport, is going to be hard pressed for an explanation. But the action probably increased the probability of survival, and that's what the precautionary landing is all about. On the other hand, there might not have been sufficient fuel.

There are times, however, when a pilot should be willing to accept aircraft damage. It is far better to sacrifice the machine if this helps to protect the safety of those inside.

Some pilots feel that scratching or bending an airplane speaks poorly of his piloting skills. But if life is preserved in the process, the converse might be true.

So when is a precautionary landing advisable? Unfortunately, there is no cut-and-dried answer. It boils down to weighing the variables and exercising judgment. If a pilot begins to fear the outcome of continued flight because the risks are expected to increase beyond acceptability, he should consider a precautionary landing before it is too late.

Adverse weather and inadequate fuel reserves are not the only reasons that might warrant a precautionary landing. Other possibilities include:

- A visible oil leak of some magnitude.
- An indication of low oil pressure, excessive and uncorrectable cylinder-head or oil temperatures, or low fuel pressure. (An alarming indication by a single instrument usually is insufficient cause for emergency action unless an additional sign of abnormality confirms that something is amiss; the problem could be a faulty gauge.)
- Partial power loss.
- Any worsening engine difficulty (in single-engine airplanes).
- Serious airframe or powerplant vibrations.
- In-flight structural damage (bird strike, broken or cracked windshield, hail damage, strut failure, and so on).
- Impending nightfall when the pilot is untrained and the aircraft is inadequately equipped.
- Being hopelessly lost when help is unavailable and fuel reserves are low.
- A partially incapacitated pilot, especially when the condition is worsening.
- Any other situation likely to become more hazardous with continued flight.

Is it legal to make an off-airport, precautionary landing? Considering only the Federal Aviation Regulations (and not state, county, and municipal laws), no regulation prohibits landing on other than an airport. Additionally, a pilot-in-command has the emergency authority (and perhaps the obligation) to do whatever appears to be in the best interest of safety.

If a pilot opts to execute an off-airport, precautionary landing instead of risking an eventual forced landing (or worse), he shifts the odds of survival strongly in his favor. With the engine still running (or the visibility still reasonable), the pilot has time to gather his wits and select a suitable landing site—something that might not be possible later. He has time to drag the proposed landing area and reject it, should it appear undesirable. With power, he can land more slowly and with the precision needed to avoid the likelihood of an under- or overshoot. With power, he can always reject the landing and try again.

But once the fuel is exhausted or the ground becomes obscured, these advantages also disappear.

Although a planned, precautionary landing is almost always survivable, the same cannot be said about forced landings or untimely descents caused by other emergencies.

If a decision is made to land at other than an airport, a pilot should make the necessary preparations while time is still available.

The first step might be to attempt notifying someone of his intentions. This radio call should include aircraft identification and type, precise location of the landing site (if possible), and the number of souls on board. If communications cannot be established with someone on the ground, attempt to contact a nearby aircraft by making a call in the blind on a frequency you would expect to be monitored in that area.

Also, turn on the ELT while airborne (if possible), and set the transponder (if available) to the emergency code of 7700.

Next, prepare both aircraft and passengers. Securing the cockpit is the easy part: turn off unnecessary systems, reduce the electrical load as much as practicable, stow loose objects, and make sure a flashlight is kept handy (at night).

Calming the passengers and gaining their confidence might not be so easy. If time allows, explain the situation in unruffled tones. Don't give them cause for unnecessary alarm. If possible, keep them preoccupied during the descent with such perfunctory chores as calling off altitudes every 500 feet or watching for traffic (even though the nearest aircraft may be 100 miles away).

Passengers also should be told how to protect their faces with pillows (or coats, blankets, and the like) during the touchdown and landing roll. Also review with them the operation of normal and emergency exits, if any.

If aircraft damage is considered possible, entertain the notion of opening a door or two prior to landing, but only if such action is known not to have an adverse, aerodynamic effect on tail surfaces. Otherwise, a twisted fuselage might make it impossible to open the door(s) on the ground. This is a particularly important consideration if the landing is to be made in water. A jammed door can prevent evacuation during the short time it takes to drown. Conversely, an open door reduces aircraft buoyancy.

Also consider having passengers remove dentures and eyeglasses.

However, if the landing is to be made on a paved, straight, miles-long highway cleared of traffic, much of this is unnecessary.

Ideally, the landing should be made on a level, smooth surface and into the wind. But try to select a site from which a subsequent takeoff can be made safely (with permission from the local constable, of course). Consider also that landing uphill considerably reduces landing roll distance, a rather convenient arrangement, especially if conditions later allow a downhill departure.

Unfortunately, there is not usually a wind sock available to determine wind direction, so use some savvy and look for telltale signs such as drifting smoke and dirt, or trees leaning with the wind. Or, look for a herd of cattle. These bovine beasts usually stand with their backsides into the breeze (or so I've been told). This presumably is an instinctive habit that allows them to see enemies approaching from ahead and smell those who approach from behind.

Once the landing site has been chosen and time permits, drag the field at least once to confirm that you've chosen wisely. Fly parallel to the "runway" at approach speed with the flaps partially extended. This allows for a relatively nose-low attitude and provides better visibility to search for potholes, ditches, wires, and other hazards that might not have been visible from a higher altitude.

When on a heading parallel to the direction of intended landing, set the heading indicator to 360 degrees. This is especially important if the approach is to be made during curtailed visibility, because it helps to standardize the "traffic" pattern and find the "runway" should the pilot become temporarily disoriented.

A book could be written to describe the techniques recommended to land on various types of terrain. Consequently, space permits only a few generalizations to be included here.

- When landing on a broad field of snow or in water, depth perception can be poor. Use a power-on descent to the point of touchdown.
- When ditching in a river, land downstream unless strong winds dictate otherwise. This reduces the relative touchdown speed between aircraft and water, thereby reducing damage potential.
- When landing on highways or roads, land with the traffic and be on the alert for wires and other man-made obstacles.
- If a tree landing must be made, attempt to allow both wings and the fuselage to contact the tree crowns simultaneously (and pray that the trees are not tall and widely spaced).
- In mountainous terrain (good luck), try to select an uphill slope. Avoid a situation where an excessively long landing roll would bring the aircraft to either a sharp dropoff or an area of severe lateral twist that might force the aircraft to perform a wingover into a canyon. When about to land on a steep upslope, maintain enough airspeed to convert the descent profile angle into a steep climb angle that closely matches that of the upslope gradient.
- In most cases, damage and injury are minimized by touching down as slowly and with as reduced a sink rate as is possible and practical.

Most of the time, however, pilots are not confronted with these extremes. Usually, it is a simple matter of finding a long field and landing parallel to the furrows. Or it might be as mundane as squatting on a dirt road in the desert.

But if the aircraft is damaged during the landing, be sure the fuel selector valve, master switch, and magnetos are turned off. (It is recommended that these items not be turned off prior to touchdown because this would eliminate the option of executing a last-minute go-around.) Then, with premeditated calm, evacuate the machine and lead the passengers safely away. Do not return until the probability of fire or an explosion is nil.

In the final analysis, there can be no precise determination as to the causes and circumstances that dictate executing a precautionary landing. In each case, a pilot must evaluate all factors on a balancing scale. If one side tips in favor of a precautionary landing, then, objectively and philosophically, he should exercise the option to land as soon as possible, airport or no.

Section 7

Multi-Engine Flying

The advantages of a multi-engine airplane are redundant systems, additional performance, and the ability to continue flight following the failure of one engine. The margin of safety that these provide, however, demand that the pilot be proficient and knowledgeable beyond that required to obtain a multi-engine rating. These three chapters provide some of that additional insight.

Chapter 37 **Engine-Out Approaches**

Ask the average pilot to describe the most hazardous aspect of multi-engine flying and he most likely will answer, "Engine failure after takeoff." Although this emergency receives the greatest attention and probably is the most difficult to manage, landing accidents following an engine failure at altitude are the most prevalent kind of accident, according to a study published by the National Transportation Safety Board.

NTSB studied light twin-engine accidents involving engine failure that occurred during a recent five-year period. During that time, 87 accidents (of which 23 were fatal) occurred during takeoff and initial climb as a result of engine failure; but during that same period, 442 accidents (of which 70 were fatal) occurred when a pilot attempted to land an aircraft with an inoperative or malfunctioning engine. In other words, more than five times as many accidents and more than three times as many fatalities occurred when pilots attempted to land with a failed engine than when departing with one.

This is not as paradoxical as it might seem. After all, a pilot is exposed to the possibility of an engine failure during takeoff and initial climb for only a minute or two during each flight. According to NTSB, most engine failures occur during the enroute phase of flight. What is not readily understood, however, is why 78 percent of the resultant accidents occur during the subsequent landings and why 57 percent of these are fatal.

This is particularly puzzling, because a single-engine approach and landing in a twin generally is not regarded as a difficult maneuver. Perhaps part of the problem is that, during training, the maneuver is made to appear easy and not much different from a normal approach with both engines running. The student executes a few approaches and quickly develops the skill and confidence needed to satisfy a flight-test examiner. But here is the rub: this engine-out approach is almost always conducted with the "dead" engine developing zero thrust and rarely at night or during IFR conditions. The pilot may not have an opportunity to learn that an actual approach and landing with a propeller feathered can be much more difficult than one performed in a training environment. After all, if anything goes wrong when an instructor is aboard, the problem is resolved by firewalling both throttles and leaving the problem behind. This option obviously is not available when one engine has genuinely failed.

The minimum experience required during multi-engine training can breed a complacent attitude toward engine-out approaches. Consequently, multi-engine pilots are not sufficiently aware of the need to either maintain or develop additional proficiency in single-engine approaches. They also seem to be reluctant to practice engine-out emergencies whether they own their own aircraft, rent, or practice in simulators. I interviewed 23 noncommercial multi-engine pilots and was shocked to learn that only four had practiced the maneuver since obtaining their multi-engine ratings; only seven had had any recurrent training in multi-engine airplanes during the previous two years.

Pilots who own their twins are particularly reluctant to practice engine-out emergencies because of the damaging effect that rapid power changes (shock cooling) have on engine life. But renter pilots are not as concerned about engine life as they are about the cost of renting a light twin for training purposes. In other words, the cost of multi-engine proficiency seems to take precedence over safety.

NTSB also recognizes that pilots allow their multi-engine skills to erode. "Accidents following engine failure in light twins generally involve a lack of proficiency in responding to these emergencies. These accidents often involve some degree of panic, probably related to inadequate immediate recall of the exact emergency procedures or lack of confidence in one's ability to execute the emergency procedures. These symptoms are indicative of insufficient recurrent training in engine-failure emergencies."

Since the FAA does not require certificated multi-engine pilots to maintain engine-out skills, NTSB has suggested that the FAA revise its regulations so as not to allow anyone to act as pilot-in-command of a multi-engine airplane unless he has successfully completed a flight review in such an aircraft within the previous 24 months. (From discussing this with a number of instructors, we have concluded that most general aviation pilots with multi-engine ratings take their biennial flight reviews in single-engine airplanes because it is simpler and less expensive.)

Since the engine-failure-after-takeoff emergency is given the greatest attention and since the enroute engine failure often is regarded complacently (even though it ultimately claims more lives), perhaps the latter needs to be placed in proper perspective. Even when it occurs at altitude, an engine failure is a genuine emergency that can demand all of the knowledge and skill a pilot can muster.

Another negative effect of multi-engine training is that pilots are conditioned to shut down and secure an engine as soon as the failure occurs. This is because so much emphasis is placed on an engine failure occurring shortly after liftoff, an emergency that often does dictate feathering a propeller as soon as possible. Otherwise, a light twin might be incapable of climbing or even maintaining altitude.

When an engine fails or malfunctions in cruise flight, however, the pilot need not be in such a hurry. He has considerably more time to analyze the difficulty and possibly restore power by turning on a fuel pump, switching fuel tanks, or adjusting the fuel-air mixture. Even if these or other corrections have no effect, a pilot might determine that the malfunction (such as a partial fuel-flow restriction) still enables the engine to develop more than zero thrust, the power required to simulate a feathered propeller. At such a time, the engine should be allowed to operate and be used to advantage during the subsequent approach, as long as other conditions (such as severe vibration, engine fire, loss of oil pressure) do not dictate otherwise.

Pilots operating turbocharged engines at high altitude must be particularly cautious about shutting down an engine that only appears to have failed. At 25,000 feet, for example, a turbocharger failure could be interpreted as an engine failure because the manifold pressure would be so low (less than 12 inches). Rather than hurriedly securing the engine, first consider descending to determine if manifold pressure increases in the manner of a normally aspirated engine. This may confirm that the turbocharger— not the engine has failed and that considerable power will become available at lower altitudes.

Many instructors teach that a pilot should not be in a rush to extract additional power from the operative side following an enroute engine failure. This is because airspeed is well above minimum-controllable airspeed (V_{MC}), and the aircraft probably can maintain altitude easily on one engine. Other instructors—including myself—recommend adding power anyway, even if it is not apparently or immediately needed. This reduces the likelihood of a potentially hazardous loss of airspeed while the pilot is preoccupied with attempting to resolve the problem. After all, if this additional power later proves to be unnecessary, the throttle can be retarded. Recovery from inadvertent loss of control is not accomplished as easily. (NTSB has recorded numerous fatalities caused by engine-out spins entered at cruise altitudes.)

Under no circumstances should speed be allowed to erode below V_{YSE} (best single-engine rate-of-climb speed), because if altitude cannot be maintained at this airspeed, then it cannot be maintained at any airspeed. (If descent cannot be prevented using V_{YSE}, then maintain this airspeed to minimize the sink rate.)

Once the aircraft is under control, a pilot should consider heading for the nearest suitable airport. Numerous accidents result from pilots being too anxious to land and selecting nearby airports that are unsuitable for a variety of reasons.

For example, short runways should be avoided because these do not allow sufficient safety margins. Not only does a twin with a feathered prop require a longer-than-normal landing distance, a pilot discovering at low altitude that he is about to overshoot or undershoot the runway might not be able to execute a single-engine go-around because of performance limitations.

For similar reasons, an actual IFR approach should be avoided if a VFR alternative is reasonably close, especially if the weather is near minimums or the approach requires either circling or leveling off at intermediate descent altitudes. If the engine failure occurs at night, it is best to select an airport where either an electronic glideslope or visual-approach-slope indicator (VASI) is available for assistance. An engine-out approach at night to a runway without such an aid—even in clear weather—can be more difficult than is generally appreciated.

Everything else being equal, select an airport with at least two runways. (Single-runway airports are more susceptible to closure, because of a disabled aircraft on the runway, for example.) Also, if the aircraft is particularly heavy, consider circling the airport at altitude to burn off excessive fuel and improve performance prior to beginning an approach.

In other words, don't be impatient. A pilot should take ample time, if available, to plan an appropriate course of action and stack the odds as much in his favor as possible. He also should remember that he has the option to declare an emergency so that maximum assistance and priority handling can be obtained from air traffic controllers. This also makes it easier for the FAA to understand and empathize with any regulatory deviations that might become necessary.

A well-managed approach is the key to a successful landing. The approach must be well planned and professionally executed; otherwise, the outcome might be speculative. The approach should be made to the longest, cleanest runway available. If practical, plan on a long final approach (at least 3 miles, but preferably 4 or 5) to take advantage of available descent guidance. All maneuvering prior to the final descent should be executed in a minimum-drag configuration (gear and flaps up). If possible, maintain an airspeed at least 10 to 20 knots above V_{YSE}.

One school of thought is that the descent angle should be steeper than usual to minimize the possibility of an undershoot. Although this conservatism seems logical, it has significant disadvantages. First, the temptation to come in high and fast often leads to an overshoot and an attempted go-around on one engine, an extremely hazardous (and sometimes impossible) maneuver in many light twins when attempted below 500 feet. Secondly, a pilot executing a steep descent loses some of his normal perspective; he cannot as readily detect and correct glideslope excursions as they occur.

Pilots tempted to make high, hot approaches also should consider that every 1 percent increase in airspeed and every additional 10 feet above the runway threshold increases landing distance by approximately 2 percent and 5 percent, respectively. And since an airplane with a feathered propeller decelerates more slowly and floats longer (because of reduced propeller drag), a high, fast approach can demand much more runway length than may be available.

Consequently, it is usually wiser to fly a normal descent so that the aircraft can be brought to a halt within the confines of the runway. After all, if an airplane can maintain altitude while approaching the final approach course, it certainly has the capability of being flown down a standard, 3-degree slot.

Upon intercepting the glideslope (electronic or visual), begin a normal descent and reduce airspeed to V_{YSE}, because this requires minimum power and leaves available a maximum of reserve power with which to correct glideslope excursions.

Fortunately, a pilot need not be concerned with V_{MC}, because when one propeller is feathered, V_{MC} usually is well below stall speed. By maintaining V_{YSE}, airspeed is well above the bottom of the green airspeed arc (V_{S1}) and precludes the possibility of either stalling or losing directional control (unless steep bank angles are used).

While descending on a 3-degree glideslope at V_{YSE}, most twins usually require relatively little power from the operative engine. If this is the case, extend flaps to the maximum-lift position, most often about one-fourth to one-third of maximum deflection; this should result in the need for only slightly more power.

Consider extending the landing gear at about 1,000 feet AGL, and only if the approach is proceeding normally. Do not drop the gear, however, when below the glideslope because the additional drag makes it all the more difficult to re-establish a normal slot.

Some might criticize extending the gear so early in the approach, claiming that the added drag necessitates additional power. This makes it more difficult to maintain directional control and to prevent slipping beneath the glideslope. The other side of this controversial coin is that a pilot needs to be aware of a potential landing-gear malfunction while high enough to execute a safe missed approach and then extend the gear by emergency methods.

If the drag from the landing gear is such that a safe approach cannot be continued, then by all means, retract the gear and continue inbound until extension becomes absolutely necessary. In extreme cases of limited aircraft performance, it might be preferable to intentionally land gear-up on the runway than to either undershoot the airport or risk a low-altitude, single-engine go-around. (During a recent five-year period, 78 pilots became so preoccupied during engine-out approaches that they *inadvertently* landed gear up).

Perhaps the gravest error that can be committed during an approach is to allow airspeed to erode much below V_{YSE}. If this airspeed cannot get an airplane to the airport (with maximum power from the operative engine), then no other speed will either. An attempt to stretch range by decelerating below V_{YSE} not only defeats the purpose, but might allow the aircraft to approach the single-engine stall speed.

Equally serious is not recognizing soon enough that an approach is not proceeding well and that it should be abandoned while still at a sufficiently safe altitude. Trying to go around from too low an altitude—and that depends on the aircraft, its gross weight, and density altitude—is so hazardous that the FAA no longer requires multi-engine applicants to demonstrate the maneuver. Consequently, most light-twin pilots have little or no proficiency in performing single-engine go-arounds. During an FAA seminar required of designated examiners, it was agreed that a go-around should be initiated only when above 500 feet AGL. Below this altitude, the average pilot probably would be better off undershooting the runway and landing short while under control. This option might be difficult to accept, but it is preferable to the risk of losing control and spinning the aircraft during an attempted go-around.

A single-engine go-around requires maximum-available power from the operative engine, and the pilot must have the will to sacrifice altitude while maintaining V_{YSE} and cleaning up the airplane. When the descent finally is arrested, the subsequent climb rate and angle is likely to be anemic. To appreciate the difficulty of this maneuver, pilots are encouraged to practice it periodically at altitude under the tutelage of a competent instructor.

Once the option to go around is no longer available, complete the before-landing checklist. But avoid extending the flaps fully until there is absolutely no doubt that the airplane will land on the runway. After all, the last two-thirds of flap extension adds considerable drag and very little additional stall protection. Full flaps should be used only to assist in decelerating and reducing landing distance.

As the runway threshold passes beneath the aircraft and power is reduced, be alert for a yawing moment toward the operative engine caused by the windmilling drag of its propeller. Also be aware that the feathered propeller on the other side reduces total aircraft drag and causes the airplane to float more than it normally would. So if runway length is critical, sacrifice finesse and get the aircraft on the ground as soon as possible. If it appears that the airplane cannot be stopped before reaching the end of the runway, consider a ground loop, consider colliding with a fence or ditch at 20 or 30 knots, consider praying, but do not consider applying power and pulling the aircraft off the ground. You'll never make it.

Pilots who periodically and diligently rehearse engine-out procedures usually are well equipped to manage an actual engine failure. Those who are complacent and ignore the need for recurrent training are unprepared. For someone in this latter and unfortunately large group, the operative engine does little more than take him to the scene of the accident. Consequently, it comes as no surprise that the fatality rate following an engine failure in light twins continues to be more than four times as great as it is following an engine failure in single-engine airplanes.

Chapter 38 **Engine-Out Driftdown**

Many light twins (especially those without turbocharging) have poor single-engine performance. Consider, for instance, that the engine-out service ceiling of a Beech B55 Baron is only 6,400 feet while the Piper Seminole is limited to a relatively meager 4,100 feet MSL.

One conclusion drawn from these specifications is that an engine failure while cruising over mountainous terrain converts a perky twin into little more than a powered glider that is compelled to descend toward the high-rise granite. Such a situation, however, is not that dire. By allowing a twin to drift down gradually, a pilot is afforded considerably more time and distance than he might imagine. In all but extreme cases, such a crippled twin can hobble to an airport and perform a safe landing even when that airport is above the aircraft's single-engine ceiling.

To begin with, the failure of an engine does not necessitate descending to the single-engine service ceiling. At this altitude, after all, the aircraft is capable of climbing 50 fpm. The aircraft eventually will descend, however, to its single-engine absolute ceiling, which is above the service ceiling. For example, an engine-out Beech Duchess has a service ceiling of only 6,170 feet, but an absolute ceiling of 8,000 feet.

Secondly, these altitude limits apply only when the aircraft is at maximum-allowable gross weight, an improbable condition considering fuel burnoff during climb and cruise. An aircraft weighing less enjoys dramatically higher service and absolute ceilings.

Consider, for example, a heavily loaded Beech Duchess cruising at 16,000 feet over the 14,000-foot peaks of Colorado. The aircraft will not "fall out of the sky" following an engine failure. At 16,000 feet, the Duchess can be held to a sink rate as low as 228 fpm. When the aircraft reaches 14,000 feet, sink rate is only 180 fpm. This provides lots of time to head for lower terrain.

At 10,000 feet, the rate of descent is a mere 60 fpm because of increased power available from the operative engine. Considerably more than an hour after engine failure, the aircraft finally settles at and maintains its absolute ceiling of 8,000 feet. Surely, however, the Duchess will have burned off considerable fuel and weigh much less than its maximum-allowable weight, giving it an absolute ceiling of 9,000 feet or higher.

According to manufacturer's data, the Duchess has a still-air range of 50 nautical miles while drifting down from 14,600 to 10,200 feet on one engine. From 14,000 to 9,000 feet, engine-out range during driftdown is 80 nautical miles even though the aircraft is well above its published single-engine service ceiling.

Although published single-engine service ceilings do reflect practical climb limits, they obviously are well below the altitudes to which "single-engine" twins can descend and maintain. In this respect, airframe manufacturers are conservative. Often, a twin powered by only one engine can maintain an altitude twice as high as its engine-out service ceiling.

During my research of this subject, I opted to investigate the driftdown characteristics of the Piper Seminole because of this aircraft's minimal single-engine altitude capability. The results of this flight test are reflected in Figure 82.

While the plane was cruising at 14,000 feet, the left engine was throttled and feathered. Rudder trim was applied, and the aircraft stabilized in a descent. The first 1,000 feet of altitude loss took 3 minutes and 36 seconds, an average sink rate of 254 fpm. Almost 6 minutes elapsed while drifting down from 13,000 to 12,000 feet, an average sink rate of only 168 fpm—not bad for an aircraft that was only 260 pounds under gross at the time of "engine failure."

Altitude Loss	Elapsed Time per 1,000 ft.	Cumulative Time	Average Sink Rate	Driftdown Range per 1,000-ft. Loss	Cumulative Distance	Descent Gradient	Equivalent "Glide Ratio"	True Airspeed
14,000 to 13,000	3:56	3:56	-254 fpm	7.2 nm	7.2 nm	1.3°	44:1	110 kt
13,000 to 12,000	5:58	9:54	-168 fpm	10.7 nm	17.9 nm	0.9°	65:1	108 kt
12,000 to 11,000	6:34	16:28	-152 fpm	11.7 nm	29.6 nm	0.8°	71:1	107 kt
11,000 to 10,000	8:32	25:00	-117 fpm	14.9 nm	44.5 nm	0.6°	91:1	105 kt
10,000 to 9,000	12:19	37:19	-81 fpm	21.1 nm	65.6 nm	0.4°	128:1	103 kt
9,000 to 8,000	22:46	60:05	-44 fpm	38.5 nm	104.1 nm	0.2°	234:1	102 kt

Figure 82. Driftdown characteristics of a Piper Seminole

It took fully an hour to drift down to 8,000 feet, where the sink rate was only 44 fpm. Extrapolation shows that the Seminole eventually would have leveled at 7,600 feet, almost twice as high as the published single-engine service ceiling of 4,100 feet.

It also is interesting to note that the still-air range during this descent was 104 nautical miles; average sink rate during the 5,000-foot loss was less than 100 fpm.

Using this data and aeronautical charts of the Rocky Mountain states, it can be shown that no matter where in the 48 contiguous states such an engine failure might occur, the Seminole would almost always be within driftdown range of a suitable airport.

Certainly this indicates that once any light twin has climbed to some minimum safe altitude, an engine failure—even when above the published service ceiling—rarely dictates the need to make an off-airport, single-engine landing.

Unfortunately, manufacturers of light twins do not provide specific recommendations for drifting down to a single-engine absolute ceiling following the failure of one engine. Thankfully, however, the procedure is relatively simple, and applies to any multi-engine airplane (including turbocharged models) being flown above its engine-out ceiling.

When the ailing engine rolls over and dies, the prescribed shutdown checklist should be completed. But don't be in too much of a hurry lest ye shall join the elite ranks of those who have feathered the wrong engine. Simultaneously, maintain altitude while the airspeed bleeds to V_{YSE}, the best single-engine rate-of-climb speed. Then allow the aircraft to descend while maintaining this airspeed with the operative engine developing maximum power. It is important to recognize that V_{YSE} results in the minimum sink rate (when above the absolute ceiling) or the maximum climb rate (when below the absolute ceiling). Under no circumstances, therefore, should the airspeed be allowed to vary either above or below V_{YSE}. Otherwise, driftdown performance suffers due to an increased rate of descent.

In other words, if maintaining V_{YSE} does not result in a climb or the ability to maintain altitude, accept the sink rate (which will diminish steadily) and drift down to an altitude that can be maintained (the single-engine absolute ceiling).

It is very tempting when above the absolute ceiling to attempt maintaining altitude by raising the nose excessively and permitting airspeed to decay. Not only is this futile, it is extremely hazardous because of two significant factors.

First of all, the wings of a twin have different stall speeds when a propeller is feathered. Because of the absence of propwash, the wing supporting the "caged" engine stalls several knots faster than the wing with the good engine.

Secondly, because the naturally aspirated, operative engine develops considerably less than 100 percent power when at altitude, the minimum controllable airspeed (V_{MC}) is much lower than when the aircraft is at sea level. As a result, not as much rudder force is required to prevent yaw. But more significant is that V_{MC} could be considerably lower than the stall speed of the wing supporting the inoperative engine.

Therefore, if airspeed is allowed to drop much below V_{YSE}, the "unpowered" wing probably will stall before directional control is lost. Such a stall conspires with the asymmetrical power condition to produce a most wicked spin. The maneuver is definitely counterproductive. Recovery necessitates throttling back the operative engine and sacrificing considerable altitude.

Once driftdown begins, use visual observations, sectional charts, and an ATC radar facility (if available) to determine the safest direction in which to lose altitude. Usually it is best to head for down-slope valleys that lead to lower terrain and, hopefully, a suitable airport.

But don't be in a hurry to turn. Steep bank angles produce increased sink rates. A 15-degree bank angle should be considered a maximum. Although such a shallow bank angle may seem insufficient, the turn rate this produces when flying at reduced airspeed (V_{YSE}) usually is adequate.

And if a pilot is having difficulty maintaining his sanity during an engine-out driftdown, he might consider advancing the throttle of the dead engine to silence the gear-warning horn.

Also during descent, try to hold a steady pitch attitude to maintain the desired airspeed; chasing the airspeed needle is inefficient and increases average sink rates. If an autopilot is available, by all means, use it to decrease cockpit workload (but only after the rudder has been trimmed properly). While descending at so slow an airspeed, be sure to maintain a watchful eye on the cylinder-head temperature of the operative engine (which is developing maximum possible power). As altitude is lost, ambient temperature usually increases, as does the power output of the engine. This usually results in warmer cylinder-head temperatures, but these probably will not become excessive at intermediate altitudes. If the CHT needle does creep toward the red line, however, reduce rpm slightly. This reduces internal engine friction without significantly affecting power and sink rate.

Since drifting down to the airplane's single-engine absolute ceiling can take well over an hour, consider the possible need to crossfeed. Yes, accidents have been caused because the only operative engine suffered a fatal case of fuel starvation while the opposite tank remained untapped.

Once the absolute ceiling is reached and a specific altitude can be maintained, the airplane continues to become lighter. Unless power is reduced, this results in a slight airspeed increase that can be used to "drift up" (at V_{YSE}) to gain altitude.

There comes a time during such an emergency when a pilot's thoughts turn to landing—as soon as possible. In most cases, this requires little more than a single-engine approach to a low-lying airport. But if man and machine are over (or between!) the Rocky Mountains, the nearest suitable airport might be near or above the airplane's single-engine ceiling. Such a problem requires considerable planning and cool heads-upmanship.

First of all, if an airport can be seen in the distance, it most likely is within range even if an initial appraisal indicates otherwise. Consider for example, the data in Figure 82. Notice that the descent from 12,000 to 11,000 feet resulted in an effective "glide ratio" of 71 to 1, which is considerably better than could be expected from the world's most efficient sailplane. The descent from 10,000 to 9,000 feet resulted in a "glide ratio" of 128 to 1, which is equivalent to a descent gradient of only 0.4 degree.

Properly interpreted, this means that, yes, if an airport can be seen, it probably is possible to get there safely and execute a landing no matter how far away it appears to be. But to be certain, watch the airport carefully from afar. If the landing area moves up with respect to a point on the windshield, you might not make it. Consider, however, that during driftdown, the descent angle becomes much shallower (and eventually becomes horizontal), which might confirm the ability to reach an airport previously rejected. If and when the landing area moves down with respect to a point on the windshield, you've got it made.

The approach to such a high-elevation airport must be executed carefully. Very carefully. Since a missed approach is virtually impossible because of the inability to climb (or even maintain altitude), the pilot is afforded only one opportunity. Fortunately, the maneuver does not require any fancy footwork.

To begin with, establish a long final approach. The aircraft should be lined up with the runway when at least 3 miles out. Use a normal, 3-degree approach slot. Since the engine-out twin has such an outstanding "glide ratio" on one engine, there is no real problem even if the aircraft dips somewhat below the slot. Just maintain V_{YSE} and sufficient power to recapture the "glideslope." A normal slot, after all, descends at 3 degrees while a single-engine twin can be held to a descent slope of less than 1 degree. Eventually, the descent path of the aircraft will merge with the normal approach slot.

A slight excess of airspeed (about 10 knots), however, is recommended until on short final approach.

When landing is assured, extend the landing gear and flaps. During the flare and while reducing power, anticipate the need to apply rudder toward the dead engine to compensate for opposite rudder trim that had been applied earlier, as well as the drag created by the now windmilling propeller of the good engine.

Occasionally a departure is made from an airport with a density attitude that is above the single-engine ceiling of a light twin. An engine failure after takeoff, therefore, would result in a compulsory driftdown.

One way to avoid this is to load lightly because of the substantial effect this has on raising the single-engine ceiling. Instead of topping off the tanks before departure, for example, consider an enroute landing for fuel at an airport with a lower elevation. Otherwise, be mentally prepared to descend should an engine failure spoil the climbout. If the aircraft has reached at least 1,000 feet AGL, a return to the airport might be possible because of the minimal sink rate that can be maintained when below 10,000 feet MSL. If a return is not practical, accept the notion of an off-airport landing. By maintaining V_{YSE} and maximum-available power from the operative engine, the outstanding "glide ratio" should offer a considerable choice of landing sites even when at a relatively low altitude.

Statistics indicate, however, that a multi-engine pilot is psychologically unable to accept the reality of an off-airport landing as long as one engine is developing power. This stems from the erroneous belief that having two engines is an insurance policy against a forced landing due to the failure of one engine. He attempts to climb or maintain altitude even when conditions dictate that such performance is impossible. More often than not, the result is an asymmetrically powered spin that punctuates the flight quickly and with finality.

If maintaining V_{YSE} results in a descent, and lower terrain is not within range, accept a forced landing while maintaining control of the aircraft. This is much preferable to a spin and dramatically increases the probability of survival.

Chapter 39 **Minimum Controllable Airspeed and Advice**

Pilots of multi-engine aircraft who suddenly experience an engine failure recognize the urgent need to maintain directional control. But many do not realize that, if the wings are held level and the slip/skid ball is centered during certain critical phases of engine-out flight, they might unwittingly lose the ability to keep the airplane pointed straight ahead. This might seem incongruous to those trained to maintain a wings-level attitude following engine failure. Nevertheless, it is true.

Various publications do point out that a wings-level attitude does erode engine-out performance and controllability because this causes the airplane to slip sideways through the air. Although this is accurate, no explanation is offered to help pilots understand why or visualize how this occurs. Some pilots even refuse to accept the possibility. But a little imagination can help to resolve this perplexing concept.

Imagine that a light twin is parked on an extremely slippery sheet of ice. Two men wearing spiked shoes, one at each wing tip, are pulling the airplane forward. Suddenly, the man tugging on the left wing has a cardiac arrest and falls down on the job. Since the man at the Figure 83 right wing tip is still working, the airplane veers (or yaws) left, simulating a failed left engine. The remaining worker yells for help, and a third man appears. But instead of replacing the ailing man on the left, the newcomer arrests the left turn by pushing against the right side of the tail (simulating right-rudder application). As shown in Figure 83, this causes the airplane to move forward at a constant heading (zero yaw).

But, this example also demonstrates that the airplane moves sideways (or is sideslipping) toward the left, a result of the two applied forces. Notice that this happens even though the wings are level and the slip/skid bail on the instrument panel remains centered.

Sideslipping occurs in flight for the same reason. The side force created by a properly deflected rudder moves the airplane toward the dead engine, even though the wings are level, and the airplane is held on a constant heading. It is one of those phenomena that must be accepted on faith because it normally cannot be detected from inside of the cockpit.

Such a sideslip can be observed, however, by taping a yaw string to the outside of the windshield or on top of the nose. It must be located in an area

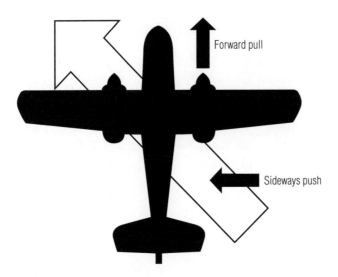

Forward pull

Sideways push

Figure 83. Sideslipping with one engine inoperative

of undisturbed airflow where reliable sideslip indications can be obtained and where it is visible from the cockpit. In nonslipping flight, the yaw string—little more than a piece of yarn—is blown straight back by the relative wind. But during a sideslip to the left, for example, the yaw string moves right.

Another way to observe an engine-out sideslip is to fly precisely along a runway centerline on a calm day with one engine shut down and the wings level. To be safe at such a low altitude, powerplant failure should be simulated by allowing the "failed" engine to develop only enough power to overcome its own drag (zero thrust). To maintain track along the centerline, the pilot must crab toward the operating engine. Otherwise, the airplane will sideslip (or drift) toward the dead engine.

Allowing a twin with asymmetric power to sideslip results in two negative effects. The first is an obvious rise in drag resulting from moving sideways through the air. Slips, after all, sometimes are used intentionally to create additional drag, a procedure that enables a pilot to descend rapidly without gaining airspeed when on an excessively high final approach. But, when a twin is flown on one engine, performance might be so anemic that the additional drag created by an unintentional and unnoticeable sideslip cannot be tolerated. This can make the difference between climbing and sinking helplessly.

The other disadvantage is not so obvious. Figure 84 shows a light twin in a wings-level sideslip toward the dead engine. Notice that some of the relative wind, which approaches the airplane from the left, pushes against the left side of the vertical stabilizer. This force compounds the problem of directional control because it adds to the effect of asymmetric thrust; both forces try to yaw the airplane toward the dead engine. Consequently, the rudder must work harder to keep the airplane pointed straight ahead.

At a time when additional yaw control is required, however, the amount of available rudder power actually erodes. This is because the vertical stabilizer prevents some of the relative wind from reaching the rudder, obviously decreasing control effectiveness. Finally, the airflow that does reach the rudder during a sideslip brushes by the control surface at a relatively small angle, further reducing rudder effectiveness.

Since sideslipping dramatically reduces rudder power, it is necessary to increase airflow across the rudder to prevent the airplane from yawing toward the dead engine. One way to do this is to maintain a faster airspeed, one that might be 10 or 20 knots above the published V_{MC}, (minimum single-engine control speed). This might even require an airspeed in excess of V_{YSE} (best single-engine rate-of climb speed).

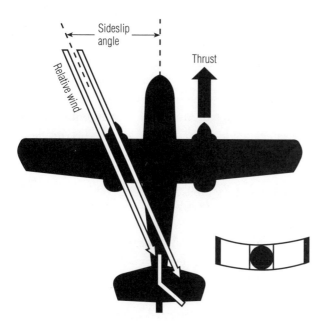

Figure 84. Wings-level sideslip toward the dead engine

Such a high V_{MC} can place a pilot between a rock and a hard place. If, just after takeoff, an engine fails and airspeed is below the actual V_{MC} but faster than the published V_{MC}, a pilot will believe that directional control is possible at a time when it is not. Failing to understand this, he becomes astonished when full rudder application fails to arrest the persistent yaw. Seemingly with a will of its own, the airplane continues its deathly spiral toward the dead engine.

The pilot's only recourse is to retard both throttles and accept the consequences of a possible forced landing (even though airspeed exceeds the published V_{MC}).

If sufficient airspeed is available to maintain directional control, the power of one engine may be insufficient to hold altitude because of the excess drag created by a sideslipping airplane. Most light twins—especially when heavy or at a high density altitude—then are destined for a downhill slide.

The only alternative is to fly the crippled twin properly. This demands eliminating most or all of the negative effects caused by wings-level sideslipping. Since a sideslip is an undesirable consequence of rudder deflection, the cause cannot be eliminated without centering the rudder and sacrificing directional control. But the force that produces a sideslip can be neutralized by creating an approximately equal force in the opposite direction. As shown in Figure 85, this is accomplished by banking the airplane toward the operating engine and tilting the direction of wing lift. The resultant horizontal component of lift acts opposite to the sideslipping force produced by the rudder.

When the airplane is prevented from sideslipping, rudder effectiveness improves substantially, because the yaw force created by the relative wind striking the vertical stabilizer is eliminated. Also, a greater amount of airflow contacts the rudder at a larger angle. The bottom line is that increased rudder power allows directional control to be maintained at the slower, published V_{MC}.

Performance improves, too. This is because the airplane can be flown at a slower, possibly more efficient airspeed (at V_{YSE} instead of above it). Also, the drag created by moving an airplane sideways through the air is eliminated. With less power required to maintain altitude, more excess power is available for climb (or reducing sink rate).

As mentioned earlier, the type of sideslip resulting from flying wings-level with an inoperative engine cannot be detected with a slip/skid ball; it remains centered. But when the sideslip is arrested by banking toward the operative engine, the ball will slide toward the lowered wing. This false indication of a slip can be ignored. Many multi-engine pilots do not realize that

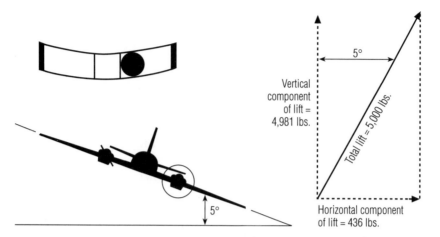

Figure 85. Bank the airplane toward the operating engine, and tilt the direction of wing lift to prevent sideslipping

the value of V_{MC} determined by the airframe manufacturers is obtained by flying the airplane in a zero-sideslip condition. In other words, the factory test pilot is allowed to bank the airplane up to 5 degrees toward the good engine. This reduces V_{MC} to the slowest possible airspeed. When the wings are level and the airplane is sideslipping, V_{MC} rises unacceptably.

To maintain directional control following engine failure, it is imperative that a pilot similarly bank toward the operative engine. Otherwise, the red radial on the airspeed indicator that represents V_{MC} (as determined during certification flight testing) has little more than decorative value.

It is possible, of course, to have too much of a good thing. An excessive angle of bank erodes climb performance; and it could be at a time when a pilot needs additional altitude as soon as possible. For this and other reasons, the FAA allows airframe manufacturers to obtain and publish the V_{MC} resulting from no more than 5 degrees of bank.

Such a shallow bank might not seem particularly significant, especially when a pilot is fighting to keep the airplane upright. But even though 5 degrees of bank is barely noticeable on the attitude indicator, it has a profound effect.

Consider, for example, the 5,000-pound airplane in Figure 85. The amount of lift developed by the wings also is about 5,000 pounds. When the airplane is banked 5 degrees right, the horizontal component of lift represents a sizable 436-pound force that usually is enough to offset the rudder force causing the sideslip in the first place.

The vertical component of lift is barely affected by the slight angle of bank. It amounts to 4,981 pounds, which represents a mere 19-pound loss.

The importance of banking toward the operative engine cannot be over-stressed. Failing to heed this requirement results in an excessively fast V_{MC} and potentially inadequate performance. Some pilots have trouble remembering which way to bank. (A bank in the wrong direction is worse than none at all.) Although mnemonics are not satisfactory for everyone, the following may be helpful to some. After all, "dead foot, dead engine" probably has saved more than a few lives. Consider, "leaning on the good engine for support" or "raise the dead (engine) to stay alive."

Pilots are quick to recognize that lightly loaded airplanes perform better than heavy ones. But there is an exception to this generalization: a decrease in gross weight causes an undesirable increase in V_{MC}. Simply stated, this occurs because the wings of a light airplane (in stabilized flight) do not produce as much lift as when the airplane is heavier. Consequently, the horizontal component of lift created during a 5-degree bank is proportionately less. In other words, the horizontal component of lift, being weaker, loses some ability to offset sideslip during flight with an inoperative engine. As a result, V_{MC} rises somewhat. The slowest V_{MC}, therefore, occurs at the heaviest gross weight (for a given airplane).

Moving the center of gravity aft also causes V_{MC} to rise. This is because an airplane yaws (and rolls and pitches) about the center of gravity. The rudder (and other control surfaces) becomes increasingly less effective, therefore, as the distance (or lever arm) between it and the center of gravity decreases.

On the other hand, as an airplane with normally aspirated engines (no turbocharging) gains altitude, V_{MC} decreases. This is because the severity of asymmetric thrust diminishes as the operative engine loses power while gaining altitude.

For those bored by aerodynamic explanations, it is important only to recognize that the published V_{MC} occurs in the practical world of flight only when the propeller of the inoperative engine is windmilling, the operative engine is developing maximum horsepower, flaps are in the takeoff position, the landing gear is retracted, the center of gravity is at the aft limit, gross weight is at a maximum (usually), and the airplane is banked 5 degrees toward the operative engine.

V_{MC} increases when the angle of bank is less than 5 degrees or the aircraft is below gross weight.

V_{MC} decreases when the propeller is feathered, when power on the operative engine is reduced, or when the CG is forward of the aft limit.

Considering the variables involved, it is clear that the precise value of V_{MC} at any given time is largely guesswork. The published airspeed applies only during a specific set of circumstances and otherwise is only a crude guide.

Since failure to bank into the operative engine is most responsible for increasing V_{MC}, pilots must be particularly alert to this during initial climb. This is when indicated airspeed might be above the published V_{MC}, and yet below the actual, higher V_{MC}, that results from keeping the wings level following an engine failure. To maintain directional control and have a shot at climbing, the pilot must be prepared to bank into the operating engine as quickly as rudder is applied to arrest the yaw.

The need to develop and maintain the proficiency required to cope with an engine failure properly suggests that multi-engine pilots refresh themselves with periodic dual instruction. But this can present another kind of problem.

V_{MC} is reduced significantly below the published value when the operating engine produces less than maximum rated horsepower. Unfortunately, this occurs routinely during multi-engine training at altitude. The operating, normally aspirated engine cannot produce more than 82 percent power at 6,000 feet, for example, so V_{MC} may be dangerously close to stall. An attempt to demonstrate directional control at V_{MC} (required of applicants for a multi-engine rating) can result in an asymmetrically powered spin—a frightening, sudden maneuver that has claimed numerous lives.

(A knowledgeable, sharp multi-engine instructor widens the gap between actual V_{MC} and stall speed either by extending flaps partially, which decreases stall speed, or sticking the toe of one foot behind the depressed rudder pedal to limit rudder travel, which artificially raises V_{MC} to a higher speed.)

This demonstrates clearly that training for proficiency can be as hazardous as the lack of it—a case of the cure being worse than the ailment. Such is the nature of multi-engine airplanes.

Index

by Robert Sacks

Boldface page numbers refer to figures.

The Proficient Pilot, Volume 2
Contents

Section 5 Systems Management
Gear-Up Landings
Operating the Pressurization System
Electrical System Failure
Flaps, Slats, and Slots

Section 6 More About the World of Instrument Flight
Time-Saving IFR Shortcuts
Another Way to Practice IFR Approaches
Missed Approaches
Two-Way Communications Failure
Communicating for Survival
Structural Icing

Section 7 Advanced Adventures
Fly to Europe—Yourself
Ditching
Formation Flying
World Aviation Records and How to Set One
Brainteasers

Flying Wisdom
The Proficient Pilot, Volume 3
Contents

Section 5 Flying for Fun and Profit

Banner Towing
Towing Gliders
Flying on Skis

Section 6 Special Treats

The Ultimate Cross-Country Flight: Around the World
My Favorite Airplane
My Favorite Flight

About the Author

Barry Schiff, with more than 25,000 hours in 250 types of aircraft, has received worldwide recognition for his wide-ranging accomplishments. He was a rated Airline Transport Pilot at 21, and has earned every FAA category and class rating (except airship) and every possible instructor's rating. As a 34-year veteran of Trans World Airlines, he currently flies the Lockheed 1011. Captain Schiff holds five world speed records (one captured from the Soviet Union) and has received numerous honors for his many contributions to aviation safety. These include a Congressional Commendation, the Louis Blériot Air Medal (France), Switzerland's Gold Proficiency Medal, an honorary doctorate in aeronautical science, and AOPA's L. P. Sharples Perpetual Award.

An award-winning journalist and author, he is well known to flying audiences for his numerous books and 1,000 articles published in some 90 aviation periodicals, notably *AOPA Pilot*, of which he is a contributing editor. Many of his articles discuss personally developed concepts, procedures, and techniques that have received international acclaim. Schiff also developed and worked to have adopted the concept of providing general aviation pilots with safe VFR routes through high-density airspace.

These credentials have not diminished his passion for flying lightplanes, which he has used to span oceans and continents. He continues to investigate and report to the aviation community various aspects of proficiency and safety, and remains a vigorous and outspoken advocate for general aviation.